Praise for *Crafty Screenwriting*

"I wish more writers knew what makes a script worth producing—not just how to structure a plot and write good dialogue, but how to come up with a story that people want to see on the screen. *Crafty Screenwriting* explains all of that in a clear and often hilarious way. I hope a lot of writers read this book; then I'll get more screenplays I want to make into movies."

—Paul Colichman, president of Regent Entertainment, producer of *Gods and Monsters*

"This is that rare kind of book about screenwriting that is truly helpful. It tells you how to write not merely a script that shows you off, but a script that convinces producers to make it into a movie."

—Eleanor Bergstein, screenwriter of *Dirty Dancing*

"*Crafty Screenwriting* explains what no one else seems to be explaining: how to write a screenplay that's not only a good read, but a good movie project that a producer can make into a good movie. Shrewdly realistic and funny."

—Pieter Kronenburg, producer of *The Hotel New Hampshire*, *Treasure Island*, and more than two dozen other films

"*Crafty Screenwriting* is an invaluable tool for anyone attempting to penetrate the dangerous thickets of Hollywood with an idea in their hand and not much else. This book gives you an actual, workable road map that, if followed with a strict loyalty to your own creativity, will guide you through the often terrifying journey of confusion and rejection toward the bright realization of your singular talent!"

—Henry Jaglom, writer and director of *Deja Vu*, *Eating*, and *Always*

CRAFTY
SCREENWRITING

CRAFTY SCREENWRITING

Writing Movies That Get Made

ALEX EPSTEIN

AN OWL BOOK
HENRY HOLT AND COMPANY • NEW YORK

Owl Books
Henry Holt and Company, LLC
Publishers since 1866
175 Fifth Avenue
New York, New York 10010
www.henryholt.com

An Owl Book® and ® are registered trademarks of
Henry Holt and Company, LLC.

Distributed in Canada by H. B. Fenn and Company Ltd.

Library of Congress Cataloging-in-Publication Data

Epstein, Alex.
Crafty screenwriting : writing movies that get made /
Alex Epstein.—1st ed.
p. cm.
"An Owl book."
Includes index.
ISBN-13: 978-0-8050-6992-1
ISBN-10: 0-8050-6992-5
1. Motion picture authorship. I. Title
PN1996 .E77 2002
808.2'3—dc21 2002017207

Henry Holt books are available for special
promotions and premiums. For details contact:
Director, Special Markets.

First Edition 2002

Designed by Victoria Hartman

Printed in the United States of America

7 9 10 8 6

To Lisa Hunter . . . you told me so

Contents

Acknowledgments

This book owes a tremendous debt to:

Angel Gulermovich Epstein, who has an unerring eye for what is right or wrong in a story, and who encouraged me to keep writing through the most frustrating times;

my beloved parents, who never repressed my tendency to smart off;

Kenneth Koch, who will probably be horrified to learn that I did after all become a television writer;

Molly Pollack and Wayne Adamson, two of the best English teachers in the world;

Betsy Amster and Deb Brody, a better agent and editor I could not ask for;

Margie Mirell, for all her wise advice;

and the directors and screenwriters with whom I've had the good fortune to work and the executives and producers who have been kind enough to read, comment on, and occasionally pay me money for my writing.

Thank you.

1

HOOK

What's a screenplay? Good question. After all, if you're going to write one, you ought to know the answer. Right?

You probably already know *an* answer. A screenplay is writing intended to be turned into film. It's a hundred-odd pages held together by brass brads, in which you have written down whatever you want the audience to see and hear in your movie.

If it gets made, the director will come up with a whole new vision, the actors will change your dialogue, the editor will concoct another way to order the scenes, and it won't be "your movie" anymore. That's okay. A screenplay is not a complete work. It is not intended to be appreciated on its own. If a movie were a building, a screenplay would be the blueprint. Nobody settles down in front of a roaring fire with her beloved, a bottle of Chianti, and a nice blueprint. Nobody takes a couple of good screenplays out to the beach—outside of show business, anyway.

That means *there is no point writing a screenplay if it isn't going to get produced.*

We all know that, somewhere in the back of our minds, but most of the thousands of screenplays I've read in ten years as a development executive were never in any danger of being made into a movie. From the moment the writer conceived them, they were *doomed*. They may have been well crafted or poorly crafted, but they were all missing what they needed in order to get made.

This book is about writing movies that get made. Not just popular movies. Art films get made, too. Writing a screenplay that will make a brilliant movie is a good part of writing a movie that will get made, and that's what *most* of this book is about. But that's not all of it. So it's important to understand what *else* a screenplay is, if you're going to go to all the trouble of writing one, because if you don't, the odds are you're wasting your time.

A Screenplay Is Part of a Package

A screenplay is the first element in what the movie business calls a package. A package is a combination of

- some material—a book, a screenplay, even just a concept, plus
- a star actor and/or a star director

that movie people are betting the audience will want to see in movie theaters or on their TVs.

A screenplay is an *element* in a *deal*.

Show business has a split personality. It is a *business*, which means people are not in it for their health. When movies flop, people lose their jobs. Unsuccessful directors have to go back to shooting commercials. Unsuccessful actresses have to go back to waiting tables, or marry carpet salesmen. Unsuccessful producers have to go back to selling carpets.* It's not surprising how crassly commercial the movies are. What's surprising is that they're not *more* crassly commercial.

Very few people go into the motion picture industry because they want above all to make a lot of money. The money's great if you're working, but really, if you just want to make money, you might as

---

*Unsuccessful studio executives receive lavish "golden parachute" severance packages with guaranteed funding for their pet movie projects, but that's showbiz, Punky.

well be selling Porsches or oil-drilling equipment. Practically everyone in the business got into it because they love movies. Screenwriters want to tell stories. Producers want to put good movies on the screen. Actors want to indulge their most extreme emotions in front of a crowd of people, so think twice about dating one. Practically everyone in the motion picture industry is trying to make good movies. They're not all trying to make great art, but if they had the choice, most of them would rather make a movie that will last.

Every motion picture project starts with a bit of commerce and a bit of art.

In theory, a motion picture project begins when someone working in development at a motion picture studio or production company reads a wonderful screenplay. *Development* is the stage of the movie-making process when screenplays get optioned, bought, rewritten, rewritten, rewritten, and usually buried. This reader is likely someone called, believe it or not, a "reader"—often a recent film school grad who gets paid $40 a pop to write two to five pages of synopsis and scornful commentary. If the reader likes it, he might alert a story editor, who brings it to the attention of a development executive, who gives it to a production executive at a studio or a producer at a production company.

Once a deal is struck, the production exec or producer sends the script out to a director, who, hopefully, sparks to the material and agrees to direct the script. Then the script goes to stars. Once a big enough star agrees to do the picture, the studio agrees to fund the picture, and we're off to the races.

Your screenplay does not get made into a movie until all of these people say yes: the reader, the story editor, the development exec, the production exec, the director, and the star. If the production exec, the development exec, the story editor, or the reader got out of bed on the wrong side that morning, your project is dead at that studio or production company.

(If Tom Cruise sends in a friend's screenplay, then it skips to the top. The production exec reads it and *automatically* likes it, it gets optioned, and if Tom agrees to star in it, it gets made. More about that in a bit.)

A screenplay is a *selling tool.* It is a salesman for the movie. It sells your story to people you've never met, whom you'll never meet, some of whom are in a permanently bad mood because you can write and they can't. It has to sell to a twenty-two-year-old reader who thinks he knows everything about what makes a great movie. It has to sell to a story editor up past midnight trying to finish her stack of scripts so she can make love to her boyfriend before he goes into REM sleep. It has to sell to a production exec who brought home two scripts: yours, and one Tom Hanks wants to do. It has to sell to an actor who is terrified of getting old. It has to convince all of these cranky people that *it is a movie* just dying to be made.

So, a screenplay is a blueprint, an element in a deal, and a sales tool.

What gets your screenplay through the gauntlet? If you read most screenwriting books, the answer is something like this:

Structure	A good, fresh, well-told story that makes sense
Characters	Interesting, fleshed-out characters with the breath of life in them
Dialogue	Good, realistic dialogue that gives voice to the characters
Pacing	Rising tension that reaches a dramatic climax

Nah.

These things don't get you past the gatekeepers. Sure, you'll want to have 'em in your screenplay. But what actually gets you through is a *great hook.*

The Hook

A hook is the concept of the picture in a nutshell. Not just any concept. A hook is a fresh idea for a story that instantly makes show business people interested in reading your script, and then makes the audience want to see your movie.

Here are some good hooks:

- A man is about to commit suicide when an angel shows him what his town would be like if he had never lived. (*It's a Wonderful Life*)
- Two people who hate each other meet anonymously and fall in love. (*The Shop Around the Corner*, *You've Got Mail*)
- A bunch of unemployed Brits decide to put on a striptease act to earn some money. (*The Full Monty*)
- A cynical advertising executive suddenly develops the power to read women's thoughts. (*What Women Want*)
- A lawyer suddenly loses his ability to lie. (*Liar Liar*)
- Some Jamaicans decide to enter the Olympics as a bobsled team, although there is no snow in Jamaica. (*Cool Runnings*)
- A strange genius discovers a number that may be the name of God. (π)
- Three filmmakers went into the woods to tape a documentary on a legendary witch. These are the tapes we found after they disappeared. (*The Blair Witch Project*)
- A puppeteer finds a secret tunnel into John Malkovich's brain. (*Being John Malkovich*)
- There's a bomb on a crowded city bus. If the bus slows below 50 miles an hour, the bomb will go off. (*Speed*)
- A man discovers he has been replaced by his clone. (*The Sixth Day*)
- A journalist finds a heart-wrenching love letter in a bottle. She tracks down the man who wrote it and falls in love with him. (*Message in a Bottle*. I didn't say a film with a great hook had to be *good*, did I? I only said you need a great hook to get your screenplay *made*.)

Some of these were made into big Hollywood productions, and some were independent pictures. ("Independent" is a huge misnomer. "Independent producers" are dependent on practically everybody. A better term might be *codependent producers*.) What all these movies have in common is that you want to see how they're going to turn out. What happened to those kids up in those woods? How do a bunch of gnarly, inhibited British guys put on a striptease show? You have to read the screenplays to find out.

Sometimes the hook is not even what the movie is really about. The hook for *Free Enterprise* might be, "two aging Trekkies bump into William Shatner, who longs to write and star in a rap version of *Julius Caesar*." The story is mostly a romantic comedy about an aging Trekkie who meets the perfect Trekkie girl and almost screws it up. But if that were the only hook, the movie wouldn't have got made. "Trekkies meet Captain Kirk" sells the movie.

At this point, you may be thinking, "But most movies don't have great hooks." In fact, if you look at the Internet Movie Database's list of the top 250 movies according to viewer ratings (see http://www.imdb.com), almost none of the top movies have great hooks.

I never said *any* screenplay needs a great hook to get made. I said that *your* screenplay needs a great hook to get made.

These days, movies are driven by bankable elements. A bankable element is any creative element—star, director, material it's based on—you can bank on getting people to come to see the picture. Or to put it another way, Harrison Ford is starring in my picture, and now I am going to deposit my big fat check in the *bank*.

How Hookless Pictures Get Made

Here are some ways hookless pictures get made:

- Steven Spielberg reads a novel about a Nazi Party member who saved thousands of Jews from the Holocaust. Steven Spielberg hasn't had a flop in ages, so he's a bankable element. (*Schindler's List*)
- A producer gets the cinematic rights to the hit Broadway show *Evita!* "The rise to power of the widow of Argentina's dictator, Juan Perón" is not a good hook. "Hit musical written by Andrew Lloyd Webber" is a bankable element.
- Kevin Costner talks with a friend who's got an idea about a Civil War hero sent to a remote outpost, where he meets

Indians and slowly goes native. Kevin promises his friend that if he'll write the novel first, Kevin will get the picture made. Kevin was the bankable element here. (*Dances With Wolves*)

- Some guys with a digital camera make a film for $10,000 and it rakes in $80 million in box office. They want to do another film. They are instant bankable elements, at least until their second picture flops. (Whatever picture the *Blair Witch* guys do next. Applies equally to the latest nine-day-wonder, e.g., Kevin Smith and *Clerks* or Robert Rodriguez and *El Mariachi*.)
- A producer reads a novel about a retarded southern man whose life goes through many weird and wonderful twists that tell the story of two decades we all lived through. After the producer hires a screenwriter to adapt it, Tom Hanks decides to do the picture. Tom Hanks's movies have made over a billion dollars. Put that in your bank and smoke it. (*Forrest Gump*)
- John Grisham writes another legal thriller. Believe it or not, many of the people going to see pictures based on John Grisham's books have no clue who he is, and may not even know they're based on books at all. But his pictures are consistently successful in the marketplace, and that makes him bankable. (*The Runaway Jury*, *The Juror*, *The Client*, *The Rainmaker*, *The Firm*, etc.)
- Dimension Films decides to do *Children of the Corn* 7. The last six *Children of the Corn* movies made a profit; the series is a "franchise." If they can make the seventh one for less than they grossed on the last one, they'll make money.

A bankable element is anything that makes people with money in the bank think that people with money in their wallets will want to go see the movie they're backing. So long as the value of the elements in a picture adds up to the cost of making the movie, you're off to the races. If you have big elements, you make a big movie. Small elements, small movie. Jim Carrey is a bankable star for big-budget comedies. Jane Campion is a semibankable director for art movies. (In case you're interested, the show business industry trade paper, *The Hollywood Reporter*, publishes an annual list of who's bankable and how much they're worth, based on expert opinions, called the Star Power rankings. Another promising recent development is the Internet Movie Database's star ratings at http://www.imdbpro.com, where stars are ranked by the number of times their credits are downloaded by fans.)

If you have bankable elements, you don't necessarily need a great hook, or any hook at all. The more bankable the elements you have, the less important it is that your screenplay is even good, as far as getting it made is concerned. But if you are trying to get a star or director who's a bankable element to read your material, then you probably need a great hook. Most stars aren't stupid; the ones who are got to be stars because they know how to hire people who aren't stupid. A great hook makes everything easier all along the way.

It is *possible* to make a movie based on a script without a great hook and without bankable elements—a script so stunningly moving and brilliantly written that it draws the passion and dedication of many people to make the film with whatever money they can find and whatever actors they can afford. Don't even go there. The odds are hugely against it. When such pictures are made, there are usually other factors at work. Government tax credits for pictures shot in foreign countries account for many of these exceptions. Niche market pictures account for most of the rest: pictures made for a built-in core audience, such as *Smoke Signals*, a charming drama about Native Americans, or *Go Fish*, a clever romance about lesbians. A tiny fraction of all films released in the United States are made by daring producers who raise the money by any means necessary, often maxing out their credit cards. For each one of those, there are ten or twenty that never got released at all. No one writes news stories about those, or about their producers who are now declaring bankruptcy.

> If your story does not have a hook, you are probably wasting your time writing the screenplay.

Assuming you do not have a bankable element attached, and you're not bankable yourself, you need a great hook or your screenplay is just not going to get made. If your story does not have a hook, you are probably wasting your time writing the screenplay.

As with any rule, there are exceptions to this one, and there are also ways around it. But if your objective is to get a picture made, and if you are not pals with influential people in show business, then it is a rule you should pay attention to.

It's worth saying again: If your story does not have a hook, you are probably wasting your time writing the screenplay. You may enjoy the process of writing, you may get an agent, you may get invited to meetings in nice air-conditioned offices. But you aren't likely to sell your screenplay, and if you do, it's not likely to get made.

So: how do you come up with a great hook?

How You Come Up with a Hook

Great hooks are pretty rare. Once a movie is made, no one else can use that hook, at least not until everyone forgets the movie. Use once and dispose. So how do you come up with new ones? Is there some magic method?

Alas for you (and me!), I don't have a magic way to coming up with great hooks. No one does. Not even George Lucas does. (Ever see *Howard the Duck*?) But I have two techniques. They're not magic. In fact, they require a lot of effort. But they do work. They are:

a. Paying Attention
b. Stealing

PAYING ATTENTION

Paying attention means being aware of the real stories going on all around you, and then twisting them into a movie premise. The classic Billy Wilder picture *Ace in the Hole* tells the story of a reporter covering the story of a man trapped in a cave. It probably began with Wilder or his producer following news reports about a man trapped in a well or a cave and noticing how excited everyone was about the ongoing situation. That's not a movie—yet. But what if your journalist is cleverly *keeping* the man trapped in the cave in order to keep the story alive? What if he's a cynical, burned-out reporter trying to bring his career back to life by manipulating the situation? *That's* a hook.

In Canada, a little girl rescued some snow geese chicks after their mother was killed. But the young geese had no mother goose to show them the way to their winter territory; all they had was the little girl they'd bonded to. So the little girl's father taught her how to fly an Ultralight (a kind of motorized hang glider), and she led her goslings all the way to Florida; he wrote a book about it.

That's a hook. All it needs to become a movie is a ghost. (I'll talk more about ghosts later.) We know why the geese need to fly home, but we don't know why the little girl needs to help them. In the 1996 movie *Fly Away Home*, she's lost her own mother, and so, by saving the geese, she heals her own wound.

The *Air Bud* movies were created because the dog who stars in them got in the news. His owner had already trained him to play basketball and the right people had the thought, "A dog who plays basketball? There's gotta be a movie in this." What makes the story a movie is that it's about a kid who's lost his father, who has given up playing basketball, his favorite sport. The dog helps the kid fall in love with the game again, helping the kid get over the death of his father.

These hooks are all from books and the news, but any stories or dramatic situations will do. You just have to figure out what's missing in the story that would make it into a movie.

For example, suppose you read an article in *The New York Times* about how couples in New York often live with each other all the way through their two-plus-year-long divorces because they can't afford to move out, or because their lawyers have told them to stay in the marital residence for tactical reasons. What might make this a TV show is if they're already dating other people and reacting to each other's dates. What might make this a movie could be if they are each trying to set the other up with a new boyfriend or girlfriend so the other will move out. Do they succeed, or fall back in love again?

Paying attention means being alert when you hear or read about a dramatic situation some real people got themselves into and then figuring out how to make a movie story out of that situation.

If your story is too close to real events, you will have to buy the life story rights of the people involved, unless they are public figures or you write your story from the public record (see the section on copyright on page 227). But if you try to write the best movie possible based on the *idea*, instead of trying to be faithful to the actual events, you will likely end up with a story that is "inspired by" the true events and not based on them. In that case, you don't need to buy anyone's life story.*

(Many producers will buy people's life story rights even though they know that by the time they've finished the movie, it will hardly be the same story at all. Why? So when they go into a meeting at a studio, they have something to sell. Anybody can walk in with a concept, but a guy coming in with the rights to someone's life story has an element. It makes the project seem more real. It also makes it harder for the studio or production company to go around the producer and make a movie based on the same concept without him. You can't copyright a concept, but you can option someone's life rights. So if you're not a producer, and you intend to change the story dramatically, you may well not need to buy anyone's life rights; you can just say the film is "inspired by true events.")

Paying attention can also be a more general process. There might be an idea floating in the air, or a new technological development. Suppose you hear about Internet dating services. How do you make that into a movie? One obvious comedy premise would be to have a couple break up and start looking for new mates on the Internet, only to find each other again. A thriller premise might be a woman being stalked by a guy she met on Webpersonals.com, who told her a pack of lies about himself but knows everything about her. Of course, both of these premises are old and tired now. They might have been fresh in 1999, and too far ahead of their time in 1997.

---

*Disclaimer: I'm not a lawyer, and the above is only my layman's opinion. If you have a real legal question, for heaven's sake please talk to a real lawyer.

That's the risk of writing from trends. They move on, and your screenplay becomes old hat.

Jurassic Park arises from a combination of the eternal attraction of dinosaurs (eternal at least since I was a kid) and the trendy new technology of recombinant DNA. "A rich man hires scientists to recreate dinosaurs for his theme park. They run amok." Almost all of Michael Crichton's scientific thrillers have cool hooks; that's why practically all of them have been adapted into movies.

Bear in mind that writing about a timely subject is not the same as coming up with a timely hook. *All Quiet on the Western Front*, written by George Abbott after the novel by Erich Maria Remarque, comes from a phrase that news reports repeated daily during World War I. The phrase takes on an ironic meaning in the movie, which is about a group of idealistic young students who cheerfully enlist, only to confront the horror of World War I. *The Best Years of Our Lives* is another phrase that suggests a movie. A lot of men found that returning from World War II to civilian life was not what they'd hoped for; that, in fact, they preferred being shot at to dealing with life's little daily insults. The movie, written by Robert Sherwood after MacKinlay Kantor's novel, follows a trio of men who fly home on the same bomber, as they try to find their way back into the civilian swing of things.

Neither of these movies has a hook. They were timely pictures. *All Quiet on the Western Front* was made fourteen years after the war, when people were ready to make sense of the horror they'd been through. Both won Oscars for Best Picture. But they would have been hard to set up at a studio if they had not been based on best-selling novels, and they would have been hard to sell to the audience if they had not been packed with stars.

Mrs. Doubtfire trades on the oddly still fresh concept that divorced men love their kids as much as divorced women do and might do anything to stay by their side. *Kramer vs. Kramer* covered this territory in 1977; a father raising a son alone was enough of a hook. What made *Mrs. Doubtfire* a movie with a hook was that Robin Williams's character impersonates a British nanny in order to be close to his kids.

The idea doesn't have to be recent if no one's made a movie about it. The concept that no one can be tried twice for the same crime is enshrined in the U.S. Constitution, but it was not until 2000 that they made a movie about it, *Double Jeopardy:* "A woman is framed for killing her husband. She does her time, only to find out that he's really alive and he framed her. She can't be prosecuted for killing him a second time, so . . ."

There is one further way to come up with a hook by paying attention. As motion picture–making technology improves, it becomes possible to put spectacles into movies that were previously too expensive. In 1990, the dinosaurs in *Jurassic Park* would have been prohibitively expensive (if they were mechanical), or ridiculous (if they were guys in rubber suits). In 1995, leading-edge computer graphics technology made them possible. Now anyone can afford to put a dinosaur in his movie. Likewise, *Twister* used leading-edge technology to replicate the effect of being in a tornado. Previously, you had to use a cloud chamber (think of the tornado in *The Wizard of Oz*), which is tough to control precisely, and tougher to stick actors in. *Backdraft* used digital compositing to place its characters in the middle of realistic flames.

People go to the movies, among other reasons, to see things they've never seen before. If you can think of something exciting that no one's seen before, that can now be put convincingly in a movie, then you have the beginnings of a hook. The hard work is finding the right story to showcase the spectacle. In some movies, the story is no more than a thinly disguised vehicle for the spectacle. There was nothing particularly compelling about *Twister*'s pair of tornado scientists trying to get a measuring instrument into a tornado before a rival team did it. People went to see the movie because it had really great tornado effects. In other movies, the story really builds on the spectacle. *King Kong*'s story is far deeper and richer than the giant ape effect. That's why we still watch it, and why we may well be watching *Titanic* fifty years from now, long after the film's water effects and sinking-ship effects seem unimpressive. Roger Spottiswoode's brilliant, as-yet-unproduced adaptation of William Golding's novel *The Spire* shows a medieval cathedral's spire going up. Until recently it was probably too expensive to put a spectacle like that on film. You'd have to build a cathedral, at least a fake one, or try to put real actors convincingly into a model cathedral; with CGI (computer graphics interaction), you don't have to build the whole cathedral, just a few sets. (I think it would be exciting to see a cathedral go up.) What makes that spectacle into a compelling movie is the battle of wills between the abbot and the master builder, one wanting to build a spire, the other convinced too tall a spire will crush the cathedral.

STEALING

Stealing seems to be more popular than paying attention, probably because so few people are any good at paying attention. Stealing means taking someone else's story without paying for it and changing it into a movie. (When you pay for it, it's called adapting. When you *faithfully* adapt something you haven't paid for, it's called buying yourself a lawsuit.)

One very effective form of stealing is updating the classics. *Clueless* is a comedy about a popular girl at Beverly High who decides to do a total makeover on a "clueless" new girl, only to discover that it is she herself who needs the makeover—a spiritual one. The hook (and the outline of the plot) is stolen from Jane Austen's novel *Emma*. *Moulin Rouge* is a tragic romance about a poor writer who falls in love with a high-class hooker who is being kept by a rich duke. The concept and characters are stolen from the famous 1848 novel by Alexandre Dumas *fils*, *Camille*, which was also made into a famous opera, *La Traviata;* Dumas was writing from his own life (paying attention).

The hook of Shakespeare's *Romeo and Juliet* was,

A pair of star-cross'd lovers take their life;
Whose misadventur'd piteous overthrows
Doth with their death bury their parents' strife.

A boy and a girl from warring families fall in love. Their tragic death stops the war.

This hook was stolen for the hit Broadway musical *West Side Story*, which became a classic movie musical. The Montagues become a white street gang (the Jets) and the Capulets a Puerto Rican one (the Sharks) duking it out on New York's West Side. *Romeo Must Die* retold it with an Asian gang and the American mob standing in for the warring families. Director Baz Luhrmann updated Shakespeare's story without changing a line of dialogue in *Romeo + Juliet:* Verona becomes Verona Beach, and the "swords" and "longswords" become brand names for pistols and assault rifles.

Shakespeare himself stole many of his hooks. He stole *Romeo and Juliet*'s hook from the Roman poet Ovid's story of Pyramus and Thisbe—a familiar story if you know another of his plays, *A Midsummer Night's Dream*.

If the source you're stealing from is public domain, you can keep as much of the original work as you want to. (For an explanation of when a work falls into the public domain, please see page 17.) You'll probably find yourself changing quite a bit just because what audiences want now has changed from what they wanted a hundred years ago. Edmond Rostand's play *Cyrano de Bergerac* is a romance about a brilliant writer and swordsman, Cyrano, in love with a beautiful girl named Roxanne. Unfortunately, Cyrano has a ridiculously long nose. He finds himself helping his handsome friend Christian woo the girl, just so he can write her love poems and know she's reading them.

Steve Martin stole that hook in *Roxanne*, where his Cyrano is a fireman and Darryl Hannah's Roxanne an astronomer. Of course he had to explain why his Cyrano didn't get plastic surgery. But the real updating is in the ending. Rostand's hero died without ever declaring his love for Roxanne because it would sully the memory of her supposed lover, his best friend Christian. His 1897 audience, steeped in honor and tragedy, ate it up. Modern audiences wouldn't stand for such nonsense, so Martin's hero not only 'fesses up, he gets the girl.

The trick to stealing a hook is to poach what still works and find a way to update what no longer does. Francis Coppola's Oscar-winning *Apocalypse Now* is loosely based on a novel by the nineteenth-century author Joseph Conrad. *Heart of Darkness* is set in colonial Africa, where Mr. Kurtz, a white man, has gone upriver and set himself up as a mad god to African tribespeople. Marlow, the hero, is sent to bring him back. Kurtz, dying, tries to communicate to Marlow the horror of what he's seen and done, so that he can explain it to Kurtz's fiancée. In *Apocalypse Now*, Colonel Kurtz, a promising career soldier, has gone upriver and set himself up as a mad god to Cambodian tribespeople. Captain Willard, an army assassin, is sent to kill him. Kurtz, dying, tries to communicate to Willard the horror of what he's seen and done, so that Willard can explain to Kurtz's son why Kurtz did what he did. The updating is in setting the movie in the insanity of the Vietnam War. The scenes and characters are replaced but the through line and the driving question are the same.

Goldoni's classic farce *The Servant of Two Masters* is practically begging for an update: a servant decides he'll make more money if he has two masters at once. He juggles his two jobs with increasingly disastrous results. Your mission, should you choose to accept it, is to figure out what your hero would do for a living now. We don't really have servants in this society. What if a personal assistant is running a second job out of the same office, over the phone?

Another good way to steal is to take the plot of a movie and set it in a different environment. Sergio Leone's classic Western *A Fistful of Dollars* has a great hook: a gunfighter comes to a town terrorized by two rival gangs. He joins first one gang, then the other, playing them off so that they destroy each other, freeing the town from its misery. It is practically a scene-for-scene remake of Akira Kurosawa's classic samurai flick *Yojimbo*, which was, shall we say, heavily inspired by Dashiell Hammett's novel *Red Harvest*. The story was again remade as a Bruce Willis picture, *Last Man Standing*.

Outland's hook is "a burned-out marshal in charge of a mining station in space tries to rouse the terrorized miners to help him confront three killers sent to murder him." It is *High Noon* in space, with the clocks all over town replaced by the space shuttle's countdown to landing.

You've Got Mail is about two booksellers who despise each other in person, but fall in love over the Internet. Ernst Lubitsch's classic comedy *The Shop Around the Corner*, written by Samson Raphaelson from a play by Miklós László, has two office coworkers who can't stand each other falling in love through the personal ads. Coincidence? Stealing? You be the judge.

Mr. Smith Goes to Washington, written by Sidney Buchman from a story by Lewis Foster, directed by Frank Capra and starring James Stewart, has a naive congressman turning the House of Representatives on its head because he won't compromise. The Eddie Murphy movie *The Distinguished Gentleman*, written by Marty Kaplan and Jonathan Reynolds, gives the Capra idea a modern twist: the new congressman is a con man, who nonetheless finds his sense of decency outraged by the far more cynical politicians.

From a legal point of view, you can always steal a hook. No one can copyright a hook. In fact, you can steal anything so long as it is an idea. You can't steal characters, dialogue, or specific bits of plot. In other words, you can write a script about a little girl who is whisked away to a magical land where, opposed by evil creatures and helped by wonderful allies, she tries to get home. But from the moment the allies include a tin woodman, a cowardly lion, or a scarecrow, you have infringed on the copyright of the L. Frank Baum estate. You also can't have the tin woodman show up in a dream sequence in a drama you wrote, unless the underlying work has fallen out of copyright (which it may have).

Adaptations

You can do a *faithful* adaptation of other material that has a great hook. Then, of course, you're not only taking the hook but the plot, scenes, characters, and possibly dialogue from the material.

You can freely do a faithful adaptation of any work that has fallen out of copyright. Copyright expires with time. When a work falls into the public domain depends on when it was created. Here are some simple rules:

- Anything published more than sixty-seven years ago is in the public domain.
- Anything published before 1978 was copyrighted for twenty-eight years. The copyright registration could be extended for up to sixty-seven years. If a book is in print, its registration has

almost certainly been extended. However, if the work is something that everyone forgot about—say, a book that fell out of print for years, or a magazine article from a defunct magazine—then it may not have been reregistered and it is now PD or in the public domain. (Apparently *It's a Wonderful Life* was never reregistered, which is why it got played so often on TV: no one had to pay for it. The colorized version is, of course, copyrighted.)

- Anything published after 1978 will be under copyright for the lifetime of the author plus seventy years, for our purposes, "forever."

If you're interested in finding out the copyright status of a work, you can check the Library of Congress (LoC) on-line at http://www.loc.gov. However, the LoC's on-line records are spotty, and the absence of a registration does not necessarily mean the material is in the public domain. For that you need a copyright search. Thomson and Thomson (http://www.thomson-thomson.com) are a copyright research firm in Washington that searches the LoC physical files and gives you a report. The reports cost a few hundred dollars and take about five business days; call (800) 356 8630. There are other companies that do copyright research; look them up on the Internet.

If fictional material isn't in the public domain, you'll have to do a deal with whoever owns the rights to it. If it's a novel, for example, you'll have to find out who controls the cinematic rights. Check the first few pages of the book to see which publishing house published it and what city they're in. Call information and get their number. Call them. Ask for the person responsible for sub rights (subsidiary rights) or movie rights for that book. The sub rights person can tell you how to reach the author's agent if the author retained control of those rights, as is common these days, or can, if the publisher has obtained the movie rights, negotiate a deal with you for them.

It's up to you to negotiate a deal to option the book that is fair to both you and to the author or publisher, and lasts long enough for you to write and sell the script. (You can also hire an entertainment lawyer to do this for you. If you don't have the money for that, you may be able to find an entertainment lawyer who will work for no money, but attach himself or herself to the project as a producer of some kind. That will cost you nothing now, but much more if your project goes forward.) Bear in mind if you option a book that it might easily take seven years to make a film out of it. There will be many, many drafts of the script, many producers who option your script and fail to set it up, many actors who get interested and then lose interest. *Forrest Gump* took over ten years to reach the screen. So don't make a one-year option unless you can renew it indefinitely. You'll lose the underlying rights before you can do anything with your screenplay.

True Stories

Material is also in the public domain if it consists of true events. Anything historical is fair game, that is, anything where everyone in the story is dead. Dead people have very few rights. Anything said in a court of law is public record, which also makes it public domain. So long as you stick exclusively to court records, you could do a movie about a certain football star murdering his ex-wife. You wouldn't want to, but you could.

If you go beyond court records, writing about people who are still alive is sticky. If you make someone look bad, you run the risk of being sued for libel, that is, writing lies about someone. If you can prove you're telling the truth about them, you might win your court case, but being in a court case is like going to war: you may win, but you'll for sure bleed.

You can also be sued for violating someone's right to privacy. Everyone except public figures has a right to privacy. Loosely that means I can't make a movie about your private life without your permission unless you make your private life into public business. You might become a public figure by running for office, going on talk shows, being an entertainer or sports star, getting arrested, or otherwise intentionally getting in the news. The right to privacy is not something I am even remotely qualified to talk about in greater detail. Suffice it to say that one exists, and if you have a doubt you should consult an entertainment lawyer. (For that matter, if you're not sure about copyright, or any other legal issue, it's probably worth talking to an entertainment lawyer for fifteen minutes before you spend six months writing a script. As a bare minimum, spend a few hours on the Internet reading through the many sites that discuss copyright law in greater depth than I've done here.) You're better off not writing nasty things about living people. You'll notice that in *Backbeat*, a lovely, semifictional movie about the Beatles in their early days, the only characters who do anything hurtful to anyone are Stuart Sutcliffe, Brian Epstein, and John Lennon. Dead, dead, and dead, alas. The movie's version of Paul McCartney just writes silly love songs, and the real one can hardly sue over that.

The rule of thumb is, stick rigorously to the provable, historical truth and consult a lawyer, or invent a fresh story inspired by real life whose characters and events are so distant from the details of real life that no real person can reasonably claim that you're writing about him or her.

OTHER HOOKS

There are lots of movies with great hooks that don't necessarily come from paying attention or stealing. The writers came up with these hooks all by themselves. Some of them come from putting opposites together, or having people pretend to be something they're not:

- "A coldhearted executive hires a prostitute for the weekend for sexual companionship, but she teaches him how to love." (*Pretty Woman*)
- "Three confirmed bachelors get stuck taking care of a baby." (*3 Men and a Baby*, a remake of Colline Serreau's much tighter *Trois Hommes et un Couffin*)
- "A tough, wise-ass Chicago cop investigates a murder in quiet, polite Beverly Hills." (*Beverly Hills Cop*)
- "A trash-talking streetwise woman masquerades as a nun to hide from gangsters." (*Sister Act*, with some inspiration from *Some Like It Hot:* "A pair of musicians dress up as women to hide from gangsters in an all-girl band.")

- "A girl's transvestite mother masquerades as her real mother to impress her fiancé's straightlaced parents." (*The Bird Cage*, a remake of *La Cage aux Folles*)

Some of them come from "what if" thoughts:

- "What if a fisherman caught a mermaid?" (*Splash*)
- "What if a conspiracy theorist uncovered a real conspiracy?" (*Conspiracy Theory*, though the film really failed to deliver on its own premise)
- "What if a rich man offered a poor man's wife a million dollars to sleep with him?" (*Indecent Proposal*)
- "What if you could talk to animals?" (*Dr. Doolittle*)

Some of them come from sheer inspiration:

- "A divorced father puts on Santa's suit and becomes Santa in spite of himself." (*The Santa Clause*)

DUPLICATE HOOKS

If you come up with a hook and then discover that a picture with more or less the same hook was made recently, or is in development somewhere in L.A., then you are probably better off abandoning the project. If five years later the project never got made, or people have forgotten about it, you can come back to it. But it is sad to write a script you love and then have it rejected because "Warner Bros. has something like that in development."

HOW LONG SHOULD I SPEND THINKING UP A HOOK?

How long is a piece of string?

How long are you willing to spend?

You may already have had a great hook in your mind when you bought this book. Or it could take you three months to come up with a good hook.

Having a less-than-thrilling hook will doom your screenplay. No one will buy it. If you're lucky, and you have a good agent, you may get to go to a half dozen meetings with development people, but it won't go any further than that. All the work you put into a screenplay with a less-than-compelling hook will be for nothing, except as practice.

Now how long are you willing to spend?

I'll tell you this: almost no one spends enough time working on his hook. It's not as much fun as writing screenplays. Most writers go with the first half-decent idea they have. But half-decent doesn't get bought. That's why I'm recommending you take three steps to testing and improving your hook. They will take you quite some time to complete, but they will save you heartache and wasted effort later:

1. Come up with a great title.
2. Pitch your idea.
3. Query.

You'll be glad you did.

Title

Before you pitch your idea, though, you need a title. Your title is the most important phrase in your entire script. A catchy title will get people to listen to your story or read your script. A dull, confusing, or pretentious title will put people off your script.

> Your title is the most important phrase in your entire script.

I'll go into much more depth about titles in the last chapter, but for now, what you need is something that

a. is catchy and
b. says something about your story.

As you develop your hook into a story, and then into a script, you should always be working and reworking your title. Almost nobody spends enough time thinking about the title, either. If you spend 10 percent of your writing time doing nothing but thinking up better and better titles for your script, your time will be well spent. You can stop when practically everyone who hears it says, "Now *that's* a good title!"

Pitching Your Idea

Okay, so you think you have a really great hook. Do you start writing the screenplay?

Not yet. Surprisingly, many of the people who think they have a fresh, inspiring, clever new story that people will want to see on the screen, *don't*.

Strange as it may seem, the best way to find out if people would be interested in a movie with your hook is to ask them.

Tell your story concept to anyone who'll listen. Tell your girlfriend, your boyfriend, your dry cleaner, your waitress, your bartender, your kids, the baby-sitter, old people on park benches. Listen closely to their reaction and watch their faces. Are they sparking to your idea? Do they want to go see your movie? Or are they just being nice and friendly?

Kids, don't try this where professional screenwriters drink their coffee, or where producers schmooze, at least not until you've written the script. People rarely steal ideas intentionally, but if they overhear you, they might convince themselves they thought of it first.

When you pitch your ideas, a few things will happen.

1. You'll find out if anyone's interested. If nobody's interested, either come up with a better idea or a better way of phrasing your idea, and try again.
2. You'll hear about the competition: all the books and movies that your idea reminds people of. There may be some you haven't tripped over. You might want to check those out to see

if there's anything you can steal. But if one of them is recent and very similar, now might not be the time to write yours.

3. If they're interested, they may interrupt with "and he's really in love with her, right?" or "and he's really evil, right?" These reactions may give you good ideas, but even if they're off base, they're telling you the sort of things your audience expects to see. You shouldn't use every suggestion—that's your call, not theirs—but you should hear what people are saying.

If you're getting really positive responses ("Wow! That's a great idea! Did you really think of that by yourself?"), then you can go on to the next step.

Query Letters

Once you know that civilians are interested, it might be a good idea to see if motion picture–industry people would be interested. I'm making the heretical suggestion that you might want to send out your query letters *before* you spend all that time writing your script rather than *after*.

A query letter is a letter you send to all the development executives in the Hollywood Creative Directory, or if you're trying to get an agent, to all the agents in the Hollywood Agent Directory. (See http://www.hcdonline.com.) It is a one-page letter that explains what your screenplay is about and asks if they'd like to read it. As a development executive, I have read thousands of query letters. If you don't know people in show business, a query letter is the natural way to get your script to people who can do something with it. No one wants to read a screenplay unless he might be able to do something with it, so if someone reads your query and asks you to send him your screenplay, he thinks you have a hook.

Now this is a step you may not want to take just yet if you're anxious that people will steal your idea. You may want to wait until you have a plot outline that you can copyright at the Library of Congress (see chapter 9). But frankly, I don't think much stealing goes on in show business, except the kind of stealing I'm recommending you do. I'm going to make the movie for millions of dollars of other people's money; out of that budget, your script is probably at most a hundred thousand bucks. Why would I steal your script and get myself into a lawsuit? I can probably option your script for a few thousand bucks, but if I want to steal your idea, I have to hire a writer to do it, and he's going to cost fifty grand. Why wouldn't I just ask to read your script, option it, and then get it rewritten if I think it needs fixing?

Okay, here's the idea. When I read a query letter, I don't actually *know* that the writer has written the screenplay already. I send back the stamped, self-addressed card and forget about it until the screenplay shows up. That's because even the tiniest, credit-challenged company listed in the Hollywood Creative Directory gets ten or twenty queries a day. You have to read fifty of these letters to find one that sounds even vaguely promising.

As a development executive, you might think I'd be peeved if people used me for free market research, but actually, I wish they would. Then I'd be more likely to find a screenplay that I could do something with.

If you send out two hundred query letters and get back two responses, you may not want to waste your time writing the script. If you get back ten, you might want to write the script. If you get twenty, stop sleeping and write the damn screenplay already.

One side benefit of writing your query first, by the way, is that you may realize that you're focusing on the wrong aspects of your screenplay.

Suppose your hook is, say, "A marine biologist falls in love with a mysterious girl who turns out to be a mermaid." Suppose in writing your story, you find yourself concentrating on the adventures of the mermaid. If you took a look at your query, you might realize you were getting off track. Or, if your gut tells you you're on the right track, you could rewrite your hook ("A mermaid falls in love with a marine biologist") and see if people are still as interested.

This is not to say, of course, that you should reduce your screenplay to the simplicity of a query letter. You need richness and depth. You need surprises and twists and turns. I am only saying that if your concept doesn't query well, then either

1. you're not getting through to people how wonderful your idea is, and you need to rewrite your query, or
2. people don't think it's that wonderful an idea, and you need a better idea.

Either way, you can now fix the problem before you write the screenplay, rather than after.

How to Write a Good Query Letter

A good query letter says in one paragraph what the story's hook is, and asks if I'd like to read it. That's all it needs to do! The story sells itself, or it doesn't.

I spend about three seconds reading the average query letter. If it doesn't grab me by the third sentence, I'm on to the next envelope. Sorry, folks, I know that sounds philistine, but I've found through years of reading query letters and scripts that if a writer can't grab me in three sentences, the script is not going to be something I can get made into a movie. Even if the idea is good, if you can't write a clear one-page letter that draws me into your story, I assume your 115-page script won't draw me in, either.

If I am interested, of course, I read the rest of the letter, and think about it, and ponder whether the idea sounds like a good movie to me.

Here is a good query letter:

> Dear Mr. Epstein:
> I have just finished polishing *Mythic*, a thriller about a dragon that attacks an isolated Alaska oil rig community; the drilling has roused it from ancient sleep.
>
> Please let me know if you'd like to read the script. I would be happy to sign a release form if you have one, or I can have my agent send you the script.
>
> Thank you.
>
> Yours very truly . . .

See how short it is? But if there's any chance I might be interested in producing a contemporary dragon movie, I'm going to ask to read the script.

(In reality, *Mythic*, a superb script by Ehren Kruger, came to me through his gifted agent Valarie Phillips, not from a query letter. We optioned it. I wonder if the company still has it? Someone make this picture, please, I'm dying to see it!)

Here's another good letter, only slightly longer.

> Dear Mr. Epstein:
> Michael Eisner suggested I contact you about my new screenplay, *Life Is Beautiful*. It's a bittersweet drama about a Jewish man in 1943 Italy who tries to hide the horrors of the Nazi occupation from his young son by pretending it's all a big game. Although the historical events are sorrowful, the story is uplifting and even comedic.
>
> My grandfather survived the Holocaust himself, and I wanted to bring to life some of the almost unbelievable stories he told me.
>
> If you are interested in taking a look at the screenplay, please let me know. An SASE is enclosed for your reply. Thank you for your consideration.
>
> Very truly yours . . .

(An SASE is a stamped, self-addressed envelope.)

The above is a made-up query letter for the hit film *Life Is Beautiful*. I have no idea if anyone ever wrote a query letter for the film. Since the writer-director was also a comedy star in Italy, probably not.

If someone in show business recommended that you write, mention that first. If you or (especially) your screenplay won an award, mention that. Awards and recommendations are the two strongest things you can put in a query letter. They mean that someone other than you thinks this is a good screenplay.

If you have some direct personal experience that touches on the screenplay, or you've done in-depth research, it's worth mentioning.

By the way, your hook in a sentence or two is often called a logline. Think of it as the sentence that would describe it in *TV Guide*.

- A dragon, awakened from ancient sleep by oil drilling, attacks a small Alaskan town.
- A Jewish man tries to hide the horrors of the Nazi occupation from his young son by pretending they are all playing a big game.

SOME DON'TS

- Don't tell me why your script will have a big audience or satisfy a need. The producer or agent or exec reading your letter knows far more than you do as to whether there's an audience for your story or not, or at least thinks she does. Just tell the darn story. The story sells itself, or it doesn't.
- Some writers (*Babylon 5* creator J. Michael Straczynski, for example) claim you shouldn't state your hook, for fear of someone stealing it. Instead you should just talk about the genre it's in, and say something like "I have a screenplay consistent with the quality of your productions." I can't imagine why anyone would bother responding to a cover letter if there's no hook in it. I never have. Also, with many of the companies you'll be sending the script to, "consistent with the quality of your productions" doesn't speak that highly of your work.
- If there is a surprise ending, you may mention that there is one, but not what it is. Sell the sizzle, not the steak.
- Don't apologize in advance for wasting my time.
- Don't tell me five stories. It suggests you're just throwing stuff up against the wall and hoping something sticks. Write five letters, and send them to different people.
- Don't write your whole query as a scene from a movie. It's been done.
- Spelling counts. I will reject a misspelled query instantly, regardless of what it says. Spell-checking is not enough. If I see "whose" for "who's" or "it's" for "its," the letter is toast.

- If you've done something really exciting in your life ("I was an AP stringer in Beirut for five years, was kidnapped by Shi'ites, and escaped after 111 days of solitude"), then let me know. If you have done years of research, let me know.
- If you have written nine earlier scripts, it doesn't help you to mention it. People in show business have sheeplike tendencies; they trust other people's judgment more than their own. They will wonder, "If no one liked the other scripts, why should I like this one?" On the other hand, if you have written scripts that have been *produced*, or even optioned, let me know!
- If you are snail-mailing a query to someone who doesn't have e-mail, use a plain white regular business envelope for the query. Don't bother with a big manila or Tyvek envelope. Be sure to include a stamped, self-addressed postcard where I can check a box that says, "Send me the script."
- If it's an e-mail query, don't send a query letter as an attached document. Send it as plain text in the message body itself. Attached documents are a pain to locate on the hard disk and often show up unreadable. There is no excuse for attaching a one-page letter.

It's all about the story. No fancy paper, fancy formatting, colored type, or a picture of you; it just looks amateurish. You're not selling yourself as a graphic designer, you're selling yourself as a wordsmith. I'll take a letter neatly typed on a manual typewriter as seriously as I'll take one from a computer.

I don't think you should offer a synopsis. That's just encouraging them to ask for the synopsis instead of the script, which creates one more step where they can say no. They may ask for a synopsis. In that case, don't send them a synopsis, which tells them everything that happens; send them a pitch. A synopsis is a working document that details the plot. A pitch is a selling document that tells them the story. See chapter 2 for how to write a pitch.

By the way, don't follow up a query letter with a call or another letter or e-mail. It is a complete waste of time. If they wanted to read your script, they would have let you know, y'know?

How to Get Your Hookless Movie Made

Suppose you have a story that you're burning to tell, and it just doesn't have a hook.

There is one way to get your hookless movie made, and that is to make your story into something that has real value in the marketplace all by itself. If you can make it into a "property" that a producer can buy from you and sell to a studio, then your story may become a movie down the road. (You can also insist on writing it.) To do that, you need to make your story into a big success *in another medium*.

Let's suppose you want to tell the story of an aging midwestern housewife who falls in love with an aging photographer visiting to shoot the local covered bridges. There's no immediate hook. What will be compelling about the story is not its concept, but the way the characters are drawn and how they react to each other and change. Much of the story is internal—the housewife's emotions awakening as the photographer reminds her what it's like to love and be loved.

Do you write the screenplay?

No, you write a novel instead. In a novel, you can give the characters tremendous depth and richness. Moments can stretch over pages. Years can collapse into a sentence. You can get inside one or even several characters' thoughts. *The Bridges of Madison County* was made into a successful movie starring Clint Eastwood and Meryl Streep. But first it was a novel. In fact, first the novel didn't do well. It took months of lonely bookstore clerks reading and recommending the book for it to get onto the best-seller lists.

The screenplay didn't have to grab people; the novel had already done that. The screenwriter didn't have to get through the gatekeepers. He was hired to adapt the book when the project was already in progress. Everyone working on the project had the book to refer to as well as the screenplay.

Novels don't even need to be long to make the transition to movies; in fact they're probably more successful if they're short. Erich Segal's very short novel *Love Story* was supposedly written on a dare in a few weeks.

Suppose you have a story about some agents in the Immigration and Naturalization Service Division Six, who dress really cool and carry really cool guns and take care of the cool-looking *real* aliens who live and work unnoticed on Earth.

Do you write a screenplay?

Although this sounds like an attractive idea, it's not really a hook. If you're thinking of *Men in Black*, you know that the aliens and guns and agents really *were* cool. But if I got a screenplay on my desk with this concept, how would I know that anything would be as cool as the screenplay promised? Movies like *Alien* and *Dark City* and *Blade Runner*, although well written, owe much of their success to their compelling visual style.

Surprisingly, screenplays don't communicate visual style at all well. Theoretically they could, if you wrote pages of extremely detailed description. The problem is that the people reading your screenplay don't much like to read big chunks of single-spaced prose. They will blip right over them to get to the story, figuring that the director will probably ignore your description anyway, which he probably will. The feeling is that screenplays should suggest a *feel* for their visual world, rather than insisting on too many details.

If you are thinking of writing a movie like *Men in Black*, you might be better off publishing it as a comic book—which is how *Men in Black* got made. Many of the most visually stylish movies started out as comic books (e.g., *Blade*, *The Crow*, the *Batman* movies). Most successful comic series (e.g., *Fantastic Four*, *Spiderman*, *Ghost*, *Sandman*) and dozens of less successful ones are already under option to movie companies for precisely the reason that when you buy the rights to a comic book series, you not only buy characters and story ideas, you buy a whole visual world.

If your story does not have a clear hook, but you are dead set on making it into a movie, see if what attracts you to the story isn't something that is best conveyed in another medium. Novels are good for the inner lives of characters and the passage of time. Comics are good for visual style. Other media—plays, the Internet—may allow you to communicate stories successfully that might not make it onto the screen if written directly as a screenplay. Once you have a best-selling book, comic, hit play, or popular website, *then* you may be able to parlay your story into a movie.

As a general rule, if the story doesn't scream, "I wanna be a movie!" then it probably wants to be in a different medium, at least at first.

Crafty Screenwriting

Having read through this chapter, by now you may be pretty steamed. All this effort to find out if you should write your screenplay at all—whatever happened to the thrill of discovering your story as you write it, huh? Whatever happened to writing what you know, telling the truth, and not worrying about selling it until it's done?

That's not crafty screenwriting. This book is called *Crafty Screenwriting* because screenwriting is a craft, not an art.

Artists create to please themselves. A painter can put whatever he likes up on the canvas, and people can buy the painting or move on. The artist is free to do what he likes. So long as he can afford paint, canvas, and cigarettes, he's golden.

A craftsman creates to please himself *and his client*. A cabinet-maker makes cabinets to fit someone else's room and someone else's taste. But he tries to give the cabinets a sense of grace and beauty and truth. The drawers have to slide in and out easily, and the proportions and finish also have to feel right. A finely crafted cabinet says something about the room it's in, and gets your clothes off the floor.

A movie is a work of craft. Dozens or hundreds of people work on it, and it costs millions of dollars. It has to entertain. It has to make money. It also should carry a theme, a subtext, say something eternal in a new way. Or to put it another way, if you make it only to please others, it will have no soul and it probably won't please anyone. But if you write your movie only to please yourself, with no regard for other people, you are unlikely to get it made.

If your screenplay isn't delightful and doesn't give insight, it's a waste of trees. In theory everybody knows that, but too many screenplays, pale mimics of movies we've already seen, don't take you anywhere and don't give you any insight; they just introduce you to people you've seen a million times. That's hack work.

But the best movies are crafty. They teach, they delight, and they move us. They open up new worlds and they pack the audiences into the multiplexes. They have a great hook that gets them past the gatekeepers, and they have rich, compelling stories filled with fascinating characters and dialogue that rings true. They are commercial, but they don't sell out. The truth is the audience wants to see great movies, and a commercial movie is simply any movie that a lot of people want to go see.

As a crafty screenwriter, your job is to craft your screenplay so it satisfies all these criteria.

PLOT

> "Persons attempting to find a motive in this narrative will be prosecuted; persons attempting to find a plot will be shot."
>
> —Mark Twain, *Huckleberry Finn*

Telling Stories

Now that you've got your hook, you'll want to start writing your screenplay, or at least an outline for your screenplay. Right?

Writing things down is the last thing you want to do. Well, almost the last.

I am about to give you the most powerful tool I know for writing screenplays. If you come away with only one technique from this book, this tool is it. It has nothing to do with writing things down. Practically no one I know uses it, because it's hard to get yourself to use it. But there is no one single thing you can do that's more useful to your screenwriting.

Listening?

Tell your story.

Tell your story out loud, to friends, to coworkers, to your mom, to your kids.

Think up your story in your head, and tell it to anyone who will listen. Tell it over and over again, fleshing it out, making it deeper and richer and sadder and funnier with each telling.

If you must write down notes to yourself while you're inventing it, then you must. But then put your writing aside and tell the story out loud as often as you and your listeners can stand it.

Writing things down takes you away from your audience. When you tell a story out loud, it comes alive. It grows in the telling. As you tell it to each new person, you'll find better and more memorable ways to turn your simple hook into a good story.

When you write things down, they tend to freeze that way. That is, after all, the point in writing them down: so you won't have to remember them. But when you're remembering your story on the fly, you are free to reinvent every twist and turn in the story. In any creative process you must be willing to "kill your darlings." Writing your story down makes it harder to kill your darlings. When you reinvent your story each time you tell it, your darlings vanish painlessly.

When you tell your story, constant reinvention is not the only thing you get. You remember how pitching your story got you an immediate response to it? How you could immediately judge their interest by the look on their faces? When you tell your story, you immediately get a reaction to every part of it, not just the parts your reader sees fit to remark on. You see whether you're drawing your listener in or leaving her behind. You see if you're getting too complicated, or if your story is too simple, or not fresh enough.

You'll also hear it yourself. Sometimes you will get bored with what you're saying. Sometimes you yourself will get confused. At that moment you know your story is boring or confusing.

When you write a story down, the sheer force of your writing can carry you over narrative bumps. Your choice of words can sound convincing even when your story itself is unconvincing. But the words and sentences in your outline are irrelevant to the movie you eventually write from it. Only the plot and characters are actually going to survive into the movie. Even if you put dialogue directly into your outline (and I don't think you should), you'll almost certainly change it once you get to writing your scenes, because the kind of dialogue an outline needs isn't the same dialogue a scene needs.

One final benefit you get when you tell your story out loud is that it forces you to write a story so simple and clear and logical that you can remember how each step, each scene, each sequence, flows into the next.

A good movie is almost always a very simple story.

There are exceptions to this rule, of course. Robert Altman makes amazing films that intercut between multiple stories and multiple characters who may or may not ever run into each other. It would be practically impossible to tell the story of *Nashville* or *Short Cuts* out loud in the right order. (I'd be surprised if the scene order in the scripts has much to do with the eventual scene order of the edited picture.) But you would also be hard-pressed to get *Nashville* made today, unless you had Robert Altman attached to direct.

Telling a story out loud forces you to remember what comes next. If your scenes flow logically from one to the other, this won't be hard at all. If nothing is connecting one scene to another, it is going to be much harder for you to remember the second one. That means you'll have to come up with a more convincing way to connect the two, whether it's a logical connection (the murderer drops off the body, the police find the body) or a thematic juxtaposition (while Joe is boozing it up with the showgirl, his wife is in church praying).

Incidentally, in the movie industry, writers tell stories all the time, to try to get development money to go and write them. Sometimes the studios are commissioning screenplays; sometimes the development money dries up and they only want to buy spec screenplays. It's a cycle, sort of like the weather. There's no particular reason why some years you can sell a story and other years you need to write it first.

The guys who wrote *While You Were Sleeping* pitched their story for *five years* before they figured out that it should be the guy in the coma and not the girl. If they'd written the script first, what do you think the odds would have been that they'd have been willing to toss out the entire screenplay and rewrite it from scratch once they figured that out? They would have tried to hold on to the work they'd done and "improve it." Once you've written something down, you have a *thing*, and it is devilishly hard to dispose of things you're fond of. A story you tell is just a story, and you can change it around one way on Tuesday and change it back around on Wednesday.

So, telling your story out loud

- helps you flesh it out inventively
- gives you instant feedback from your listener
- gives you instant feedback from your own ear
- forces you to write a simple story

So why doesn't everybody tell stories? Partly it's a fear of being plagiarized. Partly it's because people have a notion that the "artist" should go off and create by himself and only present his work when it's a finished product; that the participation of other people in the process will only dilute his creative vision.

That may be true for novel and poetry writing. But a novel or a poem *is* the words on the page. Once you've read the words, you can judge the novel. A screen *story*, on the other hand, is *not* the words on the page. A screen story is the sketch for the screenplay, which is only a blueprint for the movie itself. You don't go ahead with a blueprint until you get the sketch right.

But I think the real reason writers don't like to tell their stories is that inventing a story is, for most writers, scary. You are taking something from your soul and heart and putting it out into the wild world, where it will get hurt. If you tell your story to people and they don't like it, you'll get rejected right there in the room. If you hand them some pages and go away, you don't have to see them yawn when they read it. They'll probably tell you it was "very nice" or "interesting."

Get over it, eh?

Okay, okay. Let's suppose you don't want to do this. (Can't say I didn't try.) Still, do as much as you can. Write down your story first. Then put it away and tell it to someone without looking at your pages.

Or, tell it to yourself in the car.

Or, write the beats of the story down on index cards, shuffle them, and try to put them back together in the best possible order, which may not be the order you originally had.

Or, write it out, then hide the pages and write it all over again from memory. Now put that away and rewrite it from memory again.

Every time you take a story off the page and put it on its feet, by writing it from memory, or better, by telling it to someone out loud, it will get smoother and smarter and more logical and fresher and, well, more like a good story. Isn't that worth trying?

Adapting True Stories and Novels

Exceptions aside, a movie is a short story. A movie has one central character (maybe two in a romantic comedy) who has one goal and a few obstacles to that goal.

That's why, incidentally, you can almost always tell a movie adapted from a beloved novel. A good novel tempts people to adapt it faithfully. There are scenes so well realized in the novel that you want to keep them in the screenplay no matter what. When you see a really enjoyable, beautifully realized scene that has no business in the movie, that has nothing to do with the protagonist achieving his or her goal, you can bet dollars to doughnuts the picture was adapted from a book.

A good novel uses all the power of its medium. It exposes the internal life of its characters. It also has an unlimited "budget." A novelist can write, "The valley was filled with ten thousand horses," and there they are, kicking up dust. A novelist can write, "The earth split in two like an orange, the rind of continents hanging loose and ragged in a vacuum." It doesn't cost a cent more than writing, "She went home. She had a lot to think about." A novel can expand and contract time. A moment can unfold over five pages. Five years might rush past in a sentence. A novel has room for dozens of characters, each fleshed out and made real by the pages of description the novel form allows. Each character can have his own point of view.

That's why great novels almost never make great movies. It's too hard to be ruthless to the scenes and characters we know and love. Trashy novels, on the other hand, often make great movies because no one feels obliged to keep anything that doesn't work. The creators can be faithful to the goal of making a good movie, rather than being faithful to a work of art created for another medium.

It's said that Hitchcock used to adapt a book by reading it once, and then never looking at it again while he worked with his writer on the script. If he couldn't remember a scene, it didn't belong in the movie.

This is an excellent technique to use with novels. Your objective is to figure out what the hook and theme of the novel are, and then rebuild the story from there. What is it about this book that's a *movie*?

The less you rely on the written pages of the novel, the more likely you will be faithful to the *story* the novel tells, rather than the scenes and dialogue the novel contains.

Novel dialogue is not good movie dialogue, anyway. By and large you are better off trying to re-create the flavor and tone of the dialogue as you remember it than trying to use the dialogue from the book. Certainly you shouldn't go back to the book for specific dialogue or scenes until you've created your outline. If you can stand the wait, it's even better if you don't go back to the book until you've written a first draft of the script. This will result in more work, but a much better screenplay.

One of the most powerful techniques for adapting books is forgetting. If you read a book and put it away for a while, whatever you can't remember obviously wasn't *memorable*, was it? And if it isn't memorable, it isn't essential to the story you're trying to tell.

Of course your audience will demand the memorable lines from the book. You don't have to disappoint them. Once you've got a first draft, you can go back and poach memorable lines:

```
                RHETT
    Frankly, my dear, I don't give a damn.
```

When you go from medium to medium, from novel to screen, you have to rethink everything. What might be a good scene in a drawing room, full of long descriptions of moments and long exchanges of words, may be boring in a movie if it's transposed directly onto the screen as is. The same scene might play better in a movie while the two characters are playing racquetball, or it might play better as a few choice phrases in a lot of silence.

> You want to be faithful to the story, and the spirit and tone of the book, which always means being at least partly unfaithful to what the author actually wrote.

When you're adapting a true story, you have an even greater burden. Novels have themes. You can use them when you're adapting the book into a movie, though you are not obliged to stick with the one from the book. But real life doesn't have themes. It just happens. It's your obligation to find the theme in the series of real events and tell the story based on that theme.

In a historical adaptation, you probably want to do a lot of research, absorb everything you can about the events you're writing about, and then lock up all your research materials while you write. Write from your theme and the broad outline of events, not from the particulars, or you'll get bogged down in them. Once you have your pitch, or better yet a whole script, then you can go back and see if you missed anything important. Bet you haven't.

If you want to say that something is A True Story, or Based on a True Story, then you have a higher standard of faithfulness to meet, especially where the historical events are well known, or precious to a group of people, or where they involve living people. If you are telling a story about Jesus Christ, and you depart from the Gospels, you will have to answer to a lot of angry Christians, and it may be tough to get your movie made. If you are writing a movie about Martin Luther King, it will matter to a lot of people that you tell the truth. If you get important facts wrong, they will get righteously angry. For that matter, if you get important facts right, they may get righteously angry if they are uncomfortable with those facts.

That's why I prefer to write and see movies that are inspired by a true story: less of a burden of accuracy, leaving more room for the story to take wing.

With most historical stories, it is up to you how faithful you want to be to the actual events. If you are telling a story about Ancient Rome, then no one will be harmed if you twist historical events out of shape. Anyone who's truly interested in classical history shouldn't be getting their facts out of a movie. Whether the real Cleopatra was beautiful or not is irrelevant to your story. If you're telling a love story, then she was beautiful. Sure, if you look at the coins she minted, she was a thick-necked, plump woman with a bumpy nose, but who wants to see a romance starring a woofer?

If your true story involves people who are still alive, be careful. Living people will sue you if you spread unfriendly lies about them. You're probably better off telling a story *inspired by* true events rather than *based on* true events. Then you won't need a lawyer by your side as you write. *The Insider* is a fascinating picture, but the writers had to be extremely careful about what they claimed happened when a tobacco industry insider blew the whistle on illegal practices by his company; fortunately much of the story is available in court records, as it is in the case of *Erin Brockovich*. Unless it is critical to you that you are telling a true story, why not tell a similar story with different names? Then you're free to write your movie however you like, staying faithful to your hook and your theme, instead of having to worry whether you've invaded someone's privacy or slandered them.

What's Wrong with Your Pitch?

The longer you can develop your story by sheer inspiration, by letting it just grow in your mind and soul, the fresher it will be. Stay away from analyzing it as long as you can. Eventually, though, you'll come to a point where something isn't working, and you're not sure what. Now is when you need to get critical.

There are some essential elements every screen story needs to work dramatically:

1. A main character
2. with a goal we care about—the *stakes*—
3. who is risking a lot—the *jeopardy*—
4. with at least one but ideally three basic *obstacles* in the way.

The essence of a movie, and I think of all drama, is this:

1. Someone wants something.
2. If he gets it, things will be better than they are, and
3. if he fails, things will be worse than they are.
4. But there are obstacles in his way.

What makes this a useful tool for analysis is that all of these elements have to be things we care about.

1. A main character

One way a movie story can fail is if we don't care about what happens to the main character.

Almost all movies are about one person. The most notable exceptions are

a. romantic comedies
b. ensemble pieces

Romantic comedies occasionally have a split point of view, where there really are two main characters, for example *Sleepless in Seattle*. One character may have more screen time, but enough of the movie happens completely outside the life of that character that you really can't say it's his movie alone. Both characters have goals, but what they are really looking for, even if they don't know it, is each other. Essentially you are writing two movies that interweave and finally come together at the end.

True ensemble pieces are rare, though many people try to write them. *The Big Chill* and *The Return of the Secaucus Seven* are good examples. In both movies, a bunch of old friends gather in a house for a weekend trying to make sense of themselves now that they've grown up, grown apart, and lost their youthful ideals. (At least I *think* that's what these movies were about.)

Ensemble pieces are hard to produce. Few directors have the knack for directing them, so there are few directors you can usefully attach to the project. You need a cast of actors who are, basically, all good. Ensemble movies are hard to keep balanced, both in the writing and the editing. They're even hard to market: you put a bunch of faces on the poster and what? Ensemble pieces apparently look easy, because I've had a lot of bad ones submitted to me. I can't recommend you write one unless you're really sure what you're doing.

Most movies have a central character. We have to care about the central character or we're not going to care about anything else that happens in the movie.

As I'll discuss in chapter 3, we don't need to *like* your central character. There are plenty of movies with unlikable protagonists. We just need to care what happens to him or her. We want Dorothy to get home to Kansas. We want the evil preacher in *The Night of the Hunter* to get his comeuppance. We want to know how the Roses in *The War of the Roses* resolve their differences. We don't necessarily want Oliver Rose to get back together with his wife. But we want to know how it turns out for him, either way.

We identify with a character either because he or his situation is familiar, or because we enjoy putting ourselves imaginatively in his situation. We identify with Dorothy because we can understand how a little girl in gray, lonely Kansas would want to go to a land over the rainbow. There's a lot of Kansas in everybody's life. We can also understand why a little girl would want to get home to her family, even if she's in wonderful, Technicolor Oz, because either we miss the family we had as a kid, or we miss the family we were supposed to have as a kid.

On the other hand, we identify with James Bond because it's fun to identify with James Bond. Don't you wish you could shoot your enemies, save the world, and run off with someone sexy? If you don't, I bet you don't go see Bond movies, either.

We might identify with a character because he is an extreme example of our darkest impulses. In *Falling Down*, Michael Douglas's character, known only as D-FENS, snaps. He's an unemployed, divorced defense engineer living at home with Mom, and his car is stuck in an impossible traffic jam. He gets out of his car and goes walking across L.A. on his way home, getting progressively more aggressive and ultimately violent, on his way to see his ex-wife and kid, with a goal that could be sweet or could be really, really bad. We all have felt like we could just *snap*. The film allows us to experience snapping, to see where that could lead, without suffering the consequences ourselves.

2. A goal (the "stakes")

Drama begins when somebody wants something. (This might be why so few protagonists in drama are Zen masters, but that's another book.)

The goal has to be something, again, that we *care about*.

The stakes might be internal. We might care about what happens because we care about the main character. Will Hamlet get his act together? Will Dorothy get home?

Or the stakes might be external—something we intrinsically care about. Will the Blues Brothers rescue the orphanage they grew up in? Will William Wallace free Scotland from the yoke of England? Will Austin Powers stop Dr. Evil from blowing up the world?

The best stakes are both internal and external. In *The Sixth Sense*, Dr. Malcolm Crowe (Bruce Willis) is trying to help Cole Sear (Haley Joel Osment) with his awkward problem of seeing dead people, but he's really trying to resolve his guilt over failing to help an old patient of his who committed suicide.

A story can fail because we don't *care about* the stakes. For example, if your main character wants to make a million dollars, who cares? It's hard to get excited about someone making a lot of dough. But if he wants to make a million dollars to save an inner-city hospital from going bankrupt, you might care about that. If he needs to make a million dollars because he owes money to the Mafia and they'll kill him, you might care about that, although some people might say it serves him right.

We might even care about our hero making a million bucks if the point is that he has messed-up priorities. In that case we *care about* his getting the money because we want him *not* to get the money. We want him to realize that he has a bad goal. But if the character is just a businessman who has the very reasonable goal of making money, it's not likely to get us involved in the story.

We don't have to necessarily be on the hero's *side*. We just have to be involved emotionally in what he's trying to do.

Tucker is the story of a car entrepreneur who has a dream of making a better, safer car. The film flopped commercially, partly because it didn't get us excited about whether he succeeded or not. Likewise, *Ed Wood* flopped because the hero was a dreamer who made very, very bad movies. We might have cared about him personally because he was such a weird guy, but the stakes were pretty much nonexistent. *Bugsy*, too, had a failure of stakes. Bugsy Siegel's vision was to put gambling casinos in the Nevada desert. We might come to care about him personally, because it's easy to love a dreamer, but it's hard to feel that he did the world a favor by creating Las Vegas.

The hero's goal helps us care about *him*. In *All That Jazz*, Joe Gideon (Roy Scheider) is a terrible person. He uses and abuses all the people around him. He's compelling because he's trying really hard to put on a great show, and he won't accept mediocrity in anything he does. In *Patton*, Patton (George C. Scott) is a son of a bitch, but he is trying very hard to kick the Nazis out of Europe. If we didn't care about the stakes (winning the war), we'd hate the guy.

The hero's goal may change during the course of the story. Dorothy wants to go over the rainbow, but as soon as she gets there, she wants to go home. We need to care about whatever goal she has *at the moment*.

If your hero is just trying to live a peaceful life until something happens, you better make sure something happens quick, because until the hero has a goal we care about, there's no drama. The stakes can be anywhere from personal (falling in love is high stakes) to universal (saving the world from a planet-killing meteor is high stakes), but there can be no part of a screenplay or movie where the main characters don't have anything important to gain.

3. Something to lose (the "jeopardy")

Poker is no fun unless you can lose your shirt, too.

Your protagonist has to be risking something we care about. In an action movie it's probably his life, in a drama it's probably his happiness, but it can be anything, provided we care about it.

In a movie about a guy who's in love with two girls, the stakes are: will he choose the right girl? The jeopardy might be that he will lose both of them. If the worst that can happen is he ends up with the other girl, then you're going to have to make us care—show us that ending up with the wrong girl is really terrible. Otherwise there's no real jeopardy, and the movie probably fails.

While we might care in a nonfiction book about a scientist trying to save us all from a deadly plague (stakes), if we're going to care about her in a movie, we want her to be risking something personal that we care about (jeopardy). She doesn't necessarily have to contract the disease herself (though someone on her team or in her family is practically guaranteed to get it before the movie's over). She could be losing her marriage because she's so devoted to her work. She might be defying conventional wisdom, trying unorthodox experiments that will get her run out of her profession if she's wrong. But she has to be risking more than "Darn, that didn't work. I guess I won't win that Nobel Prize after all."

If Hamlet was just risking being sent back to Wittenberg to finish his Ph.D., it wouldn't be much of a play. The stakes are: "Will Hamlet avenge the murder of his father?" The jeopardy is, "Will Hamlet get his butt killed?"

Jeopardy puts the hero in play. If the hero doesn't risk losing something we care about, the story fails.

4. Obstacles we care about

If there were no obstacles, the hero would just get what he wants in the first few minutes. There'd be no movie, and anyway, life isn't like that.

There are three basic kinds of obstacles.

a. external antagonist (or obstacle)
b. intimate opponent
c. tragic or comic flaw

You need at least one, but a good movie may throw all of them in the protagonist's way. Your job is to make the hero's job as hard as possible. If the hero can accomplish his goal easily, there's no movie.

If it's a romance, your most difficult task is to give the two lovers the best possible reason not to fall in love. In Jane Austen's day, being from different social classes was a good reason. In Shakespeare's, it was being from warring families. These days race and class are no longer tragic obstacles, but a love story between an Israeli and a Palestinian, or a Serb and a Croat, would be perfectly valid retellings of *Romeo and Juliet*, as was *West Side Story* in which Tony was white and Maria was Puerto Rican. There's no shortage of good reasons. In *Desert Hearts*, one of the lovers is a straight woman and the other is a gay woman; in John Woo's *The Killer*, one of the lovers is an assassin who accidentally blinded his future lover during a hit.

In life, most tasks get easier as you work on them. You have a problem. You work on it, and bit by bit you get things fixed until the problem is gone. In movies, you want the obstacles to get bigger and bigger as the story goes on, until the hero surmounts the biggest possible obstacle and the story's over. That's what keeps the tension of the movie constantly rising toward the climax.

As a rule of thumb, the hero finds himself at the end of the second act in the direst possible straits. He can't go to the police; in fact, they think he's a murderer. His allies have left him or have been killed. The antagonist is closing in on him. He is in the greatest personal danger, and any sensible man would at this point run like hell. Toward the end of the second act of *Star Wars*, Luke Skywalker's wise teacher Obi-Wan Kenobi goes down before the light saber of the evil Darth Vader, and the Death Star is heading for the rebel base.

Likewise in a romance, the end of the second act sees the two lovers, who were doing pretty well in the middle, torn apart from each other. This may be by external circumstance (Romeo's exile from Verona after killing Tybalt in *Romeo and Juliet*) or because one character feels the other betrayed him (*While You Were Sleeping*), but they are much worse off now than they were before.

The hero may defeat an external antagonist (slay a dragon, defeat an army), only to find that he has a much bigger internal problem to face (the maiden hates him, he can't deal with married life).

If the hero does find allies along his way, then the antagonist becomes much stronger. Dorothy makes it to the Emerald City with the help of her three friends, only to be sent to face the Wicked Witch of the West, who is much scarier than the Great and Terrible Wizard of Oz. *The worse you make things for the hero, the more exciting it is when the hero succeeds anyway.*

External Antagonist or Obstacle

In a mountain-climbing movie, this is the mountain.

In a war movie, these are the guys who are shooting at the hero.

In a monster movie, this is the monster. The hero is trying to prevent Godzilla from making it even harder to find a decent apartment in New York.

In a love story, this might be what keeps the lovers apart; or the antagonist might be the lover himself, as in *Beauty and the Beast*, *His Girl Friday*, and *The Runaway Bride*.

Like all the other essential elements, we have to *care about* the external antagonist or external obstacle. The megabudget 1998 *Godzilla*, written by Dean Devlin and director Roland Emmerich, failed because we did not care about the creature. It did not seem to have feelings. It was not a terrifying force of nature. It was not evil. It was not misunderstood. It was a rampaging lizard; it was a special effect. We had no feelings about it, neither terror nor pity, until the very end when the poor thing got tangled up in the Brooklyn Bridge and died.

By contrast, we have a lot of sympathy for the Frankenstein creature. Sure, in the classic 1931 picture written by John L. Balderston, Francis Faragoh, and Garrett Fort, he kills an innocent little girl. But that's because he wasn't brought up properly. We feel his pain and his rage for being cast out into the world without a mother or father. In the classic *King Kong*, we love the big ape. Sure, he's kidnapped Fay Wray, but who wouldn't?

On the other hand, in *Jaws*, the big fish scares the bejesus out of us. We want that thing turned into shark steaks. In *The Ghost and the Darkness*, the two marauding lions have crossed the bounds of nature and become malevolent, evil creatures. They're killing for fun, not food. We want them shot. Either way, whether we love the antagonist or hate it, we must care about it.

If you take the sheriff of Nottingham from two Robin Hood pictures, you can see how we care about each one for different reasons. In *The Adventures of Robin Hood*, the 1938 classic starring Errol Flynn, the sheriff is a cartoon: a cruel, effete aristocrat, wicked, greedy, and supercilious. In the 1976 film *Robin and Marian*, the sheriff is an educated man, an honorable knight, whose unpleasant duty it is to put down banditry. He understands why Robin has risen up in arms, but his duty is to the law. We hate one sheriff and sympathize with the other. But we care about both of them.

If your hero has an obstacle instead of an antagonist, we still have to care about it. If your hero is crossing the Antarctic, you have to find a way to make us feel what is grand and compelling about a lot of ice. In a movie about climbing Everest, you are going to have to make us care about a really big rock.

Intimate Opponent

An external antagonist may be enough. But you often want the hero to have someone on his side who is working at cross purposes to him. A classic intimate opponent appears in *Alien*. The antagonist is of course the alien. But someone is on board the ship who is not trying to destroy the alien; in fact he is under orders from the company to bring it back alive. That's the intimate opponent. In *Rambo* the external antagonists are the Vietnamese; the intimate opponents are the dastardly U.S. Army guys who don't really want Rambo to bring back the prisoners.

The intimate opponent can also be someone the hero is in love with. In *High Noon*, written by Carl Foreman, Gary Cooper's

Marshal Will Kane has to fight three gunmen who are coming to town to kill him. His wife, Amy (Grace Kelly), is a Quaker. She wants him to flee town and not fight. Although she is on his side, she wants to prevent him from accomplishing his goal.

Tragic or Comic Flaw

The protagonist has something in his psyche that gets in the way of his accomplishing his goal.

In *Hamlet*, wicked Uncle Claudius is the antagonist. But he alone wouldn't put Hamlet in deadly danger. It is Hamlet's indecision that destroys him, his lack of a killer instinct. In *Othello*, Iago is the antagonist, but if Othello were not a blunt soldier, blindly in love with his wife but willing to suspect her of adultery, it would be a short play. Consider what would happen if you switched the two characters. Treacherous Iago attempts to frame Hamlet's wife, Desdemona, for adultery. Clever Hamlet easily sees through his schemes and has him hanged. Meanwhile, Prince Othello comes home to discover that his uncle Claudius has murdered his father. Impulsive Othello whacks Claudius's head off with his broadsword in front of the entire court. "I'm king now. Any questions?"

In *All That Jazz*, Joe Gideon has a death wish that stops him from loving either his ex-wife or his girlfriend, and finally stops him from, well, living.

In *Annie Hall*, Alvy Singer has a deep inability to experience pleasure. He doesn't want to be with any woman who'd be willing to have a boyfriend like him. That gets in the way of him ending up happily with Annie.

In *Pride and Prejudice*, Darcy's pride and Elizabeth Bennet's prejudice are the principle obstacles to their romance. There are, in fact, no other really important obstacles, since Elizabeth Bennet's lack of money is no obstacle for rich Darcy, and they are both from acceptable families.

In a really good movie, the hero's tragic flaw is often in some way a reflection of his external antagonist or obstacle. It is only in surmounting his inward flaw that he can overcome his outward enemy.

In *Amadeus*, Salieri's tragic flaw is that he has just enough talent to know how far he falls short of Mozart's genius. That turns his love for music into a hatred of the greatest composer he will ever know. His limited talent is a pale reflection of Mozart's great talent.

In *Casablanca*, Rick wants Ilsa. He can't have her, because she belongs to Viktor Laszlo. Idealistic Laszlo, not the Nazis, is the obstacle. She has wounded Rick so badly he has become cynical. She can still belong to him—but only if he gives her back to Viktor Laszlo. He has to give up his cynicism in order to be able to do that. Rick's cynicism is a reflection of the idealism of the obstacle, Laszlo.

Is it an accident that in *Cast Away*, the hero has isolated himself from his girlfriend by his obsession with saving time at his job, only to find himself isolated on an island where he has nothing but time? On the island, he has to confront both his external loneliness and his internal loneliness. It is his willingness to die to get back to human contact that saves him from his island.

It is not any sort of *requirement* to have the hero's main flaw reflect the external antagonist. *The Terminator* is a great monster movie, and the hero, Sarah Connor (Linda Hamilton), has no flaws as such. She's just an ordinary woman trying to survive a killer robot from the future. But it can add a layer to your story.

In real life, people often have the virtues of their vices and the vices of their virtues. Napoleon destroyed himself by recklessly invading Russia. But if he had not been a risk-taker, he would never have become more than a captain of artillery. Christopher Columbus stubbornly insisted, against all the smartest scientists of his day, that he could sail thirty days west and hit Japan. He was wrong, but if he had been less pigheaded, he would never have discovered America.

Don't be afraid to give your own hero the vices of his virtues. Even his strengths may be things his enemies can turn against him.

One last thought: particularly in a drama, the protagonist may be doing exactly the wrong thing to achieve his goal. A kid who feels his family has turned against him may act out in ways that does turn his family against him. A lover who feels she's losing her beloved may reject him before she can be rejected. In essence this is a tragic or comic flaw in action. Your character has to be striving to achieve a goal, but he doesn't have to be going about it in a rational way; in fact, the more logical a character is, the less dramatically interesting.

ALL THE ELEMENTS, ALL THE TIME

Your movie should have all these elements from the very beginning. The only essential element that can come in later in the story is the hook. (The hook must come by the end of the first act, but that's only another way of saying that until the hook has come in, you haven't really finished your setup.)

From the very beginning of your movie, you need a main character with a goal and obstacles to that goal. The goal may change when the hook comes in. But until the character has a goal and obstacles, there's no drama. Until there's drama, there's no movie.

For example, if you have a movie in which the hero's daughter is kidnapped, don't spend ten minutes showing us how perfect the hero's life is. It may be a happy life, but for us to become involved in the story, give our hero something he's trying to do—maybe something he's busy doing while his child is being kidnapped. If your movie has a couple being chased by terrorists, don't show us that they have a perfect relationship and life couldn't be better. Then we won't be drawn into caring about them. Who wants to watch two people tell each other how much they love each other? Instead, show that they have a problem between them that they're dealing with, that has nothing to do with the terrorists.

I always want to know, *"What would be the movie if the movie didn't happen?"*

What makes the movie happen is sometimes called the "inciting incident." The inciting incident might happen in the first reel. In *Witness*, a man is murdered in the bathroom; a little Amish boy sees the killer leave the bathroom. It might happen before the movie begins: in a war movie, the inciting incident is essentially that the war began. It might even happen at the end of the first act. In *The Wizard of Oz*, Dorothy is trying to prevent Elmira Gulch from taking away her little dog, Toto, when a tornado picks her and Toto up and brings them to the Land of Oz. It's not really important what the inciting incident is; that's for theorists. What's important is that if there were no tornado, there would still be drama. We might not want to pay money to see the movie, but there would be drama.

In *Casablanca*, Rick is trying to run a bar in Vichy-run Casablanca when Ilsa shows up. If Ilsa never showed up, Rick would be trying to figure out what to do with the precious letters of transit, and trying to forget Ilsa.

In *Star Wars*, before the 'droids show up, Luke Skywalker is trying to figure out how to get the hell away from his aunt and uncle's boring old farm.

In *Die Hard*, Bruce Willis is coming to spend Christmas with his estranged wife. Lemme tell ya, he's lucky those terrorists took over the Fox Tower, because otherwise, between him and his wife, it could have gotten ugly.

The protagonist's initial goal may not necessarily be a driving goal. She might just be trying to finish college or find a boyfriend. But the more compelling her goal is originally, the more compelling she probably will be as a character. Also, the more urgent her original goal is, the more we value her later goal, since it's obviously more important than the goal she dropped.

I find that when a story is failing dramatically, if I come back to these essential elements, one of them is almost always missing or not working. Whether they are up front or cleverly hidden, a good story will always have them.

Theme

The theme of your story is the underlying, universal human question your story deals with. Your main character, stakes, jeopardy, and obstacles give us reasons why we care about how the story turns out. The theme gives us a reason why we *should* care. Having a theme isn't essential to making a good or even a great movie. But if you want your movie to have a lasting effect on people—if you want it to be more than sheer popcorn entertainment—then you need a theme.

For example, *Blade Runner* is a well-crafted story about a cop assigned to kill a band of artificial human beings who are, for their part, trying to escape the invisible shackles put on them when they were created. They have, in some ways, a much greater appreciation for life than he does. The theme is "What does it mean to be human?" (In the director's cut, we even get a hint that the cop himself is an artificial human.) We come away with an adrenaline rush and some interesting ideas to talk about.

A movie doesn't have to make a point to have a theme. A film might have a main character drawing one moral and a secondary character drawing an entirely opposite moral. It might undercut its own point. *A Clockwork Orange* apparently says free will is a good thing, but it also shows its main character so violently abusing his free will that you wonder if free will is such a good thing after all. What gives a picture a theme is that the major scenes in it touch in some way on the question the theme raises. It doesn't have to actually answer that question.

You don't need to have a theme to have a great popcorn movie. *Alien* is a well-crafted story about a bunch of human beings in danger of being eaten by a monster. While we find out that an evil corporation put them in danger, the movie isn't really about the danger of evil corporations. It's about people trying not to get eaten by a giant bug. We come away from the film with just the adrenaline rush.

That's fine. I've seen *Alien* four or five times. Scares the bejesus out of me every time.

Here are some themes:

Jaws	Nature is still bigger than you
The Sixth Sense	Guilt versus redemption
Chinatown	Decency is not enough to defeat corruption
Mr. Smith Goes to Washington	Decency *is* enough to defeat corruption
Braveheart	Freedom is worth dying for
Modern Times	Progress can destroy people's lives

Traffic	Drug laws are more evil than drugs
The Godfather	Family is the most important thing
Star Wars	Faith can defeat empires
Annie Hall	Relationships are painful, but we need 'em
Memento	Memory versus reality
A Clockwork Orange	Free will versus sin
The Big Chill	How do you deal with the loss of ideals?
Twelve Angry Men	Truth is more important than anger
Rashomon	Truth is relative
Almost Famous	Fame is addictive
American History X	Hatred kills
The Treasure of the Sierra Madre	Greed kills
The Matrix	Humanity matters more than progress
2001: A Space Odyssey	I must stop taking hallucinogenic drugs

If you are working with a theme, then try to make each scene tell a truth about the theme. All the main characters, with their goals and their flaws, should in some way reflect the theme. If your theme is redemption, then some characters start out fallen and are redeemed, some are fallen and are never redeemed, and some are already redeemed when the story begins. Your theme comes to light in their conflict with one another.

Themes work best when they underlie the story. They get distracting when they come to the surface. If you want to say something, choose a story that makes your point just by being the story it is. For example, if you want to say that greed is bad, tell a story in which greed destroys people's lives. You might tell a gold rush story, or a story about a yuppie who destroys his marriage and abandons his children while making his first million. If you want to say that greed is good, tell a rags-to-riches story about a poor man who comes up with a brilliant idea and becomes rich.

Let the story take care of the theme. You don't need characters to talk about the theme. In *Fatal Attraction*, the audience sees that terrible things are happening to Dan Gallagher (Michael Douglas) because he cheated on his wife. No one has to extract the moral for the audience: "Hey! Don't cheat on your wife!"

"If you want to send a message," as Samuel Goldwyn was wont to say, "call Western Union."*

Surprise and Inevitability

Your plot needs to have two apparently contradictory qualities. It has to feel *inevitable* but it has to *surprise*. A story that doesn't surprise is boring. A story that doesn't feel inevitable feels like a cheat.

In essence, the story has to be surprising as we experience it, but then when we look back on it from the ending, it all makes sense, and we realize that the ending we just lived through is the true ending to this story.

A story is unsurprising, obviously, when the audience feels they know how the story is going to go, and it goes that way. A story fails to seem inevitable when the climax of the movie feels like it is just one of many possible endings. The hero survives not because he should, but because the screenwriter listened to the marketing department, or had too much Prozac. The hero dies tragically not because the story had to go there, but because the screenwriter hates life, or is French.

You can have both inevitability and surprise because surprise is mostly about *how* and inevitability is about *what*. We know that James Bond will survive falling off the cliff (*what*), but we don't know it's because he has a parachute in his backpack (*how*). We know, somewhere in the back of our mind, that Blanche Dubois's fragile

*A company that provided a primitive form of e-mail.

courtliness will come to a terrible end in the working-class apartment of Stanley and Stella Kowalski (*what*), but we don't know what Stanley will do to her to send her over the edge (*how*).

A story fails to surprise when you have not been inventive enough. If you're telling your story out loud (and you are, right?), you'll know when you're not being surprising. For one thing, your friends will stop you and say, "Let me guess. This happens," and then they tell you your ending before you can. For another thing, you'll be bored. As veteran screenwriter Jeffrey Boam says, "If I'm bored, the audience will be."

A story fails to be inevitable when you are trying too hard to force it into the shape you wanted when you first set out to write it. A story is an organic thing. It wants to grow in a certain direction. You can't just bend the branches the way you want them to go. If it's growing in the wrong direction you have to repot it, or change the direction the light is coming from. In other words, if something is wrong at the end, you may have to change the beginning. Change the beginning, and the right ending will come naturally.

LUCK

Real life is full of luck. Good luck: that girl you had a crush on in college turns out to be living next door to you after twenty years, and coincidentally, you both just got divorced. Bad luck: your car breaks down in the wrong part of town on the day you lost your mobile phone.

Luck hurts inevitability, so it's risky to have your plot depend on luck. However, many stories depend on luck. For example, in *Casablanca*, it is luck that Ilsa Lund walks into Rick's bar: "Of all the gin joints in the world, she had to walk into mine." Well, sure, Rick, there wouldn't be a movie otherwise, would there?

You generally want only bad luck for the hero and good luck for the antagonist or obstacle. You can, for example, have the two lovers just miss meeting each other, as in *Sleepless in Seattle*. You can have the hero become accidentally separated from his partner, allowing the villain to kill his partner. You can always give the villain a lucky break, just to make life harder for the hero.

If the hero gets a break, it's because of his hard work, not luck. If someone saves the hero's life at the last moment, it's because he asked them for help before, and they said no at the time, but they thought about it and came back just in time. *The bad guys get all the lucky breaks.* If the villain makes mistakes, they are forced errors, because the hero is harrying him right and left and he blows his cool.

In science fiction, it is always okay to come up with a pseudoscientific reason why the hero can't do what he wants to, but you don't want to give the hero a pseudoscientific way to solve his problem. Generally the hero should have to come up with a clever solution that would work in our world. Similarly, in fantasy, if the invincible dragon has a secret weak spot, you have to tell us early on; but if you want the dragon to escape, you can always give him a secret magical defense.

> The further along you are in your story, the less can depend on luck.

You can safely have a coincidence in your first act. Many good movie premises depend on luck. In *It Happened One Night*, coincidence throws newspaperman Peter Warne (Clark Gable) and runaway rich girl Ellie Andrews (Claudette Colbert) together on a bus trip to New York. In *The Fugitive*, Dr. Richard Kimble is headed for life imprisonment when the prison bus gets smashed by a train, allowing him to escape. In *Shallow Grave*, the mystery tenant dies, leaving the other roommates with a briefcase full of cash. In *Chicken Run*, the hens are living in a prison camp until an American flying chicken falls out of the sky. In *Deliverance*, the main characters stumble into some very nasty inbred locals. Complications, as they say, ensue.

In the second act, you can have minor coincidences: The hero and villain meet each other by accident. But they're both looking for the same thing, so it's no surprise they're in the same place. The only accident is one of timing.

In romances, it's practically traditional to have someone accidentally overhear half of a conversation around the end of the second act. They utterly misinterpret it, and what has been a growing romance becomes a disaster as we go into Act 3. (See *The Wedding Singer*, *Shrek*, etc.)

In the third act, everything should flow sensibly from the story you've been telling up to this point. Any coincidence is likely to seem like a cheat.

The Myth of Three-Act Structure

There's one thing you *don't* need to get supercritical about.

A lot has been written in screenwriting books about three-act structure. The basic idea of drama having three acts goes back to Aristotle. In the beginning, or first act, you get your hero up a tree. In the middle, or second act, he tries to get out of the tree, but ends up even farther up the tree. In the finale, or last act, he climbs down or falls out of the tree.

That much is true, but it's not saying much. It's pretty difficult to write a story without a beginning, middle, and end.*

The terms are useful shorthand, that's all. "First act" is a convenient way to talk about the beginning of the story without someone having to ask, "Do you mean the beginning shot, the beginning scene, the first reel, the first half, what?"

For the purposes of this book,

First Act = the beginning
Second Act = the middle
Third Act = the end

*This is my beef with philosophy, by the way. It seems to break down into two basic kinds of statements: obvious and preposterous. But that's another book.

A certain popular screenwriting author claims confidently that your first act should be twenty-five to thirty-five pages long and that your second act should end around page 90. At the end of each act is a turning point where the hero's situation drastically changes, his desires change, the flow of the story turns. There is also a flex point around page 60 where the situation intensifies.

Horse puckey.

A lot of high-concept off-the-rack thrillers have hard act breaks. The turning points leap up and bite you in the butt. It's moreover true that in the majority of movies, the story is going full steam by no later than the first quarter, things get complicated in the middle half, and everything comes together for a climax in the last quarter.

But only maybe half of all truly great movies have three distinct acts, and in some of those you have to stretch to figure out where exactly the act breaks are. Where are the act breaks in *A Hard Day's Night*? *All That Jazz*? How about *Spartacus*? *Forrest Gump*? *Apollo 13*? *Annie Hall*? Or the superbly written *Wild Things*, which has about five or six major twists?

Or how about *The Wizard of Oz*? Does the third act begin when the wizard sends Dorothy after the Wicked Witch of the West? Or when Dorothy gets home to Kansas? Or when the Wizard turns out to be a fraud? What difference does it make to the story? Who cares where the third act begins?

In *The Fugitive*, written by David Twohy, does the second act begin when Dr. Richard Kimble escapes the prison bus, or when he escapes the following manhunt? When does the last act begin? When he discovers the one-armed man? When he confronts Dr. Charles Nichols at the medical convention? When Marshal Samuel Gerard begins to realize that Dr. Kimble is innocent?

Who cares? Suppose you could decide where the third act begins. How would that help you understand how the story works?

Many thrillers set up the main character in a short first act, often no more than a precipitating incident. The hero is hounded through a huge second act that keeps picking up the pace. In *Alien*, there's a well-defined first act that gets the alien on board the ship. Likewise, the first act of *Predator* gets the fireteam into the jungle. But from then on, a shrinking band of humans is fighting an alien creature. You can say the third act begins when the monster kills off the hero or heroine's last ally, or when the hero or heroine finally starts to turn the tables on his or her enemy, but then you are only finding a second turning point because you are looking for one.

A story can fail in its beginning, its middle, or its end, but knowing where you are will not necessarily help you fix the story. I believe that three-act structure is overrated. The important thing is to tell a good story and deliver the goods on your hook.

A story can certainly fail structurally. For example, in *The Arrival*, the hero discovers the truth about the aliens, and enters their big secret headquarters in the jungle, in the middle of the movie. Nothing after that is going to be as interesting, so in essence the movie's over before you get to the third act. It would have been better if the story were rewritten so that the big discovery happened at the end of the movie, or if there was an even bigger discovery at the end.

But this isn't a question of three-act structure. It's a question of giving away too much in the middle and not holding enough back for the end. Worry about whether your story is taking too long to get off the ground, or if you're introducing new characters so fast that we don't get to know them well enough. Worry about whether your middle drags, or gets too complicated, or if you are running out of complications and your hero is going to defeat his enemy too quickly and easily. Worry about whether your ending feels rushed, or if you've got more than one scene that feels like an ending.

But don't worry about having three distinct acts. You may find that a five-act structure works better for your screenplay. It worked for Shakespeare. You may have a true story that just naturally breaks down into four acts. Squeezing it into the Procrustean bed of three-act structure is just going to mangle it.

Just tell a good story that keeps people interested.

Note, however, that if you are turning in an outline to a producer, he will probably want to know where the act breaks are. Pick some plausible page numbers or events and humor him.

FLASHBACKS

One film school bugaboo is that you're not supposed to use flashbacks anymore—this, even after the huge success of Best Picture of 1994 *Pulp Fiction*, which is mostly flashbacks, not to mention *Memento*, which is told entirely in reverse, not to mention Best Picture of 1943 *Casablanca*, which has a long flashback sequence. Flashbacks are in fact one of the most powerful tools of the cinema. The problem is that they are sometimes abused in a cheesy way.

For example, your character is burying his best friend. We get a cheap replay of all the funny or poignant moments in the movie where the two were together. Do we need it? Or can you trust your actor to communicate that through his sadness? Don't use a flashback to communicate something that the film can communicate without one. Instead, give the actor a memento of the best friend to hold in his hand as he weeps, or give him a powerful eulogy to say, or just let his silence speak for him.

But don't be afraid of using flashbacks in a clear and coherent way. They can communicate things no amount of talk or linear storytelling can. In general, only your central character should have a flashback. Even if the story is not told 100 percent from the literal point of view of the central character, it is his or her story. Giving someone else a flashback may wrench us out of our identification with the central character. But like all rules, this one is made to be broken when you need to.

Writing Down Your Story

When you can't possibly make your story any better without writing the screenplay, it's time to write it down. Phew. Never thought you'd get here, did you?

If you've told and retold your story like I asked you to do, writing your story down should be almost anticlimactic. All you have to do is write down what you've been telling people. Don't try to fancy it up. Just write down what you were saying out loud.

(If you chickened out on telling your story out loud, then the process of writing down your pitch will involve more back and forth. You'll write down your story and show it to people. They'll comment, you'll revise. Then you show it to some other people, get comments, and revise. Repeat as needed. Unfortunately, when people read your story for the second time, they don't invest so much energy in it. They're jaded. Don't show anyone a new draft unless you've changed at least 33 percent since the last time you got them to read it.)

You now have a pitch. It might be three to six pages long, single spaced. If it's less than that, it's probably not very carefully worked out, and if it's longer than that, you are going into too much detail for a pitch.

In days of old, you could bring a pitch to a producer and get paid to write the script. These days you have to be rather well connected to get development money at all in the United States, let alone money to write a script based on a measly pitch.

(If you live in Canada or Europe, there may be government dough for turning your pitch into a script. For example, Telefilm Canada funds the development of scripts by Canadian citizens and landed immigrants. Check out the Internet, and *also* call the government agency in question, in case its website is not up-to-date.)

The Step Outline

Your written pitch is your story on paper.

It isn't, however, the best thing to write your script from. A pitch will often use tricks of storytelling that you'll have to get rid of before you write the script. For example, you can use shorthand to describe a series of scenes. Where you intend to show a romance growing, you might say, "The more she fights him, the more he falls in love with her." You might tell the story out of chronological order. If the hero is racing to save the heroine, and the heroine is struggling to escape, in the pitch you might tell most of the hero story and then say, "While he's been doing that, here's what she's been up to," and then tell the heroine story. In the movie, you'd cut back and forth between the two parts of the story. Or, you might bring up a minor detail only at the point where it becomes important: "By the way, all along they've been wearing these necklaces that, they find out now, fit together perfectly. They're brother and sister!"

Now you have to replace all this handwaving and put all your events in their correct order. You'll want to turn your pitch into a *beat sheet* or *outline*.

A beat sheet breaks the story down into about forty to sixty steps or beats. Each beat contains a dramatic confrontation or revelation of some sort. A beat will usually expand into a scene about 2 or 3 pages long, making the screenplay about 100 to 120 pages long. A long scene might contain more than one beat, when, for example, the revelation in one beat creates a new confrontation, or a beat might also require a short sequence of scenes to pay off.

Depending on how much work you want to do before you start writing your screenplay (or "writing pages"), you may also want to write an outline. An outline takes the beat sheet one step further. While a single beat might move from the outside of a store to the inside, and then out the alley, if it's following two people having an argument, the outline specifies every single location you're going to shoot. It uses screenplay-style sluglines `(INT. SHOCKLEY'S ROOM – DAY)` to establish where and when the scene actually takes place.

Here is one paragraph of a pitch for a hacker movie:

> With his palmtop computer, Archer injects a computer virus into the power grid. Firewall's lights are flickering wildly. Archer and Zuma bluff their way into the garage. Archer finds what he's looking for. It's an experimental self-driving Bronco with a computer you can talk to and video-camera "eyes." Maybe he doesn't know how to drive, but he can get the car to drive *for* him. Archer hacks into the Bronco's computer and starts it up.

Obviously there's a lot of handwaving here. "Archer and Zuma bluff their way into the garage" could be a five-minute sequence or a fifteen-second scene. In fact, it's a scene. This paragraph of pitch might expand into a beat sheet as follows:

12. With his palmtop computer, Archer injects a computer virus into the power grid. Firewall's power starts to fail, lights flickering wildly.
13. With the electronic door locks dead, Archer and Zuma escape into the corridors, but they run into Roarke. Archer convinces Roarke that Colonel West has ordered them to the basement to boot up the backup security systems.
14. Archer finds the experimental self-driving Bronco in the garage. He hacks into its electronic brain and starts it up.

An outline would make sure we knew where this was happening, and what time of day:

```
12. INT. ARCHER'S ROOM – NIGHT

Archer uses his palmtop to inject a computer
virus into the power grid. When the electronic
locks fail, he and Zuma beat it out of there.

13. INT. CORRIDORS – NIGHT

Archer and Zuma race down the corridors, but
run into Roarke. Archer fast-talks Roarke into
believing that Colonel West has ordered the
two of them to go to the basement and boot up
the backup security systems.

14. INT. GARAGE – NIGHT

Archer finds the experimental self-driving
Bronco. He hacks into its electronic brain and
starts it up.
```

The two seem quite similar. But with an outline, you have to specify the place and whether it's day or night, and that may reveal holes in your story logic. You may suddenly realize that you have your hero meeting his girlfriend in New York when he's already flown to Paris. You may realize that you've got two terrifying night scenes of your hero running from the hounds of hell, but there's one brief scene at the Department of Motor Vehicles in between them. Government offices are only open during the day. What's your hero doing during the rest of that day, relaxing in the tub with the crossword puzzle? "Plotholes" like these are surprisingly easy to miss in a beat sheet, but easy to catch in an outline.

You don't *need* an outline, of course. I've written screenplays based on step outlines and some based on beat sheets. But I find that with a beat sheet, you work out a few more stupid bugs in the story than with a step outline.

Oddly, the term *treatment* is often used, especially in contracts, but it has no clear definition. In my book, if a producer is asking for a treatment before he buys your project, give him a pitch; if he's paying you to write it, give him an outline. And this is my book, after all.

Reading Your Step Outline

As you develop your step outline from your pitch, you are turning the twists and turns of your story into a linear procession of steps. In this process, you have the opportunity to take a hard look at each step and each scene.

Can I get rid of this beat?

Is there something missing between these two beats?

Can I set this scene someplace more interesting or more appropriate?

At this point in the story, what if something else entirely happened? What would that be?

Remember, anything that seems at all familiar to you will seem five times as familiar to the audience. They've seen at least as many pictures as you have, and they're not paying as close attention as you are. So if anything seems even vaguely like what they've seen before, they're going to forget about the minor differences and decide it's the same thing.

What Next?

When you're sure you have absolutely the best story you know how to create that delivers the goods on your hook, you're ready to move on to writing the screenplay.

Whoopee!

Once you have a detailed beat sheet, writing the screenplay is a simple matter of expanding the steps into scenes with action and dialogue.

Ha! Simple? Just as when you adapted your pitch into a step outline or beat sheet, as you go from beat sheet to screenplay you will find that some story ideas that sounded great before just don't work when they're taken to the next level. You'll discover that you don't need certain beats or scenes or characters, and you can just plain cut them out. You have to be willing at every point to discard anything that doesn't work and, if necessary, come up with something more convincing. You'll probably be revising your beat sheet all the time you're writing your script.

In crafty screenwriting, nothing is ever finished. Every draft is a first draft. You only stop writing when you run out of ideas on how to make it better, or when they go and shoot your movie.

3

CHARACTERS

Writing compelling characters is one of the toughest challenges of crafty screenwriting.

- Characters appear to be people who are swept up in the events of your story.
- But they really are only the raw materials you use to tell your story.

Everything that a character does should grow naturally out of that character's personality—his dreams, her fears, his flaws. Your characters should have the breath of life. But they exist *only* to tell your story, and any moment they're not forwarding your story, they're slowing the movie down.

Characters who do the things you need them to do, but who don't seem real, are called flat or functional. You need to put the breath of life in them.

Characters who seem alive and exciting, but who don't move the story forward, are useless characters. They may bring life to the scenes they're in. They may even seem to be the only thing going for your screenplay, but really they're just getting in the way of the story. It's awfully difficult to start writing with a character and no plot, but if you have a plot, you can figure out from it what characters you need, and breathe life into them as you write. (In television it's often the reverse: someone developing a series thinks up some wonderful characters and a promising situation, and then comes up with one plot after another in which to involve them.)

Reverse Engineering Your Characters

Writers discover their characters by many secret paths, all of them perfectly fine if they work. Most writers, I suspect, cast about in their minds for the right characters and see what they can do with them. If their instincts are good, this works out.

A crafty way to do it is by reverse engineering. If you know what your hook is, you can figure out what characters you need to tell your story. You can begin with the protagonist and the antagonist (if you have one) and build your cast from there. Each new character comes from your hook, and from the characters you have already invented, until you've got your cast.

This approach may be screenwriting heresy because it feels unnatural. It *is* unnatural, but so is storytelling. Stories are artificial: they are made by artifice. I suspect that many writers who use more natural methods are really doing the same thing I'm doing; they're just pretending they're not. But in order for a technique to be a tool, you have to know how to use it explicitly.

Your hook will generally give you your protagonist, or hero. If your picture has an antagonist, or villain, the hook will usually give you the antagonist, too. Ideally, the antagonist (or villain) is in some ways a reflection of the hero. They can be two sides of the same coin. Batman and the Joker are both angry, violent men who dress strangely and pursue their own ends outside of the law. Batman just happens to be fighting for good and the Joker for evil. They can be opposites, as in any number of action movies where a weary, decent, battered, intuitive common man fights a cool, calculating, amoral, upper-class villain (*Die Hard*, *Who Framed Roger Rabbit*). As Othello is passionate, Iago is coldly cunning.

Your protagonist and antagonist ideally express different aspects of your theme. If your theme is, for example, redemption, then your hero redeems himself; your villain remains unredeemed. If your theme is duty, then your hero might sacrifice himself for duty's sake, while your villain uses duty as an excuse to do what he wants to other people.

Many screenplays have either a love interest or a buddy; who else is the hero going to explain himself to so we can understand what's going on in his head? Again, the hero and his beloved or buddy should be in tension with each other. If one's physical, the other's mental. If one's prim, the other's rough. If one's insanely brave, the other has a proper respect for his or her life. In drama, opposites attract. You never want two people agreeing with each other for a whole scene, so it's better if they don't get along, at least until the very end.

A love interest is someone for the hero to fall in love with. The love interest may be the second lead, right alongside the hero throughout the movie. She may be a minor character put there for the sake of having a little romance among the gunshots. (For commercial reasons, most heroes in theatrical motion pictures are men, so the love interest is usually a woman. In TV movies, because the audience is more female, the hero is typically a woman and the love interest is typically a man.) If you're writing for mainstream movies, you generally do want a love interest if your hook will allow it. A movie whose main characters are all men or all women has a strike against it in the marketplace. On the other hand, don't twist your story out of shape to have a love interest. If you're writing a World War II submarine movie, don't twist your story into knots trying to put a woman on the sub.

The love interest or buddy can and often should become an obstacle for the hero; that is, she or he sometimes functions as an intimate opponent, as seen in chapter 2. It's also good if she resonates in some way with the theme. If the theme is redemption, as above, she might be someone who is already redeemed, or she might be what the hero will win in order to be redeemed, or she might be what the hero has to give up in order to be redeemed.

If the hero is investigating or entering a world he doesn't know about, you'll need an explainer: someone who can tell him and the audience what's going on, what's at stake, who the players are. The explainer may be the love interest, especially if the hero is coming from the outside into her world (*The Big Sleep*, *Witness*), or he may be the mentor (*Star Wars*).

You may want your hero to have a sidekick; your villain might have an evil sidekick. A sidekick is often the hero or villain written small. If the hero is brave, his sidekick is a coward. If the villain is grand, his sidekick is petty. A good sidekick can express those human feelings that the hero's supposed to keep locked inside. An evil sidekick can falter, or even betray the villain.

There would be no point to making a list of all possible types of characters. Characters aren't types. A sidekick can be a love interest and an explainer. My point is only that you can work backward from your hook. Then all your major characters (1) arise out of your hook or your theme and (2) are reflections in some way of your protagonist or your antagonist, your hero or your villain.

Think of the characters as notes in a chord. The hero is the dominant. The other principal characters are the third, the fifth, the seventh, and so forth. They express different shadings of feeling, but they are all in harmony with one another.

If (God forbid) your story doesn't have a hook, then your characters will arise out of your theme. If you don't think you have a theme, you may be wrong: if you think carefully about your story, you may discover that it does have a theme that you can use as a guideline to creating your characters. If you really don't have a hook or a theme, why are you writing a screenplay? (If the answer is, "Because they're paying me"—the very best answer, by the way—then you should strive to find a theme, anyway.)

Practically speaking, though, if you don't have a hook, then whatever else is driving the project will determine the characters. If your picture is a sequel, then your starting characters are whoever survived the original. If it's a well-loved book, then your characters come out of the book, though you'll cut many of them and merge others together. But even if you're working from other material, you still want to be sure that your secondary characters resonate in some way with the point of the story and with the main characters.

Reverse engineering is not as offbeat a technique as it sounds. Essentially, you're making sure all your characters move the story forward. Rather than creating them and then finding ways to make them relate to the hook and the theme, you're creating them *out of* the hook and then making sure they feel real.

Bear in mind, by the way, that reverse engineering is just a tool. No tool is more important than the story. Tools exist to help you create a great story. If you feel you need a certain character who seems to have nothing to do with your hook or your theme, then create that character and see if he works in the story. He may turn out to have something to do with the hook or theme after all. But whether he does or not, the point is to make a good story. "Black cat, white cat," as Deng Xiaoping said, "if it catches mice, it is a good cat."

REVERSE ENGINEERING *THE MUMMY*

Let's suppose you want to write a movie called *The Mummy*. You want to make it a swashbuckling romantic action-adventure full of special effects because that's what the studio thinks people want to see, or (if it's a spec script) because that's what you're in the mood to write. The hook might be:

> Archaeologists unwittingly reawaken a mummified evil high priest of ancient Egypt. As he seeks to revive his long-dead lover, a gutsy ex-Legionnaire and a beautiful Egyptologist must stop him from becoming all-powerful and destroying the world.

The hit 1999 *Mummy* is a surprisingly crafty remake of the classic Boris Karloff 1932 *Mummy*. But the screenwriters clearly rethought the story from the beginning, so we can treat it as pure invention.

The hook gives us quite a few characters right away.

The most important character, of course, is Imhotep, the mummy himself: an evil man cursed for his crimes with a living death that will make him supernaturally powerful should he ever be revived. He's the monster, but he's vulnerable and compelling because it is his love for Pharaoh's wife that makes him do wicked things. The worst thing he could do in ancient times would be to kill his king, so that's what he does, giving us the first sequence.

Then there's Pharaoh's wife, although because she's dead for most of the movie, she won't have much to say for herself.

Then we have our hero, Rick O'Connell. It's a swashbuckling movie, so we need a romantic adventurer: brash, reckless, brave. What does he have to do with a bunch of archaeologists? He could be someone they hired to protect them from the mummy, but it's more interesting when heroes are stuck in a trap of their own making, so he should be part of the original dig. He could be just a guide, of course, but that's not a very exciting way to tie him into the plot, so let's make him a man who knows where to find Hamunaputra, the secret city of the dead, where the mummy is buried. Why should he help the archaeologists? Money would be a normal reason, but he's a hero, so he can't care about money, and it's more fun if the archaeologists save his life. Let's make him a former French foreign legionnaire, because of their reputation for being troublemakers escaping their past. If he's a legionnaire, then could he find Hamunaputra while people are shooting at him? Sure he could; and there's our second sequence, by the way.

If the hero's mainly physical, then it's good if the heroine is mainly intellectual, not only so that they get on each other's nerves, which is always fun, but so that each can do something the other can't. Of course she'll need to be able to read hieroglyphics, and the more the hero is unshaven, the more she should be prim and proper. He's practical, but uncontrollable; she's romantic, but controlled. Let's make the heroine, Evelyn, a librarian at a museum of Egyptian antiquities in Cairo.

The movie is envisioned by the studio as a big, wide-ranging adventure for the whole family, so let's throw in a few sidekicks for comic relief. The first one is Jonathan, Evelyn's brother. Because Rick and Evelyn are both, in their ways, intensely brave, Jonathan's a bit of a coward. Because they're accomplished, he's a bit of a failure. But he'll pull through in the end. He's the good sidekick.

By now we have enough characters for a good movie; this is about the size of the main cast of the 1932 *Mummy*. The creators of the 1999 *Mummy* wanted a bigger cast and a bigger scope to the picture, so they went a little further.

The mummy himself is scary and serious, so, since this is a big film for all audiences, he needs a comic sidekick, right? The hero is a strong, brave, good, romantic adventurer, and the villain is a strong, brave, evil, romantic adventurer, so let's have a cowardly, despicable, greedy adventurer: Beni Gabor. The mummy is Big Evil. Beni is Small Evil. The mummy is motivated by passion. Beni is motivated by greed.

What's he got to do with the mummy? Although the mummy is Rick's antagonist, it's hard to have a relationship with a villain who speaks only ancient Egyptian and a smattering of Hebrew. So Beni is Rick's human opponent. They might as well have a relationship that goes all the way back to the Foreign Legion. That puts Beni back at Hamunaputra, being shot at alongside Rick, which explains what he's doing on the dig.

That's not quite enough mummy bait. We want to show how powerful and evil the mummy is, so we want some people to suffer horrible fates at his hands. Of course we should get to know them before the mummy kills them, so we care when he does. Also, in a swashbuckler we want as many obstacles and opponents as possible for the hero.

Let's have a competing group of archaeologists. We don't need any more evil characters, so they are morally neutral. Let's make them a bunch of reckless American cowboy-style grave robbers who are trying to beat the heroes to Hamunaputra and are half responsible for awakening the mummy. Because they've brought the curse of the mummy onto themselves, we won't feel too sad to see them go.

See where I'm going with this? In theory, every character in your story can be extracted from the hook and from the characters that precede him or her. Of course you have options at every point; a given character can be drawn any number of ways. In a parallel universe there is a *Mummy* movie in which Beni, the evil sidekick, helps save the day in the end.

Reverse engineering is a powerful tool, but like any craftsman's tool, it has to be used with heart and talent. Creating the right characters to fulfill each need is where your heart and talent come into play. If nothing else, though, reverse engineering can be a useful technique for double-checking whether you have all the characters you need and none that you don't.

Freshness

You're not writing in a vacuum. The people reading your script will read five other scripts today, some of them all the way through. The characters you slaved over, believe it or not, seem surprisingly familiar to them.

You want to avoid that. You want your characters to be memorable and distinct. You want them to be fresh.

Raiders of the Lost Ark introduces Karen Allen's feisty character in the middle of a drinking contest she wins against a mammoth Tibetan man. She is going to be Indiana Jones's love interest, but she's clearly not your typical action-movie shrieking love interest. She's fun, she's tough, she runs a saloon in the mountains, and she can hold her liquor. She meets Indy and socks him in the jaw, knocking him flat.

It was surprising, then. Ever since, of course, it seems as if every heroine has to sock the hero in the jaw. You wonder why anyone goes into the hero business.

It's always good to make your secondary characters strong rather than weak, so they can give your hero a maximum of trouble. If they can't be strong, they should be devious or mysterious.

You're not trying to make your characters seem wacky. One of the many tough challenges of screenwriting is making your characters fresh without making them different for its own sake.

When you invent a character, you need to question all of his or her attributes. Your first idea is usually not your best one. The moment you come up with a character, spend some time thinking whether a slightly different character might be better. Should he be older? Younger? Black? Latino? A woman? A devout Catholic? A Mormon with mild Tourette's syndrome, who swears all the time and doesn't see why it should bother anyone?

Reject the obvious. Swim against the tide. If you think of something, try to remember if you've seen it in another movie. If you have, try to think up something better. If you can't, okay, but you have to try.

The Devil Is in the Details

> "You can tell a lot about a man by the way he handles three things: a rainy day, lost luggage, and tangled Christmas tree lights."
>
> —Anonymous

Whether or not you use a conscious technique to generate your characters, they can still come off flat if they appear to exist only to fulfill a dramatic function. Of course they *do* exist only to fulfill their dramatic functions. But they must *appear* to be real people who've been swept up in your story's events. If they come off as purely functional, no one will care what happens to them.

The cure for flatness is hard work. You need to

a. give your characters the breath of life;
b. take pains not to betray them.

Giving your character the breath of life means giving him the quirks and strangenesses that distinguish any real person from all the other people like him. The first steps in building character involve trying to imagine your character as a whole person. What does he do for a living? Does she have a family? Where does he live? What is she afraid of? What does he long for? What did she want to be when she grew up, and how does she feel now that she isn't? What's holding him back from changing his life?

These are all important things to know, because they define the character. But these are only the bones of your character. Life is in the details.

Let's suppose you're working up a character who is president of the United States. He would of course have tremendous ambition. He'd be likable. He might come from the South, but have gone to college at an Ivy League school, showing he's smart, not just a front man. He might be having an affair, politicians not being immune from that sort of thing.

Unfortunately the above could describe a lot of presidential candidates, assuming they're having affairs. This character has no life in him yet. You can't really have any feelings for or against him. But give our character a fondness for Big Macs even though he has a top chef working for him. Make it an affair with a neurotic, overweight intern, when he could easily have had an affair with any number of gorgeous, brilliant, *discreet* Washington women. Now you have a character you can love or hate for his human flaws.

What makes a character feel real are *specific, unusual* details that the audience couldn't predict just from knowing what the character's there to do. The details ground the character in human reality. Suppose you have two cops interrogating an informant outside a pastry shop, and the guy keeps getting distracted by the pastries in the window, and the cops have to buy him an eclair to get him to pay attention? That makes your characters human beings. Most of us don't know any cops or informants. We do know people who can't resist a chocolate eclair.

One easy trick to make a character seem real, incidentally, is to throw in a little self-contradiction. Suppose you have a character who talks poignantly about her father's death from lung cancer. She might later bum a cigarette from someone, then feel embarrassed about it, then light up anyway. A liberal might own a handgun. A conservative might be gay. Don't abuse this trick, though, because it is a trick.

Ghost

Sometimes your hero will have a ghost. The ghost is the thing that haunts him: something from his past that bothers him enough that it either drives him toward his goal, or blocks him from it. If so, it's the most important detail about his character. It might be a literal ghost; the term probably came from Hamlet's father's ghost, who insists that Hamlet, against his nature, avenge his murder by killing Uncle Claudius. Likewise, Batman's parents were killed in a robbery; revenge for that crime is what drives him to defeat crime. Luke Skywalker's father is, as far as he knows, dead; Luke's desire to be a star pilot like his father makes him restless on Tatooine. The ghost might be any other sort of wound or loss that makes someone tick. In *Psycho*, Norman Bates can't reconcile his sexual urges with the reproaches of his stuffy, rigidly Puritanical mother. In *Good Will Hunting*, Will's rage against his father's brutality prevents him from taking advantage of his own mathematical brilliance, or loving anyone. In *Casablanca*, Rick is still hurting because the love of his life left him waiting at the train station; it's why he's running a bar in Casablanca instead of running guns to the Free French.

For a happy ending, the hero will lay his ghost to rest by the end of the movie. Either achieving his goal lays it to rest, or in order to succeed at his goal he has to lay it to rest first. In an unhappy ending, it is often the hero's inability to cope with his ghost that stops him from achieving his goal.

The Secret Lives of Characters

You can take the pursuit of details too far, I believe. A lot of screenwriting teachers feel that you should know much more about your characters than your audience will. You should write full backstories for all your characters: where they went to school, what they majored in, what their moms did for a living, what they ate for breakfast, etc. (*Backstory* is movie jargon for stuff that happened before the events on-screen.) The theory is that this will help you give your characters life. It may—to you, anyway. The danger is that your audience can only see what is actually on the screen. The reader can only learn what is on the page. If something's not in the screenplay, how do we know it? Can the knowledge somehow trickle down into the character you're writing?

How will you know if it doesn't? You've got a wonderful, deep, rich, rounded character in your head. You're writing wonderfully understated dialogue, given subtle shadings by the character's unique personality.

Unfortunately what may really be happening is that you are writing characters whose deep, rich inner lives are a secret known only to you. The dialogue just sits there, and nothing will lead us to suspect the character has any inner life. Your character's offscreen life or background has no reason to exist *except to the extent* that it affects the character's presence on-screen.

Personally, I like to discover things about my characters as I write what they say and do. I let them say things, and then I say to myself, "Wow, I didn't know that about Gail. That's great. I can use that!" This means I can also give my characters backstory that is convenient to the screenplay at the drop of a hat; and it means that anything I know about the character is in the screenplay.

To give a sense of a minor character, you can often show just a hint of offscreen life. Give us a hint of what they were doing just before the scene started. If your cop is going to talk to a shop owner, you might start the scene with the shop owner trying to charm a pretty customer, or shouting at some rotten kids, or haggling with a supplier over the phone. That gives us a glimpse into his life, and also gives him an attitude coming into the scene.

Roger Zelazny, a marvelous science-fiction and fantasy writer, has an interesting technique. He writes a scene with his character that he does not put in the story. Not a whole backstory, just a scene. He then refers to the scene in the story. That gives the audience the feeling that the character has a life of his own. On his website, http://www.wordplayer.com, screenwriter Terry Rossio (*The Mask of Zorro*) discusses the same idea, quoting the original *Star Wars:* Obi-Wan Kenobi tells Luke that Darth Vader "fought with your father in the Clone Wars," although we never did learn what the Clone Wars were (at least, not until the fifth episode came out twenty-five or so years later!).

But note how this is different from a whole backstory. What makes this technique effective is the moment in the screenplay or movie where someone refers to the scene. Don't overdo it, but it may be worthwhile for your characters to refer to events outside the story. You don't have to pay off every setup.

There are characters you may not want to flesh out much. A good stock character can be great fun for the audience. The obnoxious store clerk. The befuddled grandfather. Do we really want to know their angst? No, they wouldn't be as enjoyable.

And then there are villains. Take Alan Rickman's over-the-top sheriff of Nottingham in *Robin Hood, Prince of Thieves*. Did we want to know what made him the way he is? We did not. We wanted him pure, unadulterated evil. Any explanation would have made him less fun. What makes cartoon villains and stock characters good is the sheer verve with which they're portrayed. We love to hate the Wicked Witch of the West, or any of the James Bond villains (Dr. No, Goldfinger, Dr. Ernst Blofeld, etc.). They revel in their own evil, and we get a kick out of it. The stronger an impression your villain makes, the greater the obstacle for the hero, the better the conflict, the more drama.

Don't Betray Your Characters

In fleshing out your characters, take care that you don't betray them.

You betray your character when you force him or her to do something he or she doesn't have a real motivation to do. A real person in the situation you've created wouldn't do what you're making your character do, but you're the writer, so you just write the scene that way.

That's cheating.

Put yourself in the character's shoes. Think: In this situation, what would I really do?

In nearly every horror sequel, the silly humans don't seem to have learned much from their extraordinary experiences. Me, if someone opened a gateway to hell in my house, I'd be spending my free time studying up on the occult. Not these guys. They're just trying to get on with their lives.

C'mon.

One of the neatest things about *Terminator 2* was that James Cameron did not betray his heroine, Sarah Connor. In the first *Terminator*, a machine from a hellish post-nuclear-war future tries to murder her. In the sequel, Sarah has done what a real woman would do in her situation. She has transformed herself into a survivalist nut who has tried to blow up the labs working on the prototypes for the machine that will set off the nuclear war. She is stuck in a mental ward because no one will believe her. A lesser writer might have written her as pretty much the same waitress: "She's tried to put the past behind her."

Never make your characters less intelligent than you are. If you wouldn't go back inside that house, why should your character? Your characters have seen movies, too, y'know. They know what kind of stuff goes down.

Why don't they just call the police?

Why don't the police call for backup?

This doesn't mean you can't have your characters do dangerous or stupid things, only that you need to give them strong reasons to do them. *Tremors* is a good low-budget science-fiction thriller about a small town in the California desert afflicted by big underground critters that pop out of the ground and eat people. I love that from the moment the characters realize something bad is happening, *they try to get the hell out of the town*. No "Oh, that was probably just the wind," no "Let's go see what that noise was." They do nothing but try to get out of Dodge, trying one plan after another until they finally do battle with the critters because they *have no other choice*.

The more outlandish the action you want, the harder you are going to have to work to make it a reasonable choice for the characters.

Butch Cassidy and the Sundance Kid jump off a cliff into a river because otherwise they will be shot dead or hanged. I have no problem believing they'd rather jump. William Wallace in *Braveheart* walks into a likely trap because it is the only chance for peace.

When you need your character to do something, give him the right motivation to do it. If you want a beautiful woman to fall in love with your loser male lead, then give her a reason to fall for him. Don't make her do it because you'd really like a beautiful woman to fall in love with *you*. It can be a strong motivation or a totally quirky and offbeat motivation, but it has to be a believable motivation. Structure the story and write the characters so that what you want them to do is an entirely reasonable choice, given what we know about them.

> Every character is the hero
> of his own movie.

Here's a secret. In real life, everyone thinks of himself as the star of the movie of his life. Every character is the hero of his own movie. Just as in chapter 2, you made sure that your main character had a driving goal, something to win, something to lose, and obstacles, so *every* significant character needs 'em. Their goals put them in contact with the protagonist, either as allies or opponents. Your villain obviously has the hero as his obstacle. Your love interest may have the goal of having a happy life with the hero, and she might see his need to fight the villain as an obstacle to that goal: she becomes an intimate opponent. Or she has a goal of the hero surviving the villain's evil scheme: she becomes an ally. You'll spend less time working out the goals and obstacles of your lesser characters in detail. But they should have them. That's what makes them compelling.

You probably should read through your outline once for each important character (do this later with your script, too). Read only from that character's point of view. Look at her actions only from her perspective, ignoring what the script needs her to do. Is there anything you've made her do that doesn't make sense for her? If so, you'll have to give her different things to do, or different motivations to do them.

Again, I'm working backward here. The character comes from the story. The motivation comes after you decide what the character needs to do. But that's how screenwriting differs from real life. The story is all, and everything proceeds from it.

Casting Your Movie

If you are writing a star vehicle—a big-budget movie that will star someone we've heard of—you have to be careful not to violate the unwritten rules of what stars do and don't do. Here I am using a distinction that screenwriter William Goldman makes between *stars* and *actors*. Stars are people we want to see in more or less the same role over and over. They've honed an attractive screen persona we'll pay money to see. Actors are people we go to see play different roles convincingly.

For example, Harrison Ford played a brave wiseacre for years before he started playing grown-up Boy Scouts. Robert Redford has for decades played an aging golden boy, smarter than he looks but not brilliant, caught in a situation slightly beyond him, basically decent but not about to get in a fight about it unless he can't avoid it. Mel Gibson: a likable rogue, slightly crazy, often hiding tremendous inner pain.

In contrast, actors like Dustin Hoffman, Robert De Niro, and Robert Duvall play characters who are almost always different, and often wildly different.

Although different stars have different personas, there are some consistencies. The characters stars play don't lose, for example. They may be killed, but they're never broken. The character may be dirty, but if so he'll redeem himself. He may do bad things, but never petty things.

One way to get consistency in your characters is to cast them after you write them. Try to imagine the star you've chosen acting the part you've written. You'll often realize you've written actions and dialogue that your chosen star would never do. You'll have to change the scene you've written.

Make sure you're casting the right character. I once wrote a space opera "starring" Harrison Ford. The hero was a dirty cop, a weak man who found himself in a situation where his innate decency forced him to side with the rebels even though it was suicidal and he had better offers elsewhere. We weren't supposed to know which way he would jump. Somehow the lines seemed mushy.

I should have known better: Harrison Ford never plays dirty or weak. Evil, sure, in *What Lies Beneath*, but never weak. The problem fixed itself when I "recast" the part with Kurt Russell, whose screen persona is shadier: someone you like, but don't necessarily trust. As I rewrote for Russell, the lines started to give themselves an edge. The character opened up. You didn't know which way he'd jump.

You can also, of course, "cast" your own friends or enemies, people whose reactions you know.

Don't tell anyone how you've cast the movie. Let the lines speak for themselves. If you've done your job right, everyone reading the script will know whom they'd like to see play the role.

Casting your movie is not taught in film schools, I guess because teachers fear it might kill your originality. Casting your movie is a technique of craft, not a technique of great art. But to my mind, it's easier to arrive at great art through craft than through raw intuition. Picasso studied traditional painting before he invented new ways of seeing. If he hadn't, he wouldn't have been able to control his Cubist paintings. Long after he started putting two eyes on the same side of his subject's nose, Picasso would now and then whip out a perfect realistic portrait of someone, just to remind people he knew what he was doing. Once you know how to cast a role in the mold of a star, you can break that mold when you choose, not merely by accident.

Note, however, that you cannot depend on your casting of the movie to make a character interesting or likable. We, your readers, do not have Harrison Ford in our minds when we start reading. We will not start out caring about your lead character. You have to make him so compelling that we would care about him even if he were played by, say, Jim Belushi.

Try "casting" a star you find *un*charismatic in your mind's eye. Do you still care about your hero? Then you've done well. If not, there's still work to be done.

Remember, however, your hero needs to be compelling, but not necessarily likable, which brings me to . . .

Some Development Executive Myths

Over the years, I've repeatedly heard a handful of character-related criticisms from development executives that seemed to miss the real problems the scripts had:

1. "The dialogue is flat."
2. "We don't know enough about the hero."
3. "We don't like the hero."
4. "It's episodic."

These can be useless, dangerous comments, because addressing them literally may not fix the real problems. The problems are all in character.

1. "The dialogue is flat."

The most dangerous comment is, "The dialogue is flat." Now, there are many flavors of bad dialogue, and one of them is flat: bland, listless, undistinguished dialogue. But snappy dialogue that jumps off the page is only one flavor of good dialogue, and it is only appropriate for certain characters and certain scripts. If you're writing *When Harry Met Sally . . .* or *You've Got Mail* or anything else for Meg Ryan, your dialogue probably wants to be crisp, snappy, and bouncy. But if you're writing *A Fistful of Dollars* or *Unforgiven*, or anything else for Clint Eastwood, then your dialogue wants to be spare and minimalist. Spare dialogue can easily be accused of being flat, because the development executive is reading your script in bed late at night, her eyes blurry, a pile of scripts on her night table, with her boyfriend snoring resentfully at her side. She is not putting much energy into reading your lines, so if they don't do the work for her, she will think them flat. On the other hand, the actor will, I hope, put thought, passion, and talent into the lines and the silences between them, and so your "flat" dialogue may in fact be good.

But what's really going on here is that your characters are not coming through as people we care about. If we don't know where they're coming from and don't care about them, we're not going to care about what they're saying, and the dialogue will seem flat. If we care about the character, then we'll invest his or her lines with humanity. Fix the characters, and the dialogue will fix itself.

2. *"We don't know enough about the hero."*

In theory, everyone wants a well-rounded, likable hero. When your hero does not come across well, you will often hear, "We don't know enough about the hero." This is often followed by a request to give us specific scenes that fix the problem. The classic comment is, "We don't know anything about the hero's background."

Unfortunately, when you change the screenplay so you know about the character's backstory, they then reject the script for different reasons. If you're a competent screenwriter, what "I want to know more about this character's past" really means is "I don't get your character," which is not the same.

For a good example of a silly attempt at fleshing out a character, look at *Gremlins*, in which Phoebe Cates explains that she hates Christmas because her dad died on Christmas. Little savage pointy-eared beasties are running amok. Who cares whether she likes Christmas or not?

For a refreshing reversal, the TV show *Buffy: The Vampire Slayer:*

```
                BUFFY
      Puppets give me the wiggins. Ever
      since I was eight.

                WILLOW
      What happened?
```

```
                    BUFFY
      I saw a puppet, it gave me the wiggins.
      There really isn't a story there.
```

Your movie may be about characters resolving issues from their pasts. But most hit movies, and at least half of all great movies, give their heroes a throwaway past or none at all.

For example, in *The Fugitive*, Dr. Richard Kimble has essentially no backstory. His wife is killed on-screen, and he spends the rest of the movie trying to find out whodunnit. Yet no one felt we had to know more about him, because his actions on-screen said more about who he was than any backstory could have. He repeatedly risks his life and liberty to save the lives of innocent bystanders. What more do we need to know?

What was Shane like as a lad? We don't know much, and we don't miss knowing. We know how he reacts to the sight of innocents being mistreated by outlaws, and we see what he does about it.

Make sure that everything your character does shows us who he is, and no one will ask you for the Rubber Ducky.

THE RUBBER DUCKY

I am going to rant about the Rubber Ducky theory of backstory for a bit.

The *rubber ducky* is Paddy Chayevsky's term for when the hero or villain, at a lull in the action, explains that he is the way he is because his mother took away his rubber ducky when he was three. It's always a nice scene, well acted, beautifully lit, with a powerfully written monologue that the writer spent days on.

The character's past may be crucial to your story. Batman is haunted by the murder of his parents by a mugger when he was small. That's why he likes to dress up in latex and beat the tar out of muggers. In *The Terminator*, the hero's past, which is in the future, is the hellish future of the entire human race. It sets up the stakes for the whole movie. In movies like these, we do need to know about the hero's past. You will need to keep coming back to that past, to give it the weight it deserves. Both *Batman* and *The Terminator*, in fact, start with the hero's backstory before getting into the main story.

But if all you're trying to do is give your hero more emotional depth, for the sake of emotional depth, without integrating his backstory into your story, you are running the risk of awakening the dread ducky.

The strongest way to create a sense of character is to give the character things to do and say on-screen that give us a sense of a person. If the character's personality doesn't leap off the page, readers will feel that the character is flat. Development executives will ask to know more about the protagonist's past. You will surrender to the urge to put in a rubber ducky. Then if the picture becomes a go, the actors will get attached to the rubber ducky scene, because it shows they can act. So the ducky stays in the picture.

A ducky cheapens the character. Kurt Russell's character Jack O'Neil in *Stargate* is suicidal because his young son killed himself accidentally with a pistol he left around the house. To make us care more about his otherwise unpleasant character, O'Neil delivers a small monologue to James Spader's character Daniel Jackson. It is important to the picture that O'Neil is suicidal, but not why; and given O'Neil's contempt for Daniel Jackson, it's unlikely that he would open up to him about his guilt and shame. The emotional truth of the situation is that Daniel Jackson would never know why O'Neil is so willing to die. It might have been more emotionally truthful for the movie never to relay this information. But I wouldn't be surprised if Kurt Russell wanted the audience to know that his character had a good reason for being such a bastard. Actors want you to have sympathy for them.

A good example of a ducky that never comes up is *Thelma and Louise*. It becomes clear over the course of the movie that something terrible happened to Louise (Geena Davis) in Texas; that's why the two women take the long way around to the Mexican border. You begin to realize that she must have been raped in Texas, and then disbelieved in court. But Louise never says anything explicit about it in the movie, and that makes her backstory all the stronger.

If development execs are asking you for the ducky, the screenplay isn't working for them. Don't give them the ducky, but do focus your scenes so they show the character. Go through your script again, scene by scene, and make sure that every time the hero acts, it shows us who he is. Make sure you communicate how he feels about what he's doing, and give him a fresh way of doing it, one someone else wouldn't have.

There are only two ways we know anything about a character:

- hearsay: what they say about themselves, and other people tell us about them; and
- direct observation: what we see them do, including the conversations we see them have.

Actions speak louder than words. If someone tells us he's a nice guy, and then we see him calling his daughter horrible names, we don't believe he's nice anymore.

3. "The hero isn't likable."

Development execs like to ask, "Why do we like the hero?" implying that it's a bad thing if we don't.

In response, writers like to throw in a "pat the dog" scene to appease development execs.* The pat-the-dog scene is so called because it is often a scene in which the hero is nice to a stray dog, orphan child, minority person, pet iguana, etc.—anything to show that although he's a hard-bitten squinty-eyed son of a bitch, he's warm and fuzzy inside. What makes it a pat-the-dog scene is that the scene isn't really part of the plot. Your hero is otherwise not a nice guy, but here we see his soft, human side.

If you really want your hero to come across as human and vulnerable, then it has to come out in the story. He has to behave in a human, caring way with people who are actually part of the plot. Otherwise the scene feels tacked on and doesn't really score with the audience.

---

*It's also called a "pet the dog" scene, but I've always heard people say "pat the dog," and really, what's the difference to the dog?

But it is not necessary that we like the hero. Development executives who don't find the hero compelling often complain that the hero isn't likable when really they mean they are bored by him. It is not necessary that your hero be likable so long as we are drawn to watching him.

Take *All That Jazz*, for example. Joe Gideon is not a likable guy; in fact he's a heel. But he's honest about what a heel he is. We don't care about him because he's nice. We care about him because he is passionate about dance and will sacrifice everything to his muse, and because he's honest about himself.

Give a character a *dream* we care about, and we will care about him or her.

Dorothy is miserable in gray Kansas; only her little dog, Toto, makes her happy. That might make her a little hard to sympathize with. She would just be an unhappy child who doesn't appreciate her home. But she dreams of a life "Over the Rainbow." We are willing to identify with her longing in a way that we wouldn't necessarily be willing to join in her unhappiness.

The hero's dream doesn't necessarily have to be something we would want for ourselves. In the '70s film *Dog Day Afternoon*, Al Pacino's character holds up a bank to get his gay transvestite lover enough money for the operation to make him a woman. A *weird* dream, but we understand that he is driven by it.

Another reason to care about a hero might be that he has a big *problem*. In *Some Like It Hot*, Tony Curtis and Jack Lemmon's characters unintentionally witness the Saint Valentine's Day Massacre, and now the mob wants them rubbed out.

Even the sheer *intensity* of a hero or antihero can carry him through the "likability" hurdle. In the classic '50s film *The Night of the Hunter*, the main character is a homicidal preacher. In *Moby Dick*, the hero, Ahab, is also the villain. We care about him because he is us in our worst moments, driven by an obsession to drag himself down to hell, and everyone along with him. In *Taxi Driver*, Travis Bickle (Robert De Niro) goes from being an ordinary man having a really bad life to a dangerous suicidal maniac. We don't like him, but we care about him, because we catch a glimpse of how we, too, could slide into hell.

What do you do when your hero has *no redeeming qualities*, as in, say, *Leaving Las Vegas*? Make him/her as unique, human, truthful, and fascinating as you can, and then convince a likable actor to play him. Many actors love to play unlikable characters, because they

- can pull out the stops
- think it's harder, and
- don't like themselves.

Any of these—a dream, a problem, intensity—can replace likability. In no case should your hero have a trace of self-pity.

The main point is that we don't have to like the hero, we just have to care what happens to him.

Note that this is really true for any important character. Give each character something that makes us care about him. Great anger, pain, sorrow, rage, an unstoppable appetite for life, huge ambition, terrible problems—any of these can make us care. In *Casablanca*, we care about such minor characters as

a. Senor Ferrari, because he is such a cheerfully shameless crook;
b. Louis, because he is an equally shameless womanizer and cheerful hypocrite, a cynical romantic;
c. Ugarte, because he's a frightened little rat trying to survive;
d. Sam, because he's a simple man trying to make a living in a dangerous place;
e. Major Strasser, because he is a hard, dangerous, scary Nazi who wants to hurt everybody we care about.

Some we hate, some we like, some we despise. Flaws, problems, dreams, goals: all of these make us care about your characters.

4. "It's episodic."

Oddly enough, this is not a criticism of your plot, it's a criticism of your character. Confusing, huh?

It would be confusing enough if it were a criticism of your plot. After all, movies are made of sequences, and sequences are episodes, aren't they? Especially in a road movie, the plot may be made up of distinct set pieces that follow one after another.

This criticism means to say that the movie is made up of episodes that don't seem to hang together. The script lacks inevitability. One episode follows another without forcing the next.

But the problem isn't the episodes. The problem is that no dramatic backbone unites them. The hero is being buffeted from episode to episode without sticking to his goal. The protagonist's drive to reach his goal, and his emotional reactions to his setbacks, must provide the sinew to hold together what may otherwise be an episodic skeleton.

In less fancy language, it is the hero's character that holds the episodes together. The hero's character is, primarily

a. his or her goal, and
b. his feelings about that goal, along with
c. whatever backstory haunts him and gives him his goal.

If these are not clear, or they are not clearly related to what is going on in the plot, you'll get the criticism that the script is episodic. If they are clear, you can write a road movie in which the hero meets one character after another, separately, and moves on, never seeing them again, and it won't feel episodic. Take *Thelma and Louise*, where the two heroines go from one adventure to another, meeting people we mostly never see again. Take *Head*, a silly and thoroughly enjoyable movie (written by the young Jack Nicholson!) that takes the Monkees from one adventure to another with barely a connection; but we follow the band because we like them and care about what's happening to them.

Make us care about the characters and you'll never hear that your script is episodic. I promise.

Character Names

I am really finicky about the names I give my characters. The first time you give a character a name, you give him or her flesh. Then you repeat it hundreds of times throughout the script. So make it count.

Names generally need to be real enough to be believable. It's a bit much to have someone named Daedalus, unless it's a nickname someone chose.

But names should tell us something. BOB is an ordinary guy. JOEY is an ordinary working-class guy. ERIK has an edge. There's something sexy and daring about a girl named DAKOTA (at least there was before it became the fashionable name for the five-year-old daughters of yuppies). MR. FINSTER is a kindly grocer the kids make up rhymes about. And so on.

Whether you're on a first-name or last-name basis with your character tells us a lot. Just as in real life, we'll feel more intimate with someone we know by their first name than someone we know by their last name. You'll almost certainly want your lead to go by his first name, unless he actually goes by his last name with his most intimate friends and colleagues ("Mulder?").

A handy rule: however your hero would refer to a person when speaking to a friend, that's the name you use above that character's dialogue. So, if you were adapting *Richard III*, you'd probably call Richard, Duke of Gloucester, "RICHARD," and his brother George, Duke of Clarence, "CLARENCE." If you were writing a screenplay from the point of view of one of Richard III's hired murderers, then Richard would probably be "DUKE RICHARD," and Clarence would be "DUKE CLARENCE." If the point of view belonged to King Edward, their father, they might be "RICHARD" and "GEORGE."

If you have a secondary character you're not sure we'll be able to keep track of, you might add a title to their name: DEAN WORMER. PRINCE HARRY. JUDGE HILL. DR. NO.

You don't have to give all characters names. It can be useful to leave secondary characters with a descriptive monicker rather than a name: LONER. That way the reader knows she won't have to keep track of them later.

On the other hand, never name characters VERMIN #1, VERMIN #2, or THIEF. That's just lazy. Make them FAT THIEF and SNEERING THIEF. That puts an image in a reader's head.

You may sometimes want to sucker the reader into thinking someone's unimportant by not giving him a name. Then later, when LONER—surprise!—starts dating the heroine, he becomes NICK THE LONER for a few lines until we know he's NICK. You might have a character called DARK-EYED MAN that later turns into DR. CZERNY. That gives the reader the same feeling the audience will have: who the hell is this dark-eyed guy? (If you use this crafty technique, then be careful you're not just confusing the reader by calling the same character two different things.)

This practice may give production managers ulcers when they break down the script for production, but you're writing a selling script, not a shooting draft, and anyway, they're paid to have ulcers.

Avoid giving female characters male names. I know it's fun to name a girl JOEY (*Dawson's Creek*) or CHARLEY (*The Long Kiss Goodnight*). But it's hard to remember when you're reading the script that SAM is really Samantha; and anything that confuses the reader hurts your screenplay. You don't need a boy's name to give your female character guts. Sarah Connor in *Terminator 2* could totally kick your ass, and she was still "Sarah."

Avoid KIM and LESLIE as men's names for the same reason, unless the character is a British twit.

Don't use a name that's hard to read or pronounce. It's a constant distraction. LLEWELYN is out, unless you're writing a historical piece set in medieval Wales. So is KJERSTI KYRKJEBO, a name I actually came across in a screenplay. I'm still not sure how it's pronounced.

Be careful about making up foreign names. Even when I don't know the language in question, I can usually tell when someone's made up a name from scratch. *The audience knows a lot of things it doesn't know it knows.* One of them is what names sound like, even names from strange countries. You're safer using real names. Get the names of obscure government ministers out of an almanac, or look in the *Encyclopaedia Britannica* for names from the country's history. Take one person's first name and another's last name. Slap them together. Presto! New name. Obviously, don't use famous last names like Gandhi.

A sneakier way to get foreign last names is to get a map of the country and use a place name, or to use a foreign word. No one is going to know that Arusha is a place in Masai territory and not the name of a Masai tribesman, or that Shikari is Sanskrit for "hunter."

Believe it or not, when you're writing science fiction or fantasy, you still can't get away with entirely made-up names. Names like Morthock and Gandath always sound fake, generally fakes based on *The Lord of the Rings* by J. R. R. Tolkien. So how did he make up his names? He didn't just throw syllables in the Mixmaster. He stole the names outright. Gandalf, Gimli, Glóin, and many of his other names are straight out of medieval Norse and English literature. Other names, such as Galadriel, he created using elements from High Elvish, a language he created. Tolkien was a scholar at Cambridge University. He spent years making up a lot of imaginary languages (his "secret vice"). He claimed to have written *The Lord of the Rings* to justify having spent all that time making up languages.

If you are a professional linguist, you too can make up names from scratch. Otherwise, pick out your fantasy names from African, Native American, or Asian languages like Tibetan and Uzbek.

Science-fiction names should follow foreign-language rules for human names and fantasy rules for alien names. Human names are probably not going to change a heck of a lot in the next few hundred years, any more than jambalaya is, if you think about it.

Be careful of names with literary inspiration. Many of your readers will have just as good an education as you have, and will instantly spot your references. If you name a character Janus, they will not be surprised when he turns out to be two-faced. They will be annoyed with you if he does (predictable), and they will be annoyed with you if he doesn't (then why'd you name him that?). Basically, they'll be annoyed with you.

Other readers will have no clue what you did and will think Janus is a dumb name. You don't want anything in a screenplay that you're not sure will be understood. Won't be understood is fine, will be understood is fine, but writing a screenplay is all about controlling the reader's experience, so if you don't know how the reader is going to experience what you're writing, don't write it that way.

You also don't want anything in a screenplay that throws the reader out of the experience of the movie unspooling in the reader's head. A literary reference draws attention away from the movie itself. If you must give a character a literary name for your own benefit while you write, be sure to change it before you give someone the screenplay to read.

Introducing Your Characters

Take care to introduce your main characters slowly enough that the reader has a firm grasp of each one before you introduce the next. Ideally, introduce no more than one per scene. You may, for example, want to introduce the hero alone, at the beginning of the movie. Suppose your story begins with your cop hero and his partner getting assigned a routine surveillance job that will turn into something bigger. Rather than start with the assignment itself—hero, sidekick, and their boss all at once—you may want to find a way to show the hero alone, then linking up with his partner before they both go into their boss's office.

That's why we so often meet the hero waking up in his apartment, alone. A man's home tells you a lot about him, whether he's got a happy suburban home, a loving wife and cute child, or lives in a seedy, sloppy one-bedroom with an airshaft view.

In *Lethal Weapon*, we first meet Mel Gibson's character, Riggs, alone in his trailer, contemplating blowing his own head off. It's a purely character scene; it doesn't move the plot forward, but it does move the *story* forward because we need to know that Riggs is suicidal. The scene could have come *after* we saw Riggs in action, but it was a terrific way to introduce Riggs all by himself.

You don't have to introduce your hero first. *Star Wars* spends its first reel (ten minutes) showing the two hapless robots, R2-D2 and C-3PO, escaping from a spaceship under attack, only to be captured by junk merchants on the planet surface, before we finally meet our hero, Luke Skywalker. In the meantime we've already met the love interest, Princess Leia, and the villain, Darth Vader. Very often in thrillers and action-adventure movies you'll meet the villain first, committing the terrible deed that gets the hero called in to stop him.

If you find that people are having trouble keeping your characters straight, look to how you introduce them. If too much is going on when we meet them, we may never recover from our confusion.

Rewrite!

Character is the single most difficult aspect of screenwriting. (So are hook, plot, action, and dialogue.) In a few short scenes, you need to show us everything we need to know about your characters: who they are and what they want and what they're ready to do to get it.

The key, as with every other aspect of screenwriting, is rewriting. Take each character separately and go through the script. Ask yourself how you could make your character fresher and more original. Ask yourself if a different, more surprising character could fill the dramatic functions you need this character to do.

Try to merge characters. The more time we spend with your characters, the more we care about them. If you can merge characters without losing drama, you should. If you have a character who's mostly around in the first act, and another who's mostly around in acts two and three, can you merge the two of them into one character?

Would cutting one of the characters tighten the story? In *The Big Chill*, Kevin Costner played Alex, the man whose sudden death united all the old college friends. The movie was his big break: tapes of his scenes from the rough cut of the movie made the rounds in L.A. and he suddenly had "buzz." Don't remember him in the film? That's because all his scenes were cut. *The Big Chill* wasn't about the dead guy. It was about his friends who gathered for his funeral.

Now, go through the script yet again. Make sure each scene not only moves the plot forward, but moves it forward in such a way that we get the most insight into the characters. Two people can talk to each other in a generic way, or in a way that tells us as much about them as about plot developments. Use each action and each line of dialogue to shed as much light as possible on your characters.

If you are careful and work hard at it, you should be able to make everything your characters say and do *both* move the plot forward *and* illuminate their personalities.

That's crafty screenwriting.

4

ACTION

Now you're ready to write pages. You began the process when you broke your pitch down into individual steps or story beats in chapter 2. Now you're going to expand each step or beat into one or more scenes.

When you go from a pitch to a screenplay, you are going from the medium of story, which tells the listener what happens, to a specialized form of writing intended to *create a movie in the reader's head*. Everyone knows more or less how to tell a story. Screenwriting looks simple, too. You just write down what people do and say, right? But it's a form of writing that is deceptively hard to master.

Scenes are made of action and dialogue. Action is what people and things do, and dialogue is what they say. This chapter will concentrate on action, and the next on dialogue.

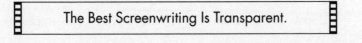

The Best Screenwriting Is Transparent.

The best screenwriting is *transparent*. That means that you don't feel like you're reading a script; you feel like you're watching a movie. One of the highest compliments I ever got on a script was when my wife asked me what movie a certain scene was from, and it wasn't from a movie, it was from a script of mine she'd read. She had a visual memory of a moment on-screen, even though she'd only seen words on a page. Most of the trick in writing transparently is in the action.

Transparency

Your objective in writing is to draw your readers into the experience of your screenplay in such a crafty way that they feel as though they're seeing a movie. The writing "leaps off the page." They don't remember the actual sentences you used to describe the action. They forget they're reading words at all. They remember characters talking and things happening.

The first step to transparency is to keep your descriptions of action clean, simple, and precise. Sentences should be short and crisp. Descriptions should be expressive without getting bogged down in details. Say as much as you can in as few words as you can. Use short, declarative, *visual* sentences.

You're not trying to paint a picture. You're trying to sketch a scene.

You want to be hyperaware of the images that your words put in people's minds.

```
While Tommy works frantically to adjust the
steam valve, Nancy keeps lookout.
```

This sentence is the written equivalent of a two-shot. A two-shot is a wide shot where both characters are in frame at once. Both characters are in the same paragraph, so in my mind's eye, they're sharing the screen. It could be more compelling to go in closer:

```
Tommy works frantically to adjust the steam
valve.

Nancy keeps lookout.
```

The white space separates the two actions.

Show, Don't Tell.

But "keeps lookout" is *telling* us what she's doing, not *showing* us. "Keeps lookout" does not give much of a visual image. Show, don't tell. The crafty way to write this is to break it up into two separate moments:

```
TOMMY

works frantically to wrench the rusty steam
valve shut.

NANCY

stares nervously out the dirty window.
```

Note how "the rusty steam valve" means we're close enough to see rust on the valve.

Only Write What You Can See and Hear

The key to transparency is to write *exactly* what you want us to see and hear, and *only* what we can see and hear.

Beginning screenplays often describe scenes without showing them to us visually. Show, don't tell. This is telling:

```
INT. O'BRIEN HOUSE – KITCHEN – DAY

The O'Brien family has just moved into their
new house, a small bungalow outside Santa
Cruz, but it hasn't helped. They've been on
each other's nerves for days.
```

That's fine for a story, but not for a screenplay. How do we know they've been on each other's nerves? How do we know it's near Santa Cruz? What do we see? What we might actually see on-screen is a kitchen, probably with some people in it. What can you show us onscreen that will let us know how long they've been in their house, or what kind of a house it is, or that they've been on each other's nerves?

I think some beginning writers put lines like that into the action to remind themselves what the scene's about as they're writing. I think this is a bad idea even if you take the lines out later, because they tend to mislead you about how much you've actually put into the scene. As with creating a long backstory for your character that doesn't appear in your screenplay, the danger with writing lines of action that aren't purely visual is that you feel you've communicated something to the reader, but you haven't communicated it to the *audience*. If it's not something you can see or hear, then it's not going to be on the screen.

A crafty screenwriter will find a way to communicate all this information in a visual and aural way.

```
EXT. O'BRIEN HOUSE – DAY

A small brick bungalow with dead grass and two
stunted palm trees. Dull green mountains in
the distance. Somewhere, SEAGULLS complain.

INT. O'BRIEN HOUSE – KITCHEN – DAY

Some boxes have been shoved to one side of the
counter, power cords hanging out of them, to
make room for three days' worth of dirty
dishes. More boxes on the floor. The faucet is
dripping. Amanda storms in, starts clattering
the dishes into the sink.

                    CATHERINE (O.S.)
          Amanda!

                    AMANDA
          I'm doing them!

                    CATHERINE (O.S.)
          Aman-da!

Amanda CLATTERS the last plate into the sink,
runs to the dining room side.
```

```
                    AMANDA
        I hate this house! I hate it! I hate
        it! Why'd we have to leave?

    She runs out the other end. The front door
    SCREECHES open and SLAMS shut.

    Catherine slumps in. Tosses her cigarette in
    the sink. To herself:

                    CATHERINE
        I hate it too, honey. But it's just
        for a little while.
```

This all takes a good deal longer than the original. But everything here can go up on the screen. We get that they've just moved into the house and they don't like it, and we have a pretty good idea why.

When you find yourself wondering if a line is showing or telling, ask yourself, "What do we see?" and "How do we know?"

Let's look at another scene description:

```
    The battle is cruel. The men fight fiercely,
    outnumbered, digging in with the little
    artillery and armor they still have.

    A dozen men hold off a half dozen tanks.
    Finally, carrying satchel charges and claymore
    mines, they hurl themselves at the tanks.
```

The first paragraph is literature, not cinema. Whether you're using archival footage or new footage or both, you have to break down each story beat into individual events we can see and hear. What will actually go on the screen? Unpack it until it is made up of individual moments. (Actually, good literature often breaks great events into small moments we can comprehend, too.)

The second paragraph is better, but it is still the *description* of some action, not an actual scene or moment. As you write a scene based on a beat like that one, you'll generally find that a single action will take the place of many actions. In other words, while your story might say that many men take out many tanks, on-screen it's probably more compelling if you focus on taking out one tank.

Here's what it might take to knock out one single tank on screen:

```
YURI

grabs a claymore mine.

               IVAN
     You'll never make it! Don't!

               YURI
     I have to try!

               IVAN
     It's madness!

Yuri ignores him, pulls the fuse, and goes
darting down the thirty yards of rubble to the
lead tank.

BOOM! A shell explodes, hurling him back. Yuri
staggers, dazed.

A GERMAN

aims. BAM!

YURI

spins, staggers. Another bullet rips through
him. He falls to one knee.

He forces himself back up.

Yuri staggers, dying, for the lead tank. He
gets close, starts to hurl the claymore at the
tank's treads –

BOOM! another shell EXPLODES and –

– Yuri's gone

IVAN

stares, stunned.

               IVAN
     God damn it.
```

```
THE LEAD TANK

rolls forward, onto . . .

. . . Yuri's claymore mine.

A HUGE EXPLOSION erupts.

And when the smoke clears, the lead tank's
right tread is destroyed, torn clean off the
wheels. The tank turns in a ragged circle, the
right wheels spinning aimlessly. This is one
piece of the Wehrmacht that isn't going home to
Berlin.
```

(Whoops. Sorry about that last sentence. You get carried away sometimes.)

Capitalize things you hear. Noises. Screams. Shouts. They should jump off the page.

Note how we no longer need to show the whole cruel battle. We don't need to show a dozen men killing half a dozen tanks. We don't even need to see a second tank get destroyed. The audience gets it.

Film is a personal medium. While a novel may talk about armies sweeping across the plains, a film will spend no more than a few shots to establish that the army is sweeping across the plain before it focuses in on a few characters. That's not only because it's expensive to shoot scenes with thousands of extras; after all, nowadays you do a little computer graphics and there's your army. It's because unlike books, movies don't present you with abstract ideas. They show you pictures of things happening. We care more when we see one guy getting clobbered with a battle-axe than when we see a hundred men getting clobbered. A book might be able to make us care about the hundred men, but on film it's going to be a hundred extras we never saw before, and we're not going to care.

The same goes for characters. I've seen more than a few characters introduced like this:

```
SALLY is in her 40s. Now a stout, jovial
woman, she used to be a track star in college.
```

```
She has a good sense of humor, but don't push
her too far or she'll bite back.
```

What we'll see on the screen is a stout woman in her forties. The part about her being a track star is misplaced backstory. The last sentence is all handwaving. We won't find out anything about her sense of humor until something makes her laugh.

To get across what Sally's like, you'll want to have her do and say things that show us. If you want us to know she's jovial, you could tell us she has a jovial *face*. Some people have obviously jovial faces, and that's something we can see. It's a small distinction, but it's the difference between giving us a sense of Sally and giving us a *visual* sense of her. A better way to do it, though, is to show her being jovial in her first scene:

```
Jack enters. Sally grins.

                 SALLY
      Hey! Look what the cat drug in!

She pours him a cup of coffee as he slides
onto a stool.
```

If you want to tell us she was a track star, you can show us a track medal on the wall in a frame, or you can have another character ask, "What happened to you, Sally? You used to do a four-minute mile!" You could even have her put on her old track shoes one rainy night to go running, only to realize she hasn't got it anymore. Any of these things we can actually see or hear.

It helps to be *really strict* with yourself about only writing things that can be heard or seen. Otherwise they tend to sneak in, not necessarily so obviously as in the examples above, but in phrases here and there:

```
Tommy sighs, remembering the conversation from
earlier.
```

Whoops! All we're going to *see* is Tommy sighing.

You might be able to cut the subordinate clause and leave it at "Tommy sighs," if it's clear enough from the rest of the scene what he's sighing about. If you want us to know specifically that he's sighing about the conversation earlier, you'll have to give us that information in a way we can see and hear. The obvious way is in dialogue:

```
Tommy sighs.

                    SARAH
          What?

                    TOMMY
          Just something Neil told me.
```

Suppose you find yourself writing something like, "She wants to cry, but her mascara would run." Whoops! This is an internal thought; there's no way to shoot it.

Crafty screenwriting means *finding the outward signs of the inner experience*. Which gesture, which expression, which words, or which sequence of images will express clearly to the audience what you want them to know? Could you show her trying to wipe away her tears without messing up her mascara, and making a worse mess? Or dabbing at her eyes with a tissue? Or just fighting back the tears? What does a woman do when she wants to cry but can't? Hyperventilate? It's your job to know, or find out, the outward gesture that will show the audience the inner state of mind.

There are crafty exceptions, of course. Take this example:

```
Jim and Bob are discussing sports when Tom
comes in.
```

No good, because if the camera's on Jim and Bob, we ought to be hearing their dialogue:

```
                    JIM
          . . . come on, Hunt Stillman's the
          best rookie pitcher the A's have had
          since Catfish Hunter.

                    BOB
          Yeah, but he can't match – oh, hey,
          hi, Tom.
```

But suppose they're talking in the back of a crowded bar, and the scene has Tom's point of view.

```
INT. BAR – NIGHT

Tom pushes the doors open. Looks around.

In the back, Jim and Bob are shooting the
breeze. Bob waves Tom over.
```

Here you don't write out the dialogue because all we actually see on-screen is two guys in the back of a bar talking to each other; we can't hear their dialogue.

You can also get away with writing action that doesn't *literally* communicate something you can see or hear, provided it is shorthand for something that you can.

```
Tommy sighs. Again?
```

We all know what it looks like when someone sighs like that. Not *again*.

```
Dylan looks the painting over, smiling. Nice.
```

Of course we don't know literally that Dylan's thinking "nice!" But it's shorthand for saying, "with a relaxed, slightly triumphant smile."

You can even get away with a teeny bit of directing the actors from time to time:

```
Jack keeps pounding at the door, crying, but
we're beginning to get the sense his heart
isn't in it.

Nathan smiles in spite of himself.

Joe starts to say something. Frowns.
Something's bothering him, but he can't quite
put his finger on it.
```

None of these are strictly describing what you can see or hear, but they give you a visual image. We know what these moments look like. So long as what you're writing puts an image in our mind's eye, you can get away with it.

```
Jack keeps pounding at the door, crying, but
we're beginning to get the sense it's all for
show.
```

Where you draw the line is up to you. A little fudging can communicate something that will work on-screen but is hard to put down on paper in precise language. But you can only cheat so much before your reader starts to wonder, "How're you going to put *that* on the screen?"

You can even sometimes get away with hype. You'll notice I cheated in the example a few pages back:

```
The tank turns in a ragged circle, the right
wheels spinning aimlessly. This is one piece of
the Wehrmacht that isn't going home to Berlin.
```

The last sentence is sheer hype. It contributes nothing to what's on the screen. It's just telling us to take a little pause and feel satisfied. The reason it's excusable here, I think, is that the sound track is going to be communicating exactly this emotion, and the audience is going to be feeling savagely self-satisfied. But if you do this more than once or twice in a script, the reader's going to feel you are telling her a story instead of showing her a movie.

How to Direct the Camera Without Seeming To

Since you want reading your screenplay to feel like seeing a movie, explicit camera directions are a bad idea. For example:

```
CLOSEUP OF FEET

walking along the floor. We TRACK ALONG WITH
the feet until they disappear behind a door.
```

You might see this in a production draft of a screenplay, when the director has asked the writer to put his notes into the script, or when the director is the writer. You might see this in a TV script written by a writer-producer who has the clout to make the director shoot it the way he wants. For example, if you look at James Cameron's scripts, you'll see "We CRANE DOWN below the wall" and " . . . TILTING DOWN to see the glow pulsing under the ice." Neither of these scripts has to sell to anyone. They're already sold. Cameron is writing as much for his film crew as for a reader.

Putting explicit camera moves into the script has the effect in the reader's mind of putting the camera in the movie with the actors. Instead of seeing a scene, the reader sees a film crew shooting a scene. The reader's internal vision of the movie is compromised. When you are watching the scene on-screen, you won't be thinking "close-up of feet . . . tracking shot." If you are, the movie is in deep trouble.

On the other hand, there are times you want to give a specific visual effect. Suppose you do want to open a scene by seeing someone's feet walking across the floor. Maybe you don't want us to know whose feet they are yet. Maybe you're being coy. Maybe you just like to look at feet up close, how should I know? There has to be a crafty way to start a scene just watching feet, right?

The solution is to show us only what you want us to see:

```
FEET

walk across the floor and disappear behind a
door.
```

I like to think of this as a *virtual close-up*. The reader "sees" only what you want her to see.

Directors will tend to ignore any explicit camera instructions you put in the script, but if you manipulate the director into imagining the movie the way you do, he may well shoot it the way you want it shot.

You *need* to do some virtual directing of the camera, or you won't communicate the visual impact of your action scenes. Here's some action:

```
JOE hits the ground rolling, firing the .45 as
he rolls. STEVE takes a slug in the gut,
smashes backward through the window, glass
```

```
shattering. He falls until he slams into a car
roof, arms sprawled awkwardly.
```

The first problem is that a big chunk of solid text is tough to read. (Yes, four consecutive lines is a "big chunk of solid text.") Remember, the reader is blitzing through your script at midnight trying to find out what the script is about so she can say something not-too-stupid about it at the 9:30 staff meeting. She's reading that paragraph like this:

```
JOE hits the ground rolling, firing the .45.
STEVE blah blah blah blah blah blah blah blah
blah blah blah blah blah blah blah blah blah
blah blah blah blah blah blah blah blah blah
blah blah blah blah blah.
```

You have to lure her into having the experience of seeing the scene as you see it in your mind's eye. Break up action sequences into individual *virtual shots*. Don't be afraid to throw in sound effects:

```
JOE hits the ground rolling, firing the .45
BAM! BAM! BAM! as he rolls—

STEVE takes a slug in the gut, smashes
backward through the window, glass shattering—

. . . falling . . .

. . . falling . . .

—THUMP! Steve slams into a car roof, arms
sprawled awkwardly.
```

If I'm doing my job, you "saw" Steve fall in slow motion. Good. That's what I wanted.

Use lots of white space. White space is your friend. Remember, you're trying to write a page a minute. A quarter page of action should take fifteen seconds of screen time. If your scenes take much less space on the page than they would take to unfold on the screen, the odds are excellent that you are describing, not showing.

You can be fairly precise about your virtual cinematography, depending on how you break up your action. As a general rule, if you want two events to be in two different virtual shots, they should be in different paragraphs. If you want them to be in the same virtual shot, they might be two sentences, but in the same paragraph:

One wide shot:

```
Tommy works frantically to adjust the steam
valve. Nancy stares nervously out the window.
```

Two quick shots:

```
TOMMY works frantically to wrench the rusty
steam valve shut.

NANCY stares nervously out the window.
```

Two longer shots:

```
TOMMY

works frantically to wrench the rusty steam
valve shut.

NANCY

stares nervously out the window.
```

The words are exactly the same, but the white space and capitalization create different virtual framing just as surely as different lenses do on the camera. Depending on the effect you're trying to achieve, any one of these might be the best for your scene.

Show, don't tell. (I'm going to keep saying this.)

Note, however, that you should *not* direct the camera, even in a crafty, virtual way, if it's not telling the story. While it's hard to communicate the excitement of an action scene without a little virtual direction of the camera, you usually don't need more than dialogue and the occasional rare parenthetical to communicate what's going on in a dialogue scene. Therefore you will likely want to keep your dialogue scenes clean of camera direction, even virtual.

Graphic Sex and Violence

Gratuitous sex and violence don't belong in a screenplay because they don't belong in a movie. In this context, *gratuitous*, a fancy word meaning "for free," means that the sex and violence are there for their own sake. They're not part of the story you're telling. They stop your story dead while we watch the characters have sex or we watch someone get beaten up.

A sex scene isn't gratuitous if it's part of the story: that is, if it's important to the story not only *that* they do it but *how* they do it. Is it an act of tenderness? Of passion? Of lust? Are they just going through the motions? Are they two teenagers doing it for the first time?

Likewise, a scene of violence isn't gratuitous if it's part of the story. In *Capone*, it's important to the story that Capone is willing to bash in the skull of one of his lieutenants in front of all his other lieutenants. If sex and violence are part of your story, you need to show it. The question is, how graphic do you want to get? Do you want to show us exactly what's happening, or do you just want to suggest it?

Less is usually more here. You should show us as little as we need to see for you to tell your story. Let our imaginations fill in the details. You don't want to jolt your reader out of the experience of seeing your movie.

The more outlandish the violence, the easier it is to take. While you can perfectly well have a zombie strangle the department store Santa under the fluorescents, less cartoonish violence, especially when directed against the weak (women, children, pets) often throws the reader and the audience out of the movie. So, for example, if you have a physically abusive husband who's going to get his just deserts later on, you probably don't need to show him beating his wife on-screen. You might instead use the point of view of their daughter, who's in bed in the next room: she wakes up and hears the noises, and we know what those noises are. Likewise, you usually don't want to show a rape on-screen. The main exception would be where the abuse or rape is the subject of the movie, as in *The Burning Bed* or *The Accused*.

But there you will have to tread a fine line in what you write so it's clear that the scene won't be too painful to watch.

You pretty much never want to show someone hurting (as opposed to frightening) a child or a pet on-screen. Personally, if someone kills a pet on-screen in a script I'm reading, I will not read another page. It is a cheap and repulsive way to get an emotional effect. You can, if you must, have a bad guy shoot a dog offscreen, and we can see the body later. Yeah, it works, but I'd just as soon the pet survive.

It is usually classier and emotionally more effective to show the aftermath of extreme violence than the violence itself. In *Conan the Barbarian*, a fine film not otherwise noted for understatement, we don't see little Conan's mother get her head whacked off by Thulsa Doom. We see little Conan's face as he holds her hand; the sword swings; her hand lets go of his; and he looks up at her with a child's bewilderment.

Using Songs and Music in Your Script

You're not publishing your script, so you don't need to own the rights to a song to put its lyrics in your script. From a copyright standpoint, nothing is stopping you from telling us that a given famous song would work well in your scene, and writing all its lyrics on the page. But it's rarely a good idea. "That Lovin' Feeling" may not speak to your reader the same way it speaks to you. You can suggest that there's a certain style of music on:

```
Somewhere, a tinny radio plays surf music.
```

or

```
The cradle is empty except for the bright
yellow tape recorder, still eerily playing the
Barney song.
```

But you can't rely on the reader's remembering that a song is playing, because you can't play a song in the background of a written scene the way you can play it in the background of the scene in the movie.

On the other hand, you may need to put a song in the *foreground* of a scene. I put Woody Guthrie's song "Pretty Boy Floyd," words and all, into a driving scene. The script was about Charles "Pretty Boy" Floyd, and in the scene, Pretty Boy was listening to a song on the radio about himself. The point was that he knew he was becoming famous, and it would not have been enough to just say:

```
Woody Guthrie is on the radio, singing "Pretty
Boy Floyd."
```

That's because the reader probably doesn't know "Pretty Boy Floyd," and my goal was to play the whole song for her.

What you must never do is tell us about the score, the music written to underlie the scene and amplify its emotional impact. Never tell us the music swells at a certain point. Of course the score underlines the emotion of the scene. That's what scores do. If your scene isn't romantic enough on the page, telling us that great music is playing won't save it.

Montages

Montage comes from the French word for editing. It describes a series of images, usually without dialogue, edited together to show a bunch of things happening in one place, or the passage of time, or two lovers having a good time in the beginning of their relationship.

Here's a sample of a montage:

```
EXT. GARDEN – DAY (MONTAGE)

Two girls are skipping rope.

A man in a top hat is riding a unicycle.

The Devil is walking down the steps, whistling
a jaunty tune.
```

Unfortunately, declaring a "montage" is a good way to make your reader aware that you are using a cinematic device. In other words, when you write the word `montage`, you push your reader out of the experience of seeing a movie and reminding her that she is reading a screenplay. What you're saying is, "Here are some images, we'll edit them together later."

There is no "later." The screenplay should be the experience of seeing the movie. Don't tell us something is a montage. Just edit the moments together yourself. *Do* the montage.

```
EXT. GARDEN – DAY

TWO GIRLS skip rope near a fountain.

A MAN IN A TOP HAT balances on a unicycle,
juggling.

THE DEVIL walks down the stone steps,
whistling a jaunty tune and twirling his
umbrella.
```

Okay I've cheated a little by adding an umbrella twirl that wasn't in the earlier examples. But montages, as such, tend to restrict your writing. You will likely find yourself trying to get all the bullet points to be about the same length.

Forget the list. Some shots may be long, some short. What if the Devil shot wants to develop into a miniscene with dialogue?

```
EXT. GARDEN – DAY

TWO GIRLS skip rope near a fountain.

A MAN IN A TOP HAT balances on a unicycle,
juggling.

THE DEVIL walks down the stone steps,
whistling a jaunty tune and twirling his
umbrella. He passes an ELDERLY WOMAN, leers
at her outrageously, tips his hat.

                    DEVIL
          Madame . . .

THE ELDERLY WOMAN backs away from him into
the railing and falls backward over it,
disappearing with a muffled YELP.
```

You can't do *that* in a montage.

Editing Your Scenes

As you adapt your outline steps or story beats into scenes, there's the question of where to start and end your scenes.

The simple answer is: get into your scene as late as you can, make your point, and get out as soon as you can.

On the simplest level, don't show the guy coming in the door.

```
INT. MAX'S OFFICE – DAY

Carl opens the door, strides over to Max's desk.

                    MAX
          Carl?

Carl slams the piece of paper on the desk.

                    CARL
          What the hell does this mean?
```

Start the scene as late as you can:

```
INT. MAX'S OFFICE – DAY

Carl slams the piece of paper on Max's desk.

                    CARL
          What the hell does this mean?
```

Then, after a page or two of brilliant dialogue ending with Max agreeing, "What could possibly go wrong?" cut straight to what goes wrong. Don't let the scene trail off with the guys shaking hands and Carl going out the door.

You may find it useful to write each scene long and then see how much of the beginning and the end you can lop off without losing the point of the scene.

One way you can tell where you can cut is to ask: Where does the conflict begin and where does it end? In the example above, the argument can't begin until Carl reveals the paper, so that's where you start the scene. Once both characters agree, there's no more conflict, so it's time to go.

(Comic books, especially the great ones, are superb at showing only the core of the scene, because they only have sixteen to thirty-two pages to tell a story. Take a look at Frank Miller's *The Dark Knight Returns* or any of Neil Gaiman's *Sandman* series, all of which are collected in graphic novel form.)

There are two main exceptions to this rule. You may begin a scene earlier than you need to if you can use the beginning of the scene to set up background information that you'll need the audience to know later.

For example, in *What Lies Beneath*, a dramatic scene between Michelle Pfeiffer and Harrison Ford takes place in Ford's lab, where he's using a drug that paralyzes rats without knocking them unconscious. The drug will come up again later in a fiendish way. You don't want to give the audience too strong a warning about that, so you don't want to give a whole scene to the drug. But you do want them to know how it works. So at the top of the scene, Michelle is given a little explanation ("exposition") of the drug's use on rats, and then we move into the scene proper.

You may also extend your scene so that it covers two steps or beats. A four-page dialogue scene might contain a confrontation that ends in one revelation ("I've been unfaithful to you, Marilyn"), which in turn triggers another confrontation ("I'm not going to listen to this!" "Yes, you are!"), which ends in another revelation ("Look, I know you cheated on me, darling. That's why I've poisoned you.") In that case you still want to get out of the first beat as soon as you've made your point, and find a nifty way to segue from there to as late as possible in the second beat.

The movies want compression. They want high points and low points, with the longueurs squeezed out. A novel can afford longueurs.

Note that this rule does not mean you can't have slow scenes. Sometimes it takes a long scene to communicate what you want the beat to communicate. If the beat is "Lawrence and the Bedouins cross the endless, broiling Nefud Desert, suffering intolerable heat," then it may take ten minutes to get across how horrible the journey is. You can't start the scene later than "Lawrence and the Bedouins set off," and you can't end it earlier than "they arrive at the oasis."

The films of Ingmar Bergman likewise contain long scenes of excruciating suffering, but the suffering is the point, so he could not have shortened them. Any trimming would have made them less effective, not more.

When you have long, *unnecessarily* slow scenes, you need to trim, or you'll end up with one of those movies about which people say, "The cinematography was beautiful."

Pacing

Although it's most obvious in action-adventure pictures and thrillers, pacing is important to any movie. Pacing refers to the speed at which events unfold. In an effective movie, events unfold slowly in the first act, pick up speed in the second act, and move as fast as they can in the third act. ("As fast as they can" in the literal sense: a drama's third act may well be slower than an action movie's first act.)

That doesn't mean a slow scene can't follow a fast scene. Even in a Joel Silver action spectacular, where there's a "whammy" every ten minutes, after each whammy there's a bit of a breather for the audience to absorb what they've seen. (A whammy is just what it sounds like, a scene or moment that goes "whammy!": an explosion, a chase, an outrageous sex scene.) For example, every new Bond film opens with a huge action sequence, followed by a quiet scene at headquarters in which M explains Bond's new mission and Q gives him his new toys. In *The Terminator*, after the Terminator (Arnold Schwarzenegger) takes out the police station and Sarah Connor (Linda Hamilton) and Kyle Reese (Michael Biehn) barely escape, they take shelter in a culvert. That's when Reese explains to Sarah Connor why the Terminator is trying to kill her, and what her as-yet-unborn son means to him.

But the later you are in the movie, the shorter the breathers are, and the bigger the whammies. If you chart the intensity of each scene in a good movie, you will see a series of waves getting bigger and bigger and steeper and steeper, until the biggest wave comes right at the end.

Pacing is therefore not just a function of timing. You can't create rising pacing just by making your scenes shorter and shorter and your events happen quicker and quicker as your story unfolds. Your scenes need to become more and more intense, too. Otherwise your story is just becoming choppy. If readers are complaining that your pacing seems off, it may mean that you are taking too long with your later scenes, but it may equally mean that some of your scenes are failing to register as intense enough. The waves are not high enough. Don't just trim scenes down. Make more bombs go off, whether they are real or emotional ones. If your third-act scene is too short to score, it may be that what you need to do is lengthen it rather than trimming it further.

THE CLOCK

If your script is a thriller or action movie, you may want to put in a clock. A clock is a deadline against which the hero is racing. The classic example is *High Noon*. Marshal Will Kane (Gary Cooper) has to mobilize his small western town before bad guys show up on the noon train to kill him. Everywhere you look in the movie, the clocks are ticking off the minutes in real time. More recently, in *Outbreak*, an American town will be bombed to ashes if the virus isn't contained by a certain time. In *Executive Decision*, a jumbo jet full of innocent passengers will be blown out of the sky by a certain time or terrorists aboard it will drop deadly poison over the entire East Coast. In *The Rock*, the bad guys are going to blow poison gas into San Francisco if they don't get their money by Tuesday. And so forth.

A clock is by no means necessary. It's not hard to come up with any number of extremely suspenseful thrillers that don't have a clock. Just to pick names out of a hat: *Basic Instinct*, *Sleeping with the Enemy*, *Wild Things*, *Single White Female*, *Rear Window*, *Gaslight*, *The Parallax View*, *Day of the Condor*, *The Conversation*, *Blow Up*, *Blow Out*, *Seven*, *Chinatown*, *Body Heat*, *Jagged Edge*, *Witness*. Nor can you say that the subgenre of action thrillers needs a clock. *The Fugitive*, *Conspiracy Theory*, *Lethal Weapon*, *The Long Kiss Goodnight:* none of these has a clock.

What all suspenseful thrillers and action thrillers do have is a tightening noose, either putting the hero in more and more jeopardy, or getting the hero closer and closer to solving the mystery, or both. For example, serial-killer movies (*The Silence of the Lambs*, *Seven*) don't really have clocks, but the detective is trying to stop the bad guy from murdering his next victim. It's not a clock because we don't know whom he'll kill next or what time he'll do it. Innocent-man thrillers such as *North by Northwest* and *The Fugitive* have the hero desperately trying to clear himself before he's caught by the cops.

If someone is asking you to put a clock into your story, it may be a sign that you are not ratcheting up the suspense as the story unfolds. Your pacing does not pick up fast enough as you approach the end of the movie. You're not tightening the noose. In this case, merely providing a clock will not automatically increase suspense. The clock provides an *excuse* for your characters to get wound up, but it doesn't wind them up *for* you. You still have to provide the suspense, the jeopardy, and the mystery.

That said, if you can create an organic reason to have a clock, it can clarify the hero's task. Clarity is a Good Thing.

If you have a clock, it is also neat to speed it up periodically. We don't have six hours—we have half an hour! Oh no!

Point of View

> "Point of view: a position from which something is considered or evaluated: STANDPOINT."

A point-of-view or POV shot is a shot that shows exactly what a character is seeing. The camera shoots what the character is seeing.

```
EXT. POOLSIDE – DAY

Sabrina slips through the crowd of guests.

EXT. POOLSIDE – DAY (TONY'S POV)

Guests milling around. No sign of Sabrina.
```

```
EXT. POOLSIDE – DAY

Sabrina surges out of the crowd, pie tin
gleaming in the sun.

TONY

sees her, SHOUTS

SABRINA

hurls the cream pie
```

You can have a shot from the point of view of a dog, a monster, or a flying cream pie.

A *point-of-view character* is a character through whose perception we watch a movie unfold. We hear only those things he hears, know only those things he knows.

We don't see only through his eyes, though. That would get irritating fast. It would also give the wrong impression. When I remember a conversation, I have a mental image of me in the conversation. So if a scene takes my point of view, it will have shots not only of the person I'm looking at, but shots of me, too. However, it won't have shots of anything I didn't know was going on.

Not every film has a single point-of-view character. In many films, the story jumps back and forth between places and characters who aren't in touch with each other. But sticking with one point of view in the film can be a powerful tool. It helps us identify with the central character, pulling us into his personal story.

The most obvious use of point of view is in a detective story. If we know only what the detective knows, then we are pulled into his experience trying to figure out the mystery. If we knew everything that was going on, we wouldn't be mystified. *Fight Club*, *Jacob's Ladder*, and *The Sixth Sense* all have mysteries at their heart; the hero's discovery of the answer is the "twist" that makes these films so effective. If we knew more than what the central characters knew—if we knew what the people around him knew—these films would be less surprising.

Keeping a single point of view is extremely useful when the central character is not someone with whom we'd usually identify. For example, *A Clockwork Orange* unfolds from the point of view of Alex, a violent young psychopath. Barely any of the film takes place outside Alex's point of view. For example, when Alex's gang mutinies, it comes as a surprise to both Alex and us. Together with a wry voice-over from Alex himself telling his own story, and some clever cinematographic tricks, we come as close as we can to empathizing with a warped, evil individual.

The classic silent film *The Cabinet of Dr. Caligari* also puts us in an odd point of view. We need almost the whole picture to realize that the central character is a maniac, because we're seeing things from his point of view. But the picture is scary precisely because his point of view is so bent.

Cinema is a literalistic medium. You can't reproduce a mental state on the screen. What are you going to shoot to mimic schizophrenia? Depression? Manic joy? The Monkees film *Head* attempts to reproduce an LSD trip on film. The Monkees go through surreal escapades; everything makes some kind of poetic sense, but not logical sense. A movie has to create a visual parallel for anything you can't actually shoot. Say you want to make us identify with a paranoid person—to see the film's events from his paranoid perspective. You can't film the *feeling* that everyone's out to get the hero. But you can make the film's events seem threatening without giving a reason why:

```
Bill walks down the alley. He passes a
Dumpster. Is that something moving in the
shadows behind it. . . ?

. . . No, just a trick of the light.

He walks faster, sweating.
```

Or,

```
                 WAITRESS
        You have a good time, now.

She winks at him, strangely, as if she knows
something he doesn't.
```

It's tricky to use this technique, because the reader has to have confidence that you're intentionally showing her something, rather than just being confused yourself. You may need to tip off the audience:

```
                    LINDA
          Why do you always think someone's out to
          get you?

                    KEVIN
          I'm not being paranoid!
```

THE FOIL

The point-of-view character does not have to be the central character. The character most central to your story might be an out-of-the-ordinary person into whose mind we can never truly enter. So the film takes the point of view of another, normal character—a "foil," or stand-in for the audience.

House of Cards and *Rain Man* both have autistic characters at their center. *House of Cards* tried to show the inner world of Sally, the autistic daughter (Asha Menina). But *Rain Man* was a more successful movie partly *because* it didn't try to get inside the mind of Raymond, the autistic savant (Dustin Hoffman). He is in a place we can never go, thank God. The camera can show the outward face of autism—or, more precisely, an actor's illumination of autism. In *Rain Man* the point-of-view character is the autistic man's brother, Charlie Babbitt (Tom Cruise). *His* mind is one into which we can enter.

In Kenneth Branagh's operatic horror film *Mary Shelley's Frankenstein*, the emotional POV leaves Viktor von Frankenstein for an extended stretch when the creature finds shelter in the shed of the peasant family, and there learns to speak and read. While the creature is suffering, we can relate to his problems. But once the creature, ejected from his refuge, swears revenge on von Frankenstein, he becomes Nemesis, killing the people von Frankenstein most loves. We can't relate to him anymore; there is no way we can empathize with him. When the creature captures von Frankenstein and asks why he was made, the scene is played from von Frankenstein's POV, as is the rest of the tragedy.

The mind of a computer, an alien, a madman, a god, a demon, a dolphin: unless you can come up with a really convincing visual metaphor, you will need to filter their stories through the POV of an ordinary character we *can* understand.

EMOTIONAL POV

Point of view can be a subtle thing. A film will often leave the central character's *literal* point of view but stay in that character's *emotional* point of view. Emotional point of view includes

a. things the character sees—his literal point of view;
b. things the character doesn't see, but will eventually know happened; and/or
c. things that directly affect the character.

To give an example of (b), in a thriller in which the main character is a detective investigating a series of murders, you may often want to show the killer at work. So long as the things we see the killer do are things that the detective *will eventually learn about*, the picture stays in the detective's emotional point of view, even though it's not in his literal point of view. Thus we can see a murder happen (as in the beginning, say, of *Basic Instinct*), and then have the detective show up and investigate the crime scene. We know what he knows, even though we saw what he didn't.

To give an example of (c), in a movie in which the hero is a woman being stalked, we might see the stalker making his preparations—say, finding out where she's escaped to, and heading over to see her. What he's doing directly affects her, so we continue to identify with her even though the camera is seeing things that she doesn't know about, and that she may never know about. The *literal* POV of the film is with the stalker, but the *emotional* POV of the film is with her.

You would break the emotional point of view of the detective in (b) if you ever showed something the detective will never uncover, or in (c) if the stalker does something that doesn't affect the woman. For example, in either example, if the stalker takes a break to have some ice cream with some little kids, then the movie's emotional POV becomes his POV.

If you want us to identify with the woman or the detective, you don't have to stick with their *literal* point of view, but don't write scenes that break their *emotional* point of view. We don't have to know only what she knows, but we shouldn't see anything that we'll never know about and has nothing to do with her. Otherwise it stops being her picture.

Sticking with an emotional rather than a literal POV enables you to create more suspense than you otherwise could. For example, in *Vertigo*, we discover Judy Barton's secret halfway through the movie. Scottie Ferguson (Jimmy Stewart) doesn't learn it until the final reel. Because we know what's being done to him, we fear for him more—we experience more suspense—than we would if we only saw the story through his literal point of view. But the *emotional* point of view isn't broken, so we keep our strong emotional attachment to Scottie.

WRITING POINT OF VIEW

A scene can be written in two different ways, with identical dialogue, but with a different point of view. For example:

```
CARRIE frowns.
```

merely shows us Carrie's facial expression. The emotional POV is either neutral or it belongs to some other character who's seeing it. But this:

```
CARRIE frowns, troubled.
```

gets us into Carrie's heart just enough for us to feel her emotions, without going so deep into her mind that it can't be filmed.

Let's suppose you have a scene where Carrie walks into a room, overhearing the conversation before she comes in. If you're writing the scene from her POV, then you start the scene with her outside the room, overhearing the conversation. If you're writing from the POV of someone inside the room, then you start the scene in the room and have her walk in. Either way, she overheard the conversation, but in the first version, we're identifying with her, and in the second, we're not.

Version 1:

INT. OLD MAN'S HOUSE – CARRIE'S ROOM – DAY

Carrie wakes up, alert.

SARA (O.C.)
I just read this *Wired* piece you wrote.

NICK (O.C.)
Oh yeah? Damn, I must've left it lying around.

Carrie sits up, eager.

INT. OLD MAN'S LIVING ROOM – DAY

Carrie pokes her head in:

Sara is unfolding a piece of paper out of her back pocket. Nick is doing the crossword puzzle on the coffee table.

Version 2:

INT. OLD MAN'S LIVING ROOM – LATE AFTERNOON

Sara comes in. Nick is doing the crossword puzzle on the coffee table. She pulls a folded-up piece of paper out of her back pocket.

SARA
I just read this *Wired* piece you wrote.

NICK
Oh yeah? Damn, I must've left it lying around.

```
He looks up. Carrie's watching them from the
doorway.
```

The rest of the dialogue in the scene might be exactly the same in both versions. Once the point of view is established, it will carry through the scene until you do something that changes the point of view.

NO POINT OF VIEW OR MIXED POINT OF VIEW

Many excellent movies are totally voyeuristic—they don't take you into any character's mind, and they don't tell you everything any one character knows. *Wild Things* is an excellent example. We first see the movie from the POV of the teacher (Matt Dillon). Later we see some of it from the POV of the detective (Kevin Bacon). But it turns out later that we don't know everything they know; and in the end, the story turns out to have been entirely motivated by another character, whose machinations have been mostly kept from us. *Wild Things* works as a voyeuristic thriller. The audience may be coming for steamy eroticism (and it gets it!), but the goods the picture delivers is the cunning manipulation of the audience. In other words, the audience is paying for the thrill of being led around by the nose.

You can use a mixed point of view as a tool to achieve certain effects you can't achieve with a single point of view. But be aware that if you play games with the audience, your film risks being emotionally cold. Only by getting us to identify with a character—seeing the world through her eyes, whether cinematically or emotionally—can you move the audience emotionally.

Style

When you tell your story in a pitch, the words and sentences you use don't matter to the movie. The flow of the story is the only thing that will end up on-screen. But your dialogue, and even your action if you write it craftily enough, will. So when you go from your pitch to your screenplay, you have the opportunity to create *style*.

A movie has style when it has a consistent approach to presenting its scenes. A film might have a choppy style if the scenes are generally short and the cuts between them are generally abrupt. A film might have an operatic style if the scenery is lush, the actors' emotions are large and unrestrained, and characters talk for a long time before being interrupted. A movie might be accused of TV style if each of its scenes is introduced with an exterior establishing shot, then goes to a master shot of all the characters in the scene, and then moves in for a series of medium close-ups. The TV style makes sense for TV, where the screen is small. On the big screen, it looks cheap.

All of these styles can be communicated craftily in a screenplay.

I'm not talking about your prose style. You pretty much always want to write action using crisp, brief visual sentences, regardless of whether you are showing the slow trek across the Nefud or two people making out in a laundry room. Even if you are writing a drawing-room drama in which all the characters are highly literate and speak exclusively in long, well-thought-out sentences, you still want to avoid adjectives, adverbs, and subordinate clauses when you write the action.

```
                    POLLY
          Without a doubt, sir, you have been
          misinformed as to the feelings you
          supposed were reciprocated. I would take
          it as a mark of great courtesy if you
          would depart without exposing my family
          to any more sensation or scandal.

     She won't meet his eyes.

     Robert eyes her. Sighs.

                    ROBERT
          I regret if I have caused you any
          unhappiness. Good day, madam.

     He turns. Goes. The Butler hands him his hat.
     He fumbles it. The Butler snatches it before
     it hits the ground and hands it to him again,
     poker-faced.
```

```
                    ROBERT (CONT'D)
              (choking up)
          You are very kind, sir.
```

The action here is all in fine old short words, though the dialogue suggests that the characters have been overdosing on the novels of Henry James.

You define the style of your movie not by using a fancy prose style, but by being extremely attentive to how you are showing your story unfolding. Suppose you have two couples having related conversations in different places. Do you show one whole conversation as a scene, and then cut to the other? Do you cut back and forth between two dialogue scenes, using them as counterpoint? Do you stage the two conversations at one restaurant, in one shot, letting each couple miraculously fall silent while the other is talking, and changing focus ("racking focus") to whoever's talking? Do you let the couples rove back and forth in front of the camera so that each couple's conversation is continuous, but we only hear part of it, though we never leave the room? Prose style won't end up on the screen. Visual style will.

Each of these approaches might be appropriate, depending on the style you've chosen. If you are crafty, you can use any of them without throwing the reader out of the experience of seeing your movie in her mind's eye.

Directors and cinematographers spend their whole lives learning how to make stylish movies. All I can tell you is that your screenplay *has* a style, and you should be aware of it and control it, just as you need to be aware of and control your plot and your characters.

Choose a style in which you are comfortable writing, and one that is right for the story you're telling. It's your call. You can write a tragedy in a gritty, realistic style, or in a quirky, self-conscious style. Each approach has its own benefits. Each says a different thing to the audience. It's up to you to choose which is right for your movie.

5

DIALOGUE

Characters appear to be people, but are really the raw materials of story. Dialogue has two similar aspects:

1. It has to move the story forward.
2. It has to be believable as something your character might say.

Dialogue also creates the style and tone of the picture, at least as much as action does.

Moving the Story Forward

A script moves the story forward through action and dialogue. Action shows what people do. Dialogue tells us what people think. Therefore, action mostly shows you *what* happens while, by and large, only words can tell you *why* things happen or what it means that they happened.

Dialogue moves the story forward in two ways.

a. Dialogue carries the drama.
Dialogue is where characters' goals come out; and characters' goals, in conflict with each other, are what drive the story forward.

b. Dialogue tells us things we need to know.
Dialogue gives information we need to understand the plot and gives us insight into the characters.

DRAMA IS CONFLICT

Drama occurs when one character wants something and another character is in his way. Dialogue becomes dramatic when one character is trying to get something from another character that the other doesn't want to give; ideally, they both are. The objective could be a thing . . .

```
                JACK
      You didn't see the keys to my place,
      did you?
```

. . . or something they want done . . .

```
                JOSIE
      No I didn't. But if you go put a new
      bulb in my hallway lamp, I bet you'll
      find your keys in a New York second.
```

. . . or something they don't want to ask for directly:

```
                JACK
      I bet I could find 'em easier if I
      stayed over. Y'know, in the morning,
      more light.
```

. . . or a refusal they don't want to make directly:

                JOSIE
      Why don't I just give you back *my* keys
      to your place?

When the characters have got what they wanted, or given up trying to get it, the scene is over. Cut to the next scene, or introduce a new conflict.

"I DIDN'T COME HERE FOR AN ARGUMENT." "YES, YOU DID!"

It's always easier and more fun to absorb information when it comes in the form of an argument.

All good dialogue is *people saying things to each other because they are trying to get something from each other*. Real people talk in order to get things from other people. Sometimes it's hard to figure out what they're after, but everyone is after something.

In screenwriting you often need to get certain bits of information out to the audience; this is termed *exposition*, or *expo* for short. But you have to be careful that your characters are not talking only in order to get information out. If you need to give the audience a bit of information, make sure to give the character his *own* reason to tell us about it. That's called making dialogue *organic* to the character.

Motivating dialogue isn't enough. For example, a scene where one cop briefs another on the case may be necessary and believable, but it can be undramatic:

```
                SPINELLI
     The prints match exactly. The DNA
     checks out. Problem is, during the
     whole hour the murder could have taken
     place, our guy was playing golf with
     Roxanne.

                O'LEARY
     Phooey.
```

Sure, there's still some interest—these guys are both trying to figure out who killed the girl on page 4. But the scene just lays there like a lox. Everybody finds it easier to follow an argument than a lecture. So draw the audience by making the scene dramatic. Just set the two characters at odds with each other:

```
                    SPINELLI
          The prints match exactly. The DNA
          checks out.

                    O'LEARY
          Then you want to explain to me why,
          during the whole hour the murder could
          have taken place, our guy was playing
          golf with Roxanne?
```

Putting your characters into an argument is also one of the best ways to get a sense of them as characters. If we see someone cooking scrambled eggs, we're not going to learn that much about him, but if we see him arguing with his dad about whether to make eggs or waffles, we'll learn a lot about him right away.

Believability versus Realism

Dialogue is not the same as talk. Talk is what real people do. Dialogue is what characters say. Dialogue might sound like talk, but it is really closer to what we *remember* people saying than to what they *actually* said.

Real talk is not intended to be written down or repeated exactly. It's full of hems and haws and uhs, sentence fragments and kinda y'knows. If you've ever seen a courtroom transcript, it's tough to read, because of the careless, lazy, vague way people actually talk.

```
                    DOUG
          So, uh, I go to the, I go to the place
          where the . . . anyway, like I was saying,
          I go, fine, and I'm gonna do it 'cause,
          like, damn, y'know what I'm saying?
```

Fortunately, we're pretty good at interpreting this mess, so if we're listening, we usually hear what people mean rather than what they say. (Unfortunately, we're a little too good at interpreting, which explains why people often hear only what they want to hear.)

Good dialogue might *sound like* this example, if you're trying for a gritty, "realistic" style, but it will carry more, and more precise, information. It will really be closer to what we *heard* Doug say than what he actually said.

REALISTIC DIALOGUE

People rarely say exactly what's on their minds. They search for words. They try to phrase things so it won't cause a big confrontation. They're not sure exactly what they want or what they mean.

We say dialogue is "on the nose" when a character says exactly what's on his mind without any of the evasiveness of real conversation.

It's usually less interesting to have your characters get right to the meat of the disagreement between them. Instead, let one of them talk in circles about something apparently irrelevant, while the other character tries to figure out what's going on. Maybe he never figures out exactly what's going on, but a chance word triggers an explosion and now they're in an argument. But they still talk at cross-purposes. They answer the questions they expected, not the questions they're being asked. They hurl accusations, they take each other's words out of context, they bring up old sins.

If you need to have one character finally say exactly what's on her mind, then it's at the climax of the scene, when she can't stand to beat around the bush anymore.

There should almost always be tension between

1. what your character is literally saying,
2. what your character intends to communicate, and
3. what your character is thinking.

Roundabout dialogue is not only more realistic. It is also much more useful to a crafty screenwriter. It can carry many more levels of information. Here's some on-the-nose dialogue. It conveys a justification ("you make me mad") and an apology:

```
                    HANK
        I'm sorry I was mean to you, Janie. I
        should have kept my temper. But you
        make me really mad. It's only because
        I love you so much.
```

But this . . .

```
                    HANK
        You're just like your mother, you know
        that? Except she didn't need a fancy
        psych degree to rip up your dad's
        heart. . . . Hey, look, beautiful . . . how
        about I take us out to some nice place?
```

. . . tells the reader that Hank knows Janie's mother; that Janie has a degree in psychology, while her mother might be uneducated, like Hank; that Janie's parents' marriage was hell; and that Janie usually cooks and they rarely eat out at a nice place. All that, and still contains the justification and the apology.

REALISTIC VERSUS SNAPPY DIALOGUE

Great dialogue is not only realistic. It is striking, fresh, and expressive. It penetrates the audience's heart, it's something we haven't heard before, and it says a great deal in few words.

Real conversation is full of clichés. We explain ourselves in the first words that come to mind, not the cleverest or freshest or most precise ones. It's a rare person who comes out with more than one sentence in ten that's striking, fresh, and expressive, and most of us never manage it at all. But no one is paying good money to hear us talk, either. There is a tension between trying to make your dialogue gritty and realistic, so it sounds like something that a real person could actually say, and trying to make it striking, fresh, and expressive, so that it conveys real emotions more purely and powerfully.

Good realistic dialogue uses the repetitions, silences, and apparent aimlessness of real talk to create an effect that is much more powerful than ordinary talk. Characters may come up with surprisingly inventive turns of speech, but they come up as if by accident. Great realistic dialogue is probably the hardest kind to write, because you're trying to make it look accidental, while still carrying rich thoughts and feelings.

```
                RICK
If that plane leaves the ground and
you're not with him, you'll regret it.
Maybe not today. Maybe not tomorrow, but
soon, and for the rest of your life.

                ILSA
But what about us?

                RICK
We'll always have Paris. We didn't have,
we, we lost it until you came to
Casablanca. We got it back last night.

                ILSA
When I said I would never leave you.

                RICK
And you never will. But I've got a job to
do, too. Where I'm going, you can't
follow. What I've got to do, you can't be
any part of. Ilsa, I'm no good at being
noble, but it doesn't take much to see
that the problems of three little people
don't amount to a hill of beans in this
crazy world. Someday you'll understand
that. Now, now . . . Here's looking at you,
kid.
```

Realistic dialogue can be lyrical, almost spoken poetry, but it must feel like the characters discovered it as they reached for their thoughts. Actual poetry almost never works outside of Shakespeare adaptations.

Dialogue does not have to be gritty, of course. Hollywood has always had a fondness for snappy dialogue, especially in romantic comedies and action adventures. Characters bounce lines back and forth far more cleverly than anyone ever did in real life since the court of Louis XIV, where some people could live by their witticisms.

Snappy dialogue doesn't pretend very hard to seem accidental. We know it's dialogue. But if it's crisp, fresh, and insightful, we don't care. We know it's a movie, too, and we came to be entertained.

To write snappy dialogue, just think of the cleverest, wittiest, funniest way each character could say what he's trying to say. What's the sharpest jab, the choicest put-down, the most devastating comeback? You know, the kind of crushingly brilliant comeback you think of the morning after the party? That's snappy dialogue.

The important thing is that your dialogue's tone should be consistent, not only with the rest of the dialogue in your picture, but with the kind of picture you're making. A serious drama probably wants realistic dialogue. A comedy probably wants snappy dialogue. An austere Western might want very spare, sparse dialogue. If you're writing snappy dialogue in your serious drama, you'd better be going for a very specific effect, or you're going to run into problems.

FINDING YOUR CHARACTER'S VOICE

Although your dialogue's overall tone should be consistent, your characters shouldn't all talk the same. In far too many beginners' screenplays, everyone has the same "voice." Either they all talk in completely standard English, or it's a cop movie and the cops, thugs, and innocent bystanders all talk like thugs. But dialogue does more to distinguish your characters from each other than anything else:

```
                    BAKER
        I'm afraid that if you don't cooperate,
        the Agency may take a dim view of your,
        ah, "extracurricular activities."

                    CELLINI
        Are you freakin' threatening me?
```

When you give a character a distinctive voice, you tell us worlds about her:

```
                ELLEN
Don't ask me to take care of him,
okay? That ain't my job anymore!
        (winces)
Isn't. Isn't. Isn't.
```

We might guess that Ellen grew up saying "ain't" and has trained herself to say "isn't"; she may be middle class now, but she was brought up working class. Sure, she could tell us about it:

```
                ELLEN
I grew up in a trailer park. But I
won a scholarship, and I never
looked back.
```

But this is just dry information *about* her character. It may or may not sink in. Her falling back on "ain't" *is* her character, and it's hard to miss. The factual information in a line of dialogue is only about one-tenth of the information the line is capable of carrying.

The key to creating a voice is simply to review each line of dialogue and question what you've written: Can I rewrite this line to make it as distinctive as possible without it sounding false or drawing attention to itself?

```
                MAX
Yes.
```

. . . could be anyone. But this is an enthusiastic glad-hander:

```
                MAX
Yeah!
```

This is the wry, ironic kind of guy:

```
                MAX
Well, it's a sight better than a poke
in the eye with a sharp stick.
```

This is the quiet sort:

```
                    MAX
          Uh huh.
```

A real joker:

```
                    MAX
          Oui, mon capitaine.
```

. . . and so on. It's a fine line to tread, of course. But it's usually possible to improve a line so it tells us more about the character and gives your actor something to chew on.

TRIM YOUR DIALOGUE

When you're writing action, you want to use as few words as possible to express as much as possible. Same goes for dialogue. You may need a character to go on for half a page to make your point if he's giving a rousing speech. But if you've written a half-page rousing speech, the odds are good that you can rewrite it to be a quarter-page rousing speech, and it will be much more effective. How much dialogue can you cut without losing the point of the scene or the line?

For example, are you saying anything twice? Are your characters saying anything that doesn't move the story forward ("forward the story"), or at least give us insight into the characters or data we need to understand the plot, if not actually being part of the hero's struggle for his goal?

Let the silences speak, not just the words.

Remember, you're restricted to 120 pages and two hours. Make every line count.

TESTING YOUR DIALOGUE

Read your dialogue out loud.

I know, you were afraid I was going to say something like that. Don't worry. You don't need to read your dialogue out loud *to* anyone but yourself.

You can write a lot of lines that look fine on the page, but once someone says them out loud, they just don't sound like someone talking. For example, this line doesn't look bad on the page:

```
                    FRANKIE
        This is it, folks. Command Central.
        We've got two goals: first, find this
        mysterious Doc Wayne, then, if possible,
        through him, track down the source of
        the saucer sightings.
```

But once you try to say it out loud, it becomes a mouthful. First of all, there's the tongue-twisting last line. That's gotta go. Second, no one really uses constructions like "this mysterious so-and-so" in spoken language. They're part of the written English language, but not the spoken English language. The only time someone actually says, "Who is this mysterious so-and-so," he's being cute. Last, Frankie's line has way too many twists and turns. Real people try to get each thought out as simply as possible, and then qualify it later, if at all.

```
                    FRANKIE
        This is it, folks. Command Central.
        There's two things we need to do. First,
        find this Doc Wayne guy. Then, if we're
        lucky, he's going to lead us to wherever
        these UFO reports are coming from.
```

Read your dialogue out loud. It will become immediately obvious if it sounds like talk or like something written down. Ever hear someone give a lecture, when you could tell he was just reading off the page? It's not just that he never looked up from the podium. It's that the words he was choosing probably looked great the night before when he was typing them into the computer, but tripped over themselves trying to come out of his mouth. That's the effect you're trying to avoid. Your ear is definitely good enough to tell the difference between spoken and written English. Just read your lines out loud, and you'll know.

Hearing your lines read out loud by someone else is even better. Suppose you get a bunch of people together to read your script out loud. You're not one of them; you're just listening, with a script in front of you. If all goes well, you'll actually hear how people are hearing your lines in their head. They're putting the stress on the wrong part of the sentence. They're reading it all wrong. Whoops! If that's how people think those lines are supposed to come out, better rewrite them.

Second, you'll see how easily you can trim without losing anything. You find yourself X-ing out half the lines on your pages: Okay! I got the point! Quit talking, already! Remember, your actors' faces will be forty feet tall on the screen. The less dialogue you have, the more effective each line will be. Trust your actors to get their feelings across with a minimum of dialogue.

Try to get your friends to read the script through once before the reading. Most civilians are terrible at reading dialogue cold. They drone on, stumble over what should be easy sentences, and pause in the wrong places. That's because they can't read any faster than they can talk, so they don't have time to absorb the lines before they have to say them, let alone create a sense of character. A cold reading is better than no reading at all, but only if you can restrain the urge to commit hara-kiri when your friends mangle your brilliant dialogue.

The best way to hear your lines is to hear them spoken by actors who have had a chance to read them beforehand. They can invest their lines with all the emotion and meaning that you wrote into them. They can create your characters. You'll get a sense of what other actors will make of your lines later, whether they're lyrical or just pompous, terse or just choppy, cool or just dead. If the lines don't work then, you'll need to rewrite. If you're associated with a play reading group, or if you know actors who will do anything for pizza, then stage a private reading. You'll learn more than you thought you would.

BAD LANGUAGE AND ETHNIC SLURS

One way you probably do not need to give your character a voice is through a lot of bad language.

There was a time in the '70s where it was refreshing to see characters in movies talking as foully as real people. It's not refreshing anymore.

Real people do use curse words all the time, but usually because they're lazy and angry. Curse words don't convey much information beyond "Goddammit, I'm cursing!" and the whole goal of crafty dialogue writing is to sneak as much information into each line of dialogue as you can.

That doesn't mean you can't have curse words. Your cops and crooks mustn't talk like altar boys.

```
                BUENDIAS
It gets weirder. Place was locked
from inside. This guy's got deadbolts
on the door to the roof, and bars on
all his windows.

                TIMMY
Golly. He sure must be one nervous
person!
```

versus

```
                BUENDIAS
It gets weirder. Place was locked
from inside. This guy's got deadbolts
on the door to the roof, and bars on
all his windows.

                TOMMY
Paranoid fuck.
```

The choice use of curse words can create a comic effect or sharpen an angry moment. When a clean-talking corporate CEO suddenly, briefly, uses foul, threatening language, it's clear the gloves are coming off. When a timid housewife finally bursts out in a rage of curse words, it becomes a turning point in a drama. But many scripts I read use swear words the way real people use them in talk: carelessly scattered anywhere the writer couldn't think up a more clever or characteristic phrase.

It generally does not help your script when business people, cops, soldiers, extraterrestrials, or demons from the maw of hell speak like juvenile delinquents.*

You should only use bad language when it creates a specific effect—when it tells us something fresh about the character, gets a laugh, moves the story forward. Never use it out of laziness or because "lots of people talk like that." No one pays money to see "lots of people" talk, either. They can see lots of people talk for free on Ricki Lake.

Ethnic slurs are a special case. When people read ethnic slurs, they don't always think about the context they're appearing in, and they react as if *you* used the ethnic slur. A lot of people find the word that rhymes with "trigger" so offensive that they don't want to see it anywhere. A school board in Oklahoma recently banned the novel *To Kill a Mockingbird* from its classes because it contains the word, even though the novel is strongly antiracist. Although African-Americans still use it on the street, I'd avoid putting it in a screenplay.

If you're making a serious drama, you may need to use ethnic slurs to create the human reality of a character. But ethnic slurs are automatically serious, no matter what kind of scene they appear in. A comic villain who uses a nasty word for Jews suddenly becomes a very not funny villain. If you're making a popcorn movie—a comedy, an action adventure, a horror movie, a thriller—why not come up with something more clever and fresh? Instead of using an ethnic slur for Russians, have your foreigner-bashing character complain about "borscht-eating bastards." It's more fun, and it doesn't get people upset at your screenplay when they should just be upset at your character.

SPARE VERSUS FLAT DIALOGUE

Dialogue can also be minimalist. The dialogue in Westerns such as *A Fistful of Dollars* and *The Good, the Bad, and the Ugly* is extremely

---

*Demons from the maw of hell, as we all know, actually speak in heroic couplets.

spare. Characters talk as little as possible and say very little when they do talk. Their few lines seem almost entirely without style.

This of course *is* a style, one especially appropriate for men who have spent their lives practically alone in the vast open West, thinking a lot but having no one to talk to; it's also right for these bleached-out morality tales.

But minimalist dialogue can easily come across as simply flat and dull dialogue if you're not careful. After all, you're not giving the reader a lot to go on.

```
              MAN
    Yep.
```

Unfortunately, you can't write:

```
              MAN
        (with a steely, slightly
        pained glint in his eye that
        makes you know that what these
        other people may have suffered
        is nothing to him, because he
        has been through hell and back)
    Yep.
```

If you're adopting this dry style for your main character or your whole script, then you have to work twice as hard to make sure that we understand exactly where the character is coming from. When you do have an opportunity to let us inside the character's head, make it count. Be doubly careful that your character does things on-screen that tell us what's going on in his mind.

The more we understand a character, the richer the lines are going to seem, no matter how dry they are on the page. The reader and the audience will add their own emotions to the lines. If you've written the action in a crafty enough way, so that everything the hero does tells us what sort of man he is, the reader will add the steely, slightly pained glint without your writing it. The audience will assume a whole emotional turmoil behind the actor's steely look.

That's why the dialogue doesn't need much help from the action.

Put the emotion in the lines, not in the action.

You don't need to say much about your character's reactions if your dialogue is well crafted. The reader will feel the character's emotions without your ever saying them. Here are two office mates who have been playing with having a love affair:

```
                    ELIZABETH
          Why are you looking at me like that?

                    NEAL
          I was just wondering why you're
          working so late. Aren't you afraid
          to go home in the dark?

                    ELIZABETH
          I'm not afraid of anything.

     She comes over to him, a little bit too close.

                    NEAL
          Maybe you should be.

                    ELIZABETH
          You're not wearing your ring
          anymore.

                    NEAL
          Maybe I took it off at the gym. . . . I
          should go.

     She is very close now.

                    ELIZABETH
          You're afraid! What are you afraid
          of?

                    NEAL
          Mary's late.
```

```
                    ELIZABETH
          What, she's picking you up here? It's
          not that dangerous a neighborhood.
          She probably just left late.

                    NEAL
          No. She's . . . late. My wife is late.

     Elizabeth stares at him. She giggles, a little
     hysterically.

                    ELIZABETH
          I thought you weren't sleeping
          together anymore. What was it you said?
          "Living as brother and sister"?
```

I don't have to tell you how either of these characters *feels*. Assuming the scenes running up to this point have given you a sense of them, your empathy will tell you how they feel. The action gives you a little important blocking (we need to know they're very close) and an unexpected reaction to the bad news (Elizabeth covers her upset with a hysterical giggle). Emotional scenes tend to be dialogue scenes, even though technically dialogue only tells you what the characters are *thinking*. Dialogue is what pulls you into the world of the characters. If you saw the scene above in a silent movie, you would know that the characters are attracted to each other and that the man drops a bombshell that upsets the woman. But you probably wouldn't *care* very much, because you wouldn't know what she was getting upset about.

Technical Considerations

PARENTHETICALS

Parentheticals are those little parenthesized instructions to the actor that come between the character name and their dialogue. They're handy when a gesture is not worth giving a whole line of action to:

```
                    JOE
              (offers his hand)
          Been a long time, huh?
```

They're also extremely useful when the emotional meaning of the line is not the way you'd normally read the line:

```
                    JOE
             (pissy)
          Glad to see you.
```

However, they are often misused, for example, to tell the reader how to interpret the line when it's obvious:

```
                    JOE
            (angry)
          You bastard! I'll kill you!
```

Duh. Of course he's angry. He's threatening to kill the guy!

They are also not to be used because the screenwriter is too lazy to come up with a line that expresses the right emotion:

```
                    JOE
              (wryly)
          Been a long time.
```

The frequent overuse of the parenthetical instruction "wryly" is why parentheticals are sometimes called *wrylies*. The line could be rewritten:

```
                    JOE
          And here I figured you'd be a dead
          son of a bitch by now.
```

Or some other wry line you prefer.

It can be quite effective to have the wryly convey the true meaning of the line, so long as you don't overuse the technique:

```
                    JOE
              ("Drop dead.")
          Glad to see you.
```

Some people have a prejudice against all parentheticals. They claim that if the line is written in a crafty enough way, you shouldn't need to tell the reader how to read it. A clever director or talented actor will figure out that Joe isn't really glad to see the guy. Many of those prejudiced against wrylies are directors who don't like to see writers horning in on their job of directing the actors. Even some writers disdain wrylies. But they are generally extremely successful writers who are paid so much for their work that everyone assumes their dialogue is brilliant and reads it much more carefully than they will read *your* script.

But you need wrylies, sometimes. Your script will, if you're incredibly lucky, run a gauntlet of a dozen readers, development assistants, development execs, execs, agents' assistants, managers' assistants, and actors. All of them are trying to get through a huge stack of mostly bad scripts, often a stack sitting on their bedside table that is an obstacle between them and sleep. They will not give your script the benefit of the doubt. They will skim it in half an hour or, if they have the slightest excuse, toss it out by page 15. They will not exert themselves much to interpret your lines. If a line is not blazingly obvious, and there's no parenthetical to tell them its tone is the opposite of its supposed meaning, they'll just be confused why all of a sudden Joe is glad to see someone they thought he hated, kind of like in a French movie where two people who hate each other are suddenly screwing like minks.

Confusion is your enemy. Most readers never recover from it, because they will almost never take the time to figure out what went wrong. They'll just keep reading on, faster and faster, so they can finish and get to sleep.

So keep the important wrylies in, but get rid of them wherever you can.

(BEAT)

A beat is a special kind of neutral parenthetical used solely to indicate a moment's silence, a short pause. Think of it as an indication of rhythm:

```
                JOE
      Hi, how the hell are you?
             (beat)
      Whoa, wait a second, you're supposed
      to be in Cleveland!
```

The beat allows time for what someone says to sink in, or for the speaker to have a new thought.

Richard Attenborough, director of *Gandhi*, with whom I had the good fortune to work, does not like "beat." He feels it's an intrusive way for the writer to force his sense of rhythm on the actor and the director. He feels that, like most wrylies, "beat" is only there to help the lazy reader.

Well, sure, but until you're working with Lord Attenborough, your script is probably not being read very carefully, and your readers are plenty lazy.

More important: you're writing the words, so why aren't you allowed to write the silences? Why shouldn't you try to control the rhythm of dialogue, just as line breaks and white space allow you to give a sense of the rhythm of your action?

The problem is that "beat" does not fill the silence, only marks it. Because it is purely technical, it draws attention to itself. When I need a heavy beat, I try to show what's happening during the beat:

```
                JOE
      Hi, how the hell are you?

Tony grins mischievously.

                JOE (CONT'D)
      Hey, whoa, wait a second, you're supposed
      to be in Cleveland!
```

That gets the pacing effect I was looking for, but doesn't feel like I'm trying to direct the scene. If I want a softer pause, where nothing in particular is happening, I sometimes use an ellipsis.

```
                    JOE
          Hi, how the hell are you? . . . Say, you
          still drinking single malts?
```

The ellipsis is less intrusive, but the reader may not give it as much weight as you would like. The above example, for instance, doesn't really score. You need the reaction shot of Tony to give the double take its weight.

FOREIGN LANGUAGE AND ACCENTS

There are four ways to handle foreign-language dialogue.

1. Foreigners speak their own language, with subtitles.
2. Foreigners speak English.
3. Foreigners speak their own language, no subtitles.
4. Foreigners speak their own language; someone translates out loud.

All of them give different effects.

1. Foreigners speak their own language, with subtitles.
Ever since *Dances With Wolves*, filmmakers seem to have stopped worrying that subtitles will scare off the audience. They are the most straightforward way to film foreign-language dialogue. These days, we get to hear Germans speaking German and Lakota Sioux speaking Sioux. We even get to hear the Mummy speaking in ancient Egyptian and Hebrew, coached by UCLA Egyptologists. This is the most "realistic" approach.

Some disadvantages of subtitles are:

a. We aren't looking at the screen when we're reading subtitles, so half the time we're reading a book, not watching a movie.
b. Subtitles have to be much shorter than spoken dialogue, since many people don't read very fast, so they can't say as much.
c. Subtitles don't handle interruptions or three-way conversations very well.

I have seen a number of systems for representing subtitles, none of them entirely satisfactory. To my mind, the screenwriter's objective is to duplicate in the reader's mind the effect the movie will have in the audience's mind. Writing "(subtitled)" every time a character speaks seems awkward:

```
                JOSEF
          (to Ilsa, subtitled)
     Take this man out and shoot him.
          (to Max, in English)
     This lady will show you to your
     bungalow.
```

You will have to write "(subtitled)" or "(in German)" each time the character speaks, or the reader will forget what you're doing. That not only looks awkward, it doesn't score. Many readers will blip over the parentheticals, so they'll entirely miss the point these lines make. Joe's lines will come across as if they're all in English, and we'll miss the point.

My preference is to establish the convention that dialogue written in parentheses is in a foreign language, subtitled. I stole this idea from Garry Trudeau's comic strip *Doonesbury*.

```
                JOSEF
     (Take this man out and shoot him.)
          (to Max)
     This lady will show you to your
     bungalow.
```

Now, each time you put a line in parentheses, it will be obvious that it's in a foreign language, but it won't be awkward to read.

If you are using subtitles, you do *not* need to write the actual foreign language in your script. That gets a little tiresome to read:

```
                    ARUSHA
          Lo imali engaphezulu bala siza us
          cishile.

          TITLE: This extra money would really help
          us out.
```

No one's going to bother plowing through *"Lo imali engaphezulu bala siza us cishile."* It will slow down the read and make the reader tired. She will put the script down and rub her eyes. She will go get a cup of coffee. She'll chat with a cute intern in the copy room. As she heads back into her office, a call will come in. When the call is over, she'll get pulled into a meeting. While she's out, someone will put five pieces of mail on top of the script. By the time she works her way back down to you, it'll be five hours later and time to go home, finally. She'll toss your script in her car for home. It will get left in the trunk for three months. It will get taken out when she needs to fit all the skiing equipment in there. "What the hell is this?" she'll say, and toss it in the big blue recycling bin, feeling good she's saved a tree.

2. Foreigners speak English.

In old movies, the Nazis often spoke English among themselves, sometimes with German accents. The part about having German accents was silly, of course, because they wouldn't seem to each other to have accents at all. But the obvious advantage to having your foreigners speak English is that we know exactly what they are saying, and catch every nuance of their dialogue.

Audiences seem to expect something a little more sophisticated these days. However, filmmakers often stretch to give characters reasons to speak in English. For example, in *The Hunt for Red October*, the Russian officers start the movie speaking in Russian, subtitled, but quickly switch into English. The excuse is that they have all learned English in order to know their enemy better, and since they are planning to defect to the United States, they don't want their Russian-speaking crew to know what they're saying.

If you do have your foreigners speak English, you may want them to speak their own language, subtitled, when the hero is around. It's a bit awkward, but at least that way you don't have to explain why the hero can't understand them when they're speaking the same language he is; or, just as important, you don't have the hero "overhear" the Chinese discussing him and miraculously understand Mandarin.

3. Foreigners speak their own language, no subtitles.

When your hero arrives in prison camp, he doesn't understand what the guards are saying to each other. You can, of course, have them speak in Japanese, subtitled, if you want your audience to know what the hero doesn't know: that they suspect he is a spy, that they are watching his every move, that they think he has a cute butt. But if you want your audience to live in the experience of your hero—to have the hero's point of view—then let guards speak their own language, without a translation. That's the tack *Dances With Wolves* took: at first Lieutenant John Dunbar (Kevin Costner) doesn't understand the Sioux, and neither do we. It's only as he begins to learn their language that we get subtitles.

The disadvantage to this approach is also its advantage: we have no idea what the other guys are saying.

One way to put this on a page is to write out the foreign language:

```
                    JEAN
              (to Elise)
        Amène cet espion au bois et coupe-le
        la tête.
              (to Max)
        This lady will take you to your
        bungalow.
```

You can also use one of the many automatic translation sites on the Internet to translate your dialogue into foreign languages. This is a bit risky, because your translated dialogue won't be at all correct, so don't do this in French, Spanish, or German, which people might know. One of the nice things about writing out the foreign language is that occasionally a word or two will crop up that the reader will recognize, just as in the movie, and the audience will catch a few foreign words they understand:

```
                  HELMUT
         Dummkopf!
```

If you don't know and don't want to fake the foreign language, write what it sounds like:

```
The Kommandant screams briefly at the soldier,
who mutters something apologetic and runs off.
```

Depending on what you're counting on your foreign language to do, this may be more effective than writing it out. Skimming over pages of foreign-language dialogue gets tiresome, and this one sentence gives the reader a clear mental picture of what happens in the scene.

Note that if you aren't going to translate for the audience, don't translate for the reader. You may *say* that this dialogue is not subtitled:

```
                  JOSEF
             (in German, no subtitles)
         Take this man out and shoot him.
             (to Max, in English)
         This lady will show you to your
         bungalow.
```

. . . but the reader will blip over the parenthetical instruction `(in German, no subtitles)` and will read the scene as if we do understand what the foreigners are saying.

4. Foreigners speak their own language; someone translates out loud. In *Children of a Lesser God*, Marlee Matlin's character speaks almost entirely in American Sign Language; Bill Hurt's character repeats everything she says, and then responds to it.

I find this approach fairly unwieldy for most purposes, but it may be useful in some cases.

You don't have to restrict yourself to one approach in your movie, or even one sequence. In the cantina scene in *Star Wars*, Chewbacca speaks Wookie without any translation. Han Solo just answers him, and we get a sense of what Chewbacca's feelings are from his groans. Greedo (the green-headed guy who hijacks Solo) speaks an alien language, with subtitles. Another bar patron groans at Luke, while his ugly friend translates, "He doesn't like your face."

ACCENTS, DIALECTS, AND SLANG

When you have a character who speaks with an accent, you want to convey the feeling of the accent while changing the spelling of words as little as possible.

```
                    HANK
          Ah 'preciate yore comin' dahn heyer.
```

That's irritating to read. Reading dialogue shouldn't be work. The line might be better written:

```
                    HANK
          I 'preciate your comin' down here.
```

A more effective and less irritating way to represent the accent is to use your choice of words to give the sense of the accent:

```
                    HANK
          I do appreciate your comin' down
          to these parts.
```

Note how I'm using a bare minimum of spelling changes that gives the flavor of the accent. If you use absolutely standard English, it might begin to lose flavor:

```
                    HANK
          I sure do appreciate your coming on
          down to these parts.
```

Here's another example of overdoing it:

```
                    JOEY
          Whaddya gonna do?
```

This might be underdoing it:

```
                    JOEY
          What are you going to do?
```

And this might be juuuuuust right:

```
                    JOEY
          What ya gonna do?
```

Especially if you use your choice of words to strengthen the effect:

```
                    JOEY
          What ya gonna do, boss?
```

The key is to give flavor without ever making the dialogue hard to read or seem like you're working too hard to get the effect. If you have a character that says things like this:

```
                    HANK
          Well . . . that sure is better than a
          kick in the head.
```

. . . we are going to hear him talk in a drawl without your ever having to transcribe the drawl onto the page.

Likewise, foreign accents:

```
                    HELMUT
          I vill not tell you zis zecret.
```

That just looks silly. But remember that German has a different grammar. If Helmut has that strong an accent, he probably also hasn't mastered English grammar.

```
                    HELMUT
          I am not telling you this secret.
```

A Russian might say "Where you go?" or "Where you are going?" instead of "Where are you going?"

You can also throw in a few words of the foreign languages for flavor, if the meaning is clear, as in *The Little Mermaid:*

```
                    CHEF
          Zut alors, I have missed one!
```

Also, a foreigner might get an English idiom wrong, or translate his native idiom literally into English, with strange results. From *Casablanca:*

```
                    MR. LEUCHTAG
          Mareichtag and I are speaking nothing
          but English now.

                    MRS. LEUCHTAG
          So we should feel at home when we get
          to America.

                    CARL THE HEADWAITER
          Very nice idea, mm-hmm.

                    MR. LEUCHTAG:
          Liebchen—sweetnessheart, what watch?

                    MRS. LEUCHTAG
          Ten watch.
```

```
                  MR. LEUCHTAG
        Such watch?

                  CARL
        Ach, you will get along beautiful in
        America.
```

Not a misspelling in seven lines, but you hear the German accents pretty well.

Incidentally, actors use a trick of starting an accent strong early in the movie or in a play, and then lightening it later. Once we know the character is talking in an accent, we don't need to be reminded so thoroughly, so you can write more standard English as you go onward.

VOICE-OVERS

There are three kinds of dialogue that aren't attached to someone talking on-screen: off-camera or offscreen dialogue, overlaps, and voice-overs.

```
                  SYBIL (O.C.)
        Nice to see you.

    Mark whirls.

    And there's Sybil, dressed in a slinky red
    gown, barefoot.
```

(O.C.) means "off-camera." (O.S.) means "offscreen." The terms are interchangeable. You only use them when it's dramatically significant that we don't catch a glimpse of the person speaking, for example, because they are just now showing up, or they just stomped out and they're already out the door, or because they've crawled under a desk.

Overlapped dialogue lets us start to hear all the dialogue in a scene before we cut into it visually, or lets us continue hearing the dialogue after we've cut out of it. In feature scripts, it's usually represented with an "(O.C.)" as well, though in TV it's sometimes represented with "(overlapped)."

```
                    LINCOLN
        Four score and seven years ago, our
        fathers brought forth upon this continent
        a new nation . . .

    EXT. GETTYSBURG BATTLEFIELD – DAY

    Here and there, white, bleached bones stick up
    out of the green grass.

                    LINCOLN (O.C.) (CONT'D)
        . . . conceived in liberty, and dedicated
        to the proposition . . .
```

Voice-over means hearing someone talking who isn't in the scene at all. We might be hearing a memory of something someone said earlier in the movie, or someone might be talking directly to us, the audience. Both of these are represented by a "(V.O.)" after the character name, but only the latter is commonly referred to as a voice-over.

Film schools seem to have a prejudice against voice-overs. A V.O. is supposed to be a cheap way to convey information that ought to be conveyed visually or through dialogue. Maybe the prejudice arises from all the times voice-over is used in cheesy or even counter-productive ways. (The V.O. at the beginning of *Dark City* gives away a mystery that the movie only reveals halfway through.) But any technique can be abused.

V.O. is the only way to truly get inside a character's thoughts if he's not talking. For example, in the novel *The Accidental Tourist*, the central character has a weird internal monologue. But in the film, there's no voice-over, so all we see is Bill Hurt playing an uptight WASP. Why is he interesting? Who cares? A V.O. could have saved that picture.

Voice-over can also quickly, convincingly set up a few facts that the movie would otherwise take a long time to set up. Preview audiences found the director's cut of *Blade Runner* to be murky and confusing. A few lines of voice-over cleared things up, turning the picture, which would later become a science-fiction classic, from being a disaster to being a mere commercial flop.

Preferring the studio cut over the director's cut is of course heresy. These days Ridley Scott's director's cut gets screened all over the place, and is even available on DVD. But most of the people who prefer the director's cut *have already seen the studio cut.* So they already know what Rick Deckard does for a living, and what replicants are, and what Roy told Deckard before he died. The second time around, you don't need the voice-over.

Voice-over is one of many techniques at your disposal. It can do things that would be otherwise hard to do. It can clarify point of view. It can make a tough private eye into the only decent man in a corrupt world. It can (as the feral boy's voice-over in *The Road Warrior* does) tell us that what we're about to see is a legend.

Don't use voice-over as a crutch, but use it whenever you need it.

Images versus Sound, Action versus Dialogue

Show people have a saying that the movies are pictures with sound, while TV is sound with pictures. Historically this has some truth. The movies were silent for their first three decades. They only added sound in 1927. Meanwhile, the very first TV shows, in the late 1940s, were little more than radio shows with a fuzzy black-and-white picture. The TV networks were radio networks that added TV stations.

What are the conclusions we can draw from this bit of history?

As far as I'm concerned, none. In the motion picture medium, sound is not some poor cousin to picture, no matter what French critics say. When producers overrun their budget and skimp on the sound, it can destroy the movie, however nice the visuals are. Likewise, dialogue is not the redheaded bastard stepchild of action. Dramas lend themselves to dialogue scenes; action movies to scenes of actors running, jumping, and falling down. Telling a story through spoken words is not, per se, inferior to telling it through images.

In his book *Screenwriting Tricks of the Trade*, screenwriter Bill Froug suggests that, as an exercise, before you write a scene, you try to imagine how you would write it if you were making a silent movie. Sometimes a single visual moment can show more than pages of dialogue. There's a story that Frank Capra hired a famous playwright to write a screenplay. After a few months, he checked in. The famous playwright had written two beautiful reels of dialogue, twenty pages that showed a marriage that had once been strong but was now fading.

Capra's response was, "Here's what we'll do. We show the husband and the wife in an elevator. The husband has his hat on. Elevator stops. A pretty girl gets into the elevator. The husband takes his hat off for the pretty girl."

Any time you can communicate the essence of twenty pages of dialogue in one scene (and better yet, one shot in an elevator!), go for it. Any time you can come up with a completely new way to write *any* scene, it's worth trying. Then you have two versions to choose from.

The corollary to Bill Froug's idea is that any time you have a scene of pure action, you should probably also try to think of how you could replace the scene with dialogue. For example, in *Blade Runner*, Rick Deckard's old boss menaces him with, "You know the rules, pal. If you're not cop, you're little people." That single line carries more threat than an entire scene of, say, Deckard getting stalked by thugs.

Dialogue is soft; it is filtered through our understanding of language. Images are hard. We absorb them without having to put them into words. Dialogue can give us more factual information, but if you really want us to know one thing, show it to us. The audience may entirely forget a line about an ice pick, but they won't forget a close-up of an ice pick under the bed.

You can use the relative softness of dialogue to filter scenes that would otherwise be too harsh to put on screen. In *Jaws*, Quint (Robert Shaw), the shark hunter, tells a story about the sinking of a U.S. cruiser in World War II. The actor conjures up the screams of the sailors as sharks tore them to bits in the water. There's no way we'd want to see that on-screen, even if you could afford to shoot it.

You should also use dialogue when what's important is how the character feels about an event, not the brute facts of the event itself. If part of your story is that a woman is raped, you may well not want to put the rape scene on-screen. Not only will the scene blow the rest of the movie out of the water, it may not be so important exactly *how* it happened. What's important is what she *feels* about it.

In *A Fistful of Dollars*, the Man With No Name rescues a family. The father asks the Man With No Name why he's risked his life for them. The Man With No Name rasps out, "Because once there was a family like yours, and there was no one to help." We don't need to see what happened to the Man With No Name's family; we only need to know how he feels about it.

Images are very good at telling us *what*. Words are very good at telling us *why*. A story can't exist without *what*, but it won't make any sense, and we won't care, without *why*. That's why two years after *The Jazz Singer* introduced talking pictures, no one in Hollywood was making silent films anymore.

6

GENRE

The term *genre* is bandied about a lot in film studies and in the business, too. The main genres people talk about seem to be

a. Drama
b. Comedy
b. Action or Action-Adventure
c. Suspense or Thriller
d. Science Fiction and Fantasy
e. Horror
f. Family or Children

Genre is the section of the video store you find the film in, right?

Unfortunately films end up in different sections depending on the video store, so that's not a good definition.

For example, suppose you have a movie about a cop trying to find a killer. (A unique hook, I know, but I'm giving it away free.) You'll find a spectrum of drama, suspense, and action in cop movies, from the pure silly action of the later *Lethal Weapon* movies or John Woo's extravagant gunplay ballets, to the slow, intense dramatics of *Seven*.

Any drama has some action, and every good action movie has drama. They all have suspense. Many science-fiction films would be action-adventure films if there were no science-fiction section, or they'd be horror films, or both. *Aliens* is arguably an action-adventure science-fiction horror film. Some stores have sections for Westerns, or Hong Kong movies, or art films, or animation, or Japanimation, and there's usually a section for classics.

So what is genre, really?

Genre is the goods you must deliver to make your audience feel satisfied. No matter how brilliant your movie is on its own terms, if you don't deliver the goods on the genre, you'll frustrate your audience and your picture will fail.

Even the most tragic picture can have moments of hysterical comedy. Even in the funniest comedy, someone may die. But in a comedy, the tragedy is there to add weight to the comedy; we don't laugh if we don't also care. In any other genre, the humor is there to add humanity to the events. Similarly, movies in any genre may have horrific moments, but only when we go see a horror movie do we pay money *specifically* to be horrified, and go home grumbling if we weren't horrified enough.

It's important to know what genre you're writing in, because when the writer is confused about what genre he's writing in, the screenplay fails. You are asking millions of people to pay their hard-earned dollars to come see your vision. You'd better give them what they came for, whether it's laughs, thrills, poignant moments, or romance.

All genres have their audiences. I, for one, am a science-fiction fan. I will go see practically any science-fiction movie, no matter whether it's a drama, thriller, action movie, or comedy, unless the Internet Movie Database (http://www.imdb.com) and Cinemascore (http://www.cinemascore.com) give it truly awful ratings. I want to see how people live in a science-fiction world, whether it's a future world or our own world with something science-fictional in it, and if the science fiction in the movie does not satisfy me, I will feel let down. The movie has to have all that other good stuff, laughs, whammies, tears, but if I think the science fiction is lame, I'll feel the movie failed. I found *Universal Soldier* in the science-fiction section, with Jean-Claude Van Damme sporting some kind of futuristic goggles, and I rented it. But it was a contemporary action-adventure movie about supposed supersoldiers who behaved just like regular soldiers. It might have been a good movie for a war movie fan, but I'm not one, so I was disappointed. *Static* showed up in the science-fiction section, purporting to be about guy who rigs a radio to talk with the dead. But it turned out that he only thought he was communicating with the dead, and the point of the movie was that he couldn't get over the death of a friend. Sorry. Not science fiction. Drama.

If nobody in *Unforgiven* had fired a six-gun, the Western fans would have gone away frustrated, even if the movie was dramatically perfect. Fortunately, Clint Eastwood is no fool, and he used the West as an environment in which to set a drama.

If your picture is an *action-adventure*, it has to deliver amazing and spectacular action-adventure scenes. The audience may laugh, they may cry, they may be moved, but if there aren't awesome action scenes, you haven't delivered the goods. The Bond films practically exist for the sake of their action scenes. We forgive them their cartoon characters and their almost total lack of drama because we get to see Bond jump his car off a rickety bridge, doing a 360-degree twist in the air before he lands wheels down on the other side of a wide canal. Whee!

An *action* movie can and should have great characters. It can have a strong theme, terrific dialogue, and touching scenes. But that's all gravy. If the action doesn't score, the picture doesn't work, at least not as an action picture.

If the picture is a *drama*, it must deliver a strong dramatic arc in which a personal, emotional question is resolved. You need to take one or more characters through a life-changing or life-illuminating experience. We have to get inside the heart and soul of one or more characters and come to understand what it's like to be them in their situation. You may give us laughs, suspense, even science fiction. But there must be drama, or the picture fails.

If a picture is a *thriller*, it must deliver *suspense*. There may be bursts of action or violence, but the action is there only to heighten or relieve the tension.

If your picture is a *comedy*, you have to deliver laughs. If you deliver enough laughs, your characters can be cartoons and your plot ridiculous.

If a picture is a *romance*, we need to see lovers in danger of losing each other. We want to be inspired romantically.

If your picture is a *horror* film, you'd better scare the pants off your audience.

Let's compare a few submarine pictures. *U-571* is an action movie, or possibly simply a war movie. The central question is, will the Americans capture the Nazi Enigma machine on the *U-571* and get it safely back home? The characters are stock types and none of them changes. They're a bunch of guys trying to do a job. Neither they nor the audience have to grapple with any moral questions: anything that helps defeat Hitler is a good thing. What's exciting is the series of submarine war scenes. We're rooting for them to win.

Das Boot, on the other hand, is a drama. It's about what it was like to be on a German submarine in the Battle of the Atlantic. We don't know until the finale if the U-boat will make it back to port. We're not necessarily rooting for the sub to make it back home, though we care what the characters are going through. We're learning what it's like to be on a U-boat, knowing the war will be lost, trying to do one's duty. What's important is that we have an emotional experience and come to understand something about human nature.

Crimson Tide is a thriller. It pits two strong characters against each other in a series of dramatic confrontations over questions of duty and morality. But what's at issue in the picture isn't whether the characters will change each other or confront their inner demons. They won't. It's not about the action, either; the action is brief and explosive, and only heightens the tension. What's at issue is whether the U.S.S. *Alabama* will launch its nukes at Russia or not. We're there to enjoy the suspense and its resolution. The feeling we come away with is one of relief: Thank God we're safe!

Down Periscope is a comedy, or at least tried to be. What's important is that we laugh. I'm sure there haven't been any romances set on submarines; and boy, are mainstream audiences ever not ready for one, unless it's a coed navy.

To get out of the water, *Saving Private Ryan* has a twenty-two-minute opening action sequence. But it's there to define the characters' world, to show the hell they're living in. The audience is not there to enjoy the action for its own sake. There's no *whoo-hoo*. The main issues in the picture are dramatic: Is it worth risking eight lives to save one? Is it possible to remain good in the middle of a war?

If you're writing a drama, the audience wants to see the inner lives of your characters. Your characters need to undergo dramatic stress. They will have to change and learn and confront their inner demons. The action is there to provide opportunities for the characters to test themselves and each other.

In *The Dirty Dozen* the twenty-minute finale has just as much action as *Saving Private Ryan*'s opening sequence, but it's there for action's sake. The rest of the movie is there for us to come to care about them deeply, so that when they die heroically, we care. The main issue is about action: Will the Dirty Dozen wipe out the Nazi officers' club?

Your action had better kick ass if you're writing an action movie. The drama is there to provide emotional underpinnings for the action; the suspense is there to give pacing.

Science fiction and fantasy are tricky genres. They set up some obvious expectations, but there are some more subtle ones.

Obviously, a science-fiction film has to have an important science-fiction element. *What if* the world were different from ours in one key aspect? Ideally it is an aspect that exaggerates something true about our own lives, and so gives us a new perspective on ourselves; but the bare minimum is to create a convincing, consistent, compelling world that's different from ours. If the world of a movie isn't different from ours in at least one way, then it's not science fiction.

Likewise, in a fantasy film, magic exists. The physical laws we're used to can be broken; creatures that can't exist, do. Ideally what is different about the fantastic world is a metaphor for something all too familiar about our own world. If magic doesn't exist, we're not in a fantasy movie.

The clearest distinction between the two genres is that a science-fiction film gives a *scientific explanation* for how the world is different from ours, whether or not we know that explanation, and a fantasy film gives none: it's just magic. Thus *Star Wars* is science fiction. Without an explanation of their powers, the Jedi knights would have magical powers. But we get an explanation, even if it's a bit mystical in *Star Wars* and utterly ridiculous in *The Phantom Menace*. *The Sixth Sense* is a contemporary urban fantasy, because ghosts don't exist in the real world and there's no explanation of why they do in the movie.

So: science-fiction movies have to have science fiction, and fantasy movies have to have magic.

But science fiction and fantasy are really only worlds in which the other genres can take place. In other words, any science-fiction or fantasy film must also be a drama, action movie, thriller, romance, horror, or comedy. Therefore any science-fiction or fantasy film has a double burden: deliver the goods on the "straight" genre—emotional catharsis in a drama, thrills in an action movie, suspense in a thriller, romantic inspiration in a romance, scares in a horror movies, laughs in a comedy—*and* create a compelling world that's different from ours, either scientifically or not.

Just because a film is science fiction doesn't mean you can be vague about which genre the picture belongs to when the science-fiction element is stripped away. I once worked with a writer who really wanted to get into the thoughts and feelings of an ambitious doctor who had perfected a technique to cure blindness, but created a psychotic monster-man with hundreds of eyes popping out all over him. The problem was that what interested him was the emotional arc of the doctor, and the morality of what she was doing. But the monster-man belonged to a horror movie. It wasn't a good horror movie because there weren't enough scares. So, once you stripped away the science-fiction element, you had neither a drama nor a horror movie; the movie was neither fish nor fowl, and it didn't work.

Oliver Stone's *Nixon* is another example of the risks of genre confusion. The protagonist is a bad man. The film leads us to develop tremendous sympathy and understanding for him, but we still are happy to see him fall. We sympathize, but we sure don't want him to win. The film is shot like a monster movie, with canted angles and dark shadows; Nixon (Anthony Hopkins) even gets lit from below. *Nixon* is a monster movie just as much as *King Kong* is. But the scares were pretty subtle for the monster-movie audience, while the opening night crowds were probably sophisticated adults expecting a political drama, so the picture did not succeed commercially.

I can't give you an exhaustive list of genres or subgenres. Are Westerns a generic environment, like science fiction, in which dramas, action-adventures, and comedies take place? Are war movies a genre? Slasher films? Animation movies? Disney animation movies? Disney animation musicals? Is anything a genre if it has its own rack in a video store somewhere?

Based on my own definition, I would argue that anything is a genre if it has an audience that comes to that kind of picture with generic expectations. For example, Hong Kong action movies are highly sentimental, over-the-top action pieces with complicated plots, where no surprise can be too incredible. (They're really brothers! He's really a girl! He wasn't crippled at all!) Sometimes a mood comes to you where only an early John Woo will do. That's enough to define a genre, and that means that if you are setting out to write a Hong Kong actioner, your script had better deliver the goods on the genre. In other words, another way of deciding which genre your story belongs to is to ask, "Who is the audience for this picture?"

Note that "historical" or "period" is *not* a genre. History is only an environment in which other genres can take place. You can have a historical action-adventure movie (*The Three Musketeers*), a historical drama (*Rules of the Game*), a historical thriller (*Dangerous Liaisons*), or a historical comedy (*Monty Python and the Holy Grail*). Films with gaudy period costumes may have an audience, but the audience has *no generic expectations* of what will happen, it just wants everyone to be dressed fancy. "Historical" doesn't tell you what goods to deliver. That's why only unsuccessful films seem to be called period pieces; successful historical movies are perceived as being in their proper genre. *Sense and Sensibility* is a romance. *Braveheart* is an action-adventure. *Rob Roy*, *Restoration*, and *First Knight* were perceived as period pieces when they were just bad pictures.

THE FIRST-REEL CONTRACT

Your genre is set in the first ten minutes of your film.

In every screenplay, the first ten pages or so tell the audience what sort of picture they're going to see. They set a tone that alerts the audience as to whether this is a movie that is going to end happily or sadly or if it is the sort of movie that could go either way. The first ten minutes creates a "contract" with the audience. If you violate this contract, no matter how good the rest of your movie is, it will fail.

In old movie projectors, each reel of film was ten minutes long, so this contract may be called the First-Reel Contract.

The contract sets up the film's tone and the generic ("genre") expectations the audience or the reader will have. Ten minutes into a good movie, you know whether you're dealing with a Hollywood romance or an art film. The rest of the movie is going to have to deliver the goods on the contract. Put a quirky art film ending on a Hollywood romance and the audience will leave feeling depressed, not uplifted; put a broad Hollywood ending on an art film and the audience feels cheated. If you set up a romantic contract, the boy had better get the girl. On the other hand, if you set up a dramatic contract, the boy can lose or give up the girl, the girl can get murdered, the boy can get murdered, or they can retire to Florida after a long, happy life, just so long as you have some kind of dramatic climax.

A comedy had better start funny. A tragic movie requires a serious opening. An action movie wants an action sequence in the first ten minutes. A romantic comedy will typically start relatively more funny and end more romantic, but it's hard to satisfy the audience if you start romantic and end funny.

You'll notice that in a lot of movies with tragic endings, the filmmakers choose to start with the tragic end, and then flash back to the beginning. If your film is a tragedy, you want your audience to be prepared for it. In the play *Romeo and Juliet*, the spoken prologue tells us that the lovers are "star-cross'd" and will be dead by the end of the play; that way you don't get your hopes up. In *Easy Rider*, we have a fragmentary flash-forward in the first reel of what we'll eventually realize is the heroes getting murdered.

More subtly than a flash-forward, the beginning can *foreshadow* the tragic ending. If your movie is about an outlaw who gets hanged at the end of the movie, you might begin with the hanging of another outlaw. *Elizabeth* ends with Queen Elizabeth sacrificing herself to England: she becomes a virgin again, denying herself personal happiness in order to rule her realm in safety. The opening sequence foreshadows that, showing three Protestant martyrs being burned for their faith.

You don't have to foreshadow your tragic ending. But if you have a lighthearted opening to a tragedy, there must be some hint of doom; otherwise the audience is going to feel cheated when the tone changes. In *All That Jazz*, the title sequence contains a brief shot of Joe Gideon, the hero, falling off a tightrope. *Cabaret* starts with a lighthearted burlesque routine, but the movie opens with a disturbingly distorted reflection of the audience watching the routine. It's enough to tell you that you're not here to enjoy the show.

I'm not saying that you should be able to predict the ending from the beginning. That would make the movie predictable—it would fail to surprise. I'm saying that the ending must be *of a piece* with the beginning. The seeds of the ending must be contained in the beginning. The ending must *deliver the goods* on the beginning.

Some Notes on Specific Genres

HORROR

I believe there are two kinds of horror movies: terror movies and true horror movies. In a terror movie, the villain violates the laws of man. In a horror movie, he or it violates the laws of nature. In a terror film, you're terrified; in a horror film, you're horrified.

In a terror movie, you're terrified of ending up dead. In a horror movie, you should be so lucky. Thus in slasher films, you're terrified the innocent characters will get hacked up by the slasher. The slasher is just a nut, like real-life psychos. We're scared of him, but we don't experience true dread.

In a zombie picture, if you're killed by a zombie, you'll become a zombie. Same thing in vampire and werewolf pictures. *Frankenstein* is a horror film because, in creating a living creature from dead flesh, Baron von Frankenstein has violated the laws of God and man. What is dead should stay dead. In the *Mummy* films, *Poltergeist*, *The Amityville Horror*, and the *Friday the 13th* movies, the dead have been disturbed and return to take their revenge.

What horror films can do that terror films don't is address a *metaphysical question* in a graphic and cinematic way. You can talk about big questions in ways that aren't too deep or heavy for the audience. For example, a vampire is an undead creature who has traded a short life in the sun for a long life in the dark. He has traded his soul for power and immortality. He can't be easily killed, but he has forsaken life among humanity. What profiteth it a man if he gain the world but lose his soul? The vampire story allows you to talk about what it means to give up your soul in exchange for power and wealth, but in a fun, easy-to-grasp way.

A werewolf is a person who is good at heart, but finds that his urges take him over so that he hurts those he loves. Isn't that everybody? In *Ginger Snaps*, the protagonist, Ginger, is bitten by a werewolf just as she gets her period for the first time. She starts having sexual urges she never had before. Her body is changing in ways she can't control. If the movie had been only about a teenage girl menstruating, who would have gone to see it? But the story finds its audience as a werewolf movie.

The *Mummy* movies seem to have turned a legend of an undead creature into a parable of undying love. The mummy is a priest of ancient Egypt doomed to a living death for adultery and murder. He returns and seeks to revive his long-lost lover at any cost. He is compelling because he is driven to be with his beloved no matter what; not so different from a lot of people.

Frankenstein's creature is a triumph of science over morality. Dr. Frankenstein gives life to dead flesh, with catastrophic results. In her novel *Frankenstein*, Mary Shelley told about her fear of onrushing technology. Anyone who's freaked out by future shock, say the way computers are taking away our privacy, can relate.

The events in horror movies are in some ways very far from our own experience. After all, unless you've worked in the entertainment industry, you've never met a vampire. But the underlying parable grounds the most powerful horror stories in our own experience. What is the real message of your horror movie? What fundamental question is it dealing with? This fundamental question is what makes the audience feel connected to your story. What we are seeing is not literally true, but it is emotionally and morally true. A horror piece with no metaphysical theme doesn't work for me, because it has no connection with my reality.

By the way: please don't start your movie with a horrifying sequence that turns out to be someone's dream. It isn't original *at all*.

SCIENCE FICTION AND FANTASY

Like the horror genre, the science-fiction and fantasy genres can talk about big issues without boring the audience. The best science-fiction and fantasy stories take something true about real life and carry it to extremes.

Themes of prejudice and suspicion and distrust of the "other" are common. In one of the classic *Star Trek* episodes, a rock monster killing the *Enterprise*'s hapless red-shirted crewmen turned out to be only trying to protect her children. *Star Trek VI: The Undiscovered Country* was about the difficulties of creating peace between old enemies.

Stories about androids and robots raise the issue: What is human? In *Blade Runner*, Rick Deckard is trying to kill six artificial humans who have escaped from their life of slavery. On the surface, the picture is just a film-noir detective movie set in a future world, but at a more elemental level it asks what it means to be a human being.

You shouldn't write only for the science-fiction and fantasy audience. Science-fiction films are too expensive to make for an exclusive audience, so why cut yourself off? If you ground your out-of-this-world story in a universal this-world human question, then anyone can enjoy your picture.

For your science-fiction movie to work for the mainstream audience, don't create a world too far removed from our own. The most successful science-fiction movies introduce one science-fiction element into our contemporary world. I believe that a science-fiction script set in this world should have no more than one science-fiction element, one that can be summed up in a few words. Dinosaurs can be cloned from fossilized DNA. An alien child is left on Earth by accident. Think of *Independence Day; Stargate; Predator; The Terminator; Terminator 2; Starman*; *E.T.: The Extra-Terrestrial; Close Encounters of the Third Kind; The Day the Earth Stood Still;* and *Star Trek IV: The Voyage Home*. ("So you're from outer space?" asks the woman, and Captain Kirk responds, "No, I'm from Iowa. I only work in outer space.") Everyone can relate to the contemporary background and characters and put themselves in the shoes of an ordinary modern person confronting something out of this world.

Avoid having two science-fiction elements in your film. For example, if you have space aliens in your contemporary movie, don't have time travel, too. It just confuses the issue.

Once you've established your science-fiction element, the farther away from our reality you take the picture, the less effective it is going to be. The audience will become, um, alienated if one thing after another takes them out of their reality. Instead, keep the rest of the story as real as possible. If dinosaur cloning exists, what will people do with the dinos? Try to make money off them, of course. Open an amusement park. Sell dinoburgers.

The standard for realism and believability is actually higher in science fiction than in realistic movies, not lower. If someone in a romantic comedy does something wildly unpredictable, I'm not worried: that's just the character. If a character in a science-fiction thriller does something unmotivated, my suspension of disbelief starts to weaken. You want to make everything as realistic as possible in every detail that does not relate to the science-fiction element.

By the way, the rules for science fiction have their corollary in thrillers. Thrillers are about extraordinary things happening to ordinary people. A thriller should have only one unlikely event in its premise; anything else unlikely is a consequence of that.

The next most successful science-fiction movies create a not-too-distant future similar to our own, but warped by one major science-fiction element. *Blade Runner* is set in a film-noir L.A. not far removed from modern Tokyo or Bangkok, except that (science-fiction element) there are superhuman androids on the run and Deckard has to retire them. *Outland* is *High Noon* retold on (sci-fi element) a mining colony on Ganymede.

As you can tell from the examples above, these movies also fall back on familiar genre plots and characters. We may not be personally familiar with the Old West, but we recognize Sean Connery's character in *Outland* from a dozen Westerns. That's what grounds these stories for the audience.

Star Trek, for example, was conceived of as "*Wagon Train* in space." It could equally be described as a futuristic version of Homer's *Odyssey:* a ship is sailing through uncharted waters and meets strange beings. The captain could have come out of any World War II movie about a U.S. Navy ship in the South Pacific. Bones was the "old country doctor" DeForest Kelley had played in a dozen Westerns. Everything you really need to know to understand the science-fiction part of the show is contained in the famous opening narration: "These are the voyages of the starship *Enterprise* . . . its five-year mission: to explore strange new worlds, to seek out new life and new civilizations, to boldly go where no man has gone before."

Incidentally, futuristic science fiction too often pretends that technology from our own time will be forgotten in the next few hundred years. The Space Marines in *Starship Troopers* use assault rifles to duke it out with giant bugs; what happened to tanks and cruise missiles? The crew in *Star Trek* get thrown to the deck whenever the *Enterprise* hits a bump; what happened to seat belts?

Whatever you do, don't do like many novice writers and create a whole world full of things named the Vogon and the planet Utapau and the Journal of the Whills and the Bendu of Ashla and so on. These movies never get made, because only hard-core science-fiction fans love to plunge wholeheartedly into a different world with a different social structure, different laws of physics, different history, and deeply meaningful names that you never heard of before:

> The REPUBLIC GALACTICA is dead. Ruthless trader barons, driven by greed and the lust for power, have replaced enlightenment with oppression, and "rule by the people" with the first galactic empire.
>
> Until the tragic Holy Rebellion of "the '06," the respected JEDI BENDU OF ASHLA were the most powerful warriors in the Universe. For a hundred thousand years, generations of Jedi Bendu knights learned the ways of the mysterious FORCE OF OTHERS, and acted as the guardians of peace and justice in the REPUBLIC. Now these legendary warriors are all but extinct. One by one they have been hunted down and destroyed by a ferocious rival sect of mercenary warriors: THE BLACK KNIGHTS OF THE SITH . . .

Oy, vey. Enough, already! The brain can only hold so many facts!

Okay. Well. These movies *almost* never get made. The quote is from something by a novice writer named George Lucas, an early draft of something then called *The Star Wars*.* Before you get all smug, though, I must point out that for many, many years no one would touch the project, because no one could make head or tail of the script. Fortunately for all of us, visionary executive Alan Ladd Jr. ("Laddie"), then boss of Twentieth Century Fox, believed on the basis of Lucas having written and directed the surprise hit *American Graffiti* that Lucas could do anything he believed in. So he commissioned the script and got the picture made, and even then, no one

---

*At least, it is from a screenplay someone has put up on the Internet *claiming* it is an early draft of *Star Wars*.

else at the studio believed it would make money, even up through the first preview screenings. (That's why they gave George the merchandising rights. Oops.)

Likewise, the Wachowski brothers didn't get to direct their script *The Matrix* until they had already hit with *Bound*.

If you have not written and directed a huge hit, and Laddie doesn't think the world of you, you may not find it all that useful to write a space opera like *The Star Wars*. As someone once told me, "There are no rules, but you break them at your peril."

If you must write a story that takes place far in the future, or in a fantasy world, at least make sure that the world is internally consistent and that the characters in it are compelling and believable within their own world. Beyond that, try to ground your story in the great myths that we're all familiar with. Arguably, *Star Wars* worked because it was an unexpected retelling of the universal-hero legend made famous by Joseph Campbell in *The Hero with a Thousand Faces*. Luke Skywalker follows a dramatic path that heroes have been following since Gilgamesh in ancient Sumer.

The moral of the story is unless you have already written and directed one surprise hit, and know a studio head, or are basing your movie on a classic TV show that became a cultural phenomenon, keep the science-fiction aspects down to what can be explained in one phrase: "Nasty aliens invade the world." "Some people can make your head explode just by thinking at you." "An Egyptologist finds an ancient portal to another solar system."

Fantasy films have requirements similar to those of science-fiction films. They are usually more successful when they take place in a world like our own, but with one fantasy element injected. *The Sixth Sense* takes place in our world, but there is a boy who can see ghosts. *Ghost* takes place in downtown New York City, but the main character becomes a ghost. *It's a Wonderful Life* is set in small-town America, but angels exist. *The Green Mile* is set in a prison half a century ago, but one inmate has magical healing powers. *Groundhog Day* is set in modern-day Punxsutawney, Pennsylvania, but Bill Murray keeps waking up to experience the same day over and over again.

Unlike science-fiction films, fantasy films can take place in the historical past. There, too, they seem to be most effective when the world is as gritty and realistic as possible, but with one fantasy element. *Dragonslayer* is set in a very realistic medieval Norwegian village beset by a dragon.

Fantasy pictures seem to have more success than science-fiction pictures in creating entire new worlds. Every now and then someone gets it right and makes a *Shrek* or *The Company of Wolves* by pillaging fairy tales, melting them down, and forging something personal and true. But by and large they are not successful unless they are based on best-selling books (e.g., *Conan*, *The Princess Bride*, *Interview with the Vampire*) or legends everyone already knows (e.g., *Excalibur*, the King Arthur story). Maybe book adaptations work because someone has already gone to the trouble of creating a coherent fantasy world in much greater depth than filmmakers do. The reality of that world might be what grounds films adapted from fantasy books. Otherwise, we get *Willow*, *Legend*, *Dragonheart*, *The Dark Crystal*, *Labyrinth*, *Dungeons & Dragons*, and other pictures that try to tell a new fairy story, and crash and burn. These pictures are not grounded in anything. They aren't based on legends that ring true for the audience. They aren't based on a universal human truth. They are *mere* fantasies.

It is very, very hard to come up with a new fairy tale.

PERIOD PIECES

Okay, I said period pieces aren't a genre. But certain rules still apply to movies set in the historical past.

Get the details right. The audience doesn't necessarily know what's right, but they know when you get it wrong. For example, William Wallace's anachronistic use of burning kerosene in his medieval battles in *Braveheart* cheapens an otherwise grand picture. (It's a pity, because the real William Wallace won Stirling Bridge by cleverly attacking the English while they were in the middle of trying to get their army *across* the bridge, which should be cinematic enough.) If you are writing a movie about Cleopatra, then don't put camels in it, because camels were not introduced to the Middle East until A.D. 1000, which is why they're not in either the Bible or the Koran. Faithfulness to historical details gives the audience a sense of being in another time.

But the story isn't *about* the details. The audience shouldn't *have* to know any more about the period to understand the story than can be put in a title card or title crawl in the beginning of the picture. (A title crawl is any text that crawls up the screen, as in the beginning of all the *Star Wars* pictures.)

One of the hardest things is getting the dialogue right. People in the sixteenth century didn't speak in old-style English; they spoke the very latest, up-to-date modern sixteenth-century English. To get the same sense of modernity, don't be afraid to use contractions and sentence fragments, just like people do now. You can and should use slang, but it must be modern-sounding slang that could have existed then. "Poxy whoreson dog" is period-accurate, but audiences won't know if them's fighting words or just kidding. "Dude" will be jarring. But "son of a bitch" is a timeless sentiment.

The key to a great period piece is to show real people we'd want to be with who operate in a world that is different from our own. The people are timeless. Their goals, and the obstacles in their way, are of the period. In *The Three Musketeers*, D'Artagnan is a romantic adventurer (timeless) who wants to save the queen's honor (period—these days he'd want to run away with her). He is restrained by his honor as a gentleman. In *Braveheart*, William Wallace is a romantic adventurer (timeless) who wants to liberate Scotland from an evil English king (period). The period is no more than a background to a human story. The period makes for a richer cloth, but the weaving must still be passions, vices, lies, hopes, frustrations, greed, love, pride, and mercy—the stuff that dreams are made of.

7

GET HELP!

Film is a collaborative medium. For a film to get made, dozens or hundreds of people need to help make it. So why shouldn't you get help making a screenplay?

Here are the best ways to get help:

1. Reading other scripts
2. Reading the right books
3. Writing groups
4. Getting feedback from friends, film fans, and industry people

Here are some others:

5. Screenwriting software
6. Writing workshops
7. Staged readings
8. Script consultants

Reading Other Scripts

One of the best ways to learn how to write scripts is to read them. There are three kinds of scripts you might be able to get hold of, and each has its advantages:

a. Scripts of great movies
b. Unproduced scripts
c. Unproduced scripts by great screenwriters

The point of reading great produced scripts is that you know they were made into great movies. So the writers must have known something, right?

The best way I know to get and read the scripts of produced movies is on the Internet. As I write, there's a great site, Drew's Script-O-Rama (http://www.script-o-rama.com), which links to dozens of scripts of produced movies. If you carefully read early and late drafts of the same picture, you'll see what writers and producers go through trying to get the script right. If you read the production draft, and compare it to the movie, you'll also learn something about how pictures get edited. For example, in *Star Wars*, the hero, Luke Skywalker, doesn't show up in the picture until we've seen a good deal of business involving the two 'droids, R2-D2 and C-3PO. The screenplay introduces Luke right away. But somewhere along the line, George Lucas decided that Luke's story didn't really begin until he met the 'droids, so he cut the early scenes with Luke.

If you know people in show business, they may be able to get you photocopies of great scripts. If you live in L.A., you may see scripts at a yard sale. It is technically illegal to photocopy a script and sell it. That's called a bootleg script. Fortunately, it is not illegal for someone who has a script legally to sell it. These scripts are called collector's copies. You find them at bookstores that specialize in the entertainment industry, such as Samuel French, Larry Edmunds, and Collectors Bookstore (all in Los Angeles and on-line).

Be sure you're reading the scripts, and not transcripts. A transcript typically won't have standard screenplay format. Worse, you may not be reading what the screenwriter wrote. Actors use their own rhythms and may ad-lib their lines. Almost all *published* scripts are transcripts. Many published scripts that are formatted like screenplays have been altered to match what the movie looks like, so they might as well just be transcripts.

When you read the script, try to forget you saw the movie. Pay attention to how the writer is telling the story. How is he envisioning the action? How does he describe the characters? And so on. Don't just use the script as a reminder of the movie. Read it as carefully as if you were a development executive getting it for the first time. Ask yourself: Who is the point-of-view character? Who is the central character (hero, protagonist)? What is his goal? The stakes? The jeopardy? The obstacles or antagonist in his way?

If you know people in show business, they may have copies of unproduced scripts they think are particularly good. In particular, try to get your hands on adaptations of books you have read and scripts by screenwriters whose other work you admire. The advantage to reading unproduced scripts is that you don't have the distraction of having already seen the movie. You can try to envision what the writer is trying to put in your mind. You can also try to guess whether it would make a good movie or not. Don't be impressed just because the writer won an Oscar for something else. Even the best writers write terrible screenplays when they didn't spark to the material. William Goldman, writer of *Butch Cassidy and the Sundance Kid*, has his name on some stinkers. Joe Esterhas, who wrote the classic erotic thriller *Basic Instinct*, also wrote *Showgirls*. Judge the script on its own merits. Does it succeed or fail? How could you improve it?

Unfortunately you are more likely to get your hands on scripts with no pedigree than scripts by top writers. For some reason, development people are more willing to hand out bad scripts than good ones. Maybe it makes them feel powerful to have something that no one else has. Most development people don't get to feel powerful very often.

When you get a script that's not by a famous writer, do what a producer or agent does: Try to figure out if there's a movie in there waiting to be made. Is there an audience for this movie? What genre is it in? Does it have a hook? Do you care about the characters? What about the stakes? What went wrong? How can its problems be fixed? If there's a good hook but bad execution, how would you retell the story with that hook?

William Goldman says in *Adventures in the Screen Trade* that "nobody knows anything" in show business. It's not really true, but everybody's wrong lots of the time. It's like baseball: even a great hitter may not get on base more than a third of the time. So you have to be your own judge of material. The more effort you invest in reading, the more you'll learn.

Books You Should Read

Well, this one, obviously.

Books will answer questions you didn't know you had.

I don't think you need to read a lot of different screenwriting how-to books. If you're reading more than two in the same year, you're procrastinating. Just put the book down and get writing. The books I find most useful are about other aspects of filmmaking: directing, editing, acting, and producing.

Many of these books may be available in your local library. You can also buy them. We authors dig that.

DIRECTING

You're directing a movie on the page. They're directing a movie on the screen. Directors mostly just like to tell war stories in their autobiographies, but every now and then they'll let an actual trick of the trade slip out. Many of these books will also fill you with the desire to be involved in the film industry, which may cause you to put the book down and go write, which is a Good Thing.

- Ingmar Bergman, *The Magic Lantern*.
- Sidney Lumet, *Making Movies*. One of the few directors who actually explain in their book what they were trying to do.

- David Mamet, *On Directing Film*. Mamet has a unique perspective on film. I think he's full of it, but any new perspective is good.
- Ken Russell, *Altered States*. War stories, but fun ones.
- Sergei Eisenstein, *Notes of a Film Director*. One of the great film theoreticians. You don't have to agree with his theories, but they get you thinking.
- François Truffaut, *Truffaut by Truffaut*.
- Peter Bogdanovich, *This Is Orson Welles*. Bogdanovich is rather too impressed with himself, but somewhat enlightening, too.
- Milos Forman, *Turnaround*.
- John Boorman, *The Emerald Forest Diary*, his journals while he was shooting *The Emerald Forest*.
- Dale Pollock, *Skywalking*, about George Lucas. This is the only straight biography (not autobiography) I've read that says anything useful.

EDITING

Editing is the art of trimming unnecessary action and dialogue, and occasionally rearranging scenes so they make a more compelling movie. Hey, kind of like rewriting!

- Ralph Rosenblum and Robert Karen, *When the Shooting Stops . . . the Cutting Begins: A Film Editor's Story*.

PRODUCING

You're trying to sell your screenplay to producers. So why not see what their lives are like? Buy a copy and an economy-sized bottle of Maalox.

- Roger Corman, *How I Made 100 Movies in Hollywood and Never Lost a Dime*. From the man who hired so many great filmmakers before anybody knew they were great (Jack Nicholson, Ron Howard, etc.) that his production company is nicknamed the Corman School of Cinema.

- Samuel Arkoff, *Flying Through Hollywood by the Seat of My Pants*. From the guy who practically invented the drive-in movie.
- Art Linson, *A Pound of Flesh*. Witty and wise.
- Robert Evans, *The Kid Stays in the Picture*. An old warrior tells war stories.

HOLLYWOOD, THE ANIMAL THAT EATS ITS YOUNG

- Hugh Taylor, *The Hollywood Job-Hunter's Survival Guide*. This is an excellent nuts-and-bolts handbook on how to get and keep your first job as an assistant to an executive, by someone who recently made it out of the trenches. The level of detail to things like what a phone sheet looks like is terrific. I wish I'd had it when I was an assistant. Why do you need to read it? Because it gives you an inside look into the people who get your script in the mail, is why.
- Jason E. Squire, *The Movie Business Book*. Forty-one filmmakers talk about what they do.
- K. Callan, *Directing Your Directing Career*. I liked this one a lot.
- David Pirie, *Anatomy of the Movies*. An overview of the 'biz.
- Hortense Powdermaker, *Hollywood*. This is a classic anthropological study, by a real live perfessor, of a strange tribe of moral pygmies, their rituals and customs. Pioneering work from the '40s that still holds true.

OKAY, ONE OTHER BOOK ABOUT SCREENWRITING. BUT JUST ONE.

- William Goldman, *Which Lie Did I Tell?* Although this pretends to be a book about Goldman's experiences in the business, it contains many useful insights into the writing process itself. In particular, he wrote half of a first-draft screenplay for the book, and then has six A-level writers (Callie Khouri, John Patrick Shanley, etc.) describe where they think the rest of the movie should go. As an antidote to the notion that there's only one best solution to any given screenwriting challenge, this section alone is worth the price of the book.

TWO INTERESTING BOOKS YOU MIGHT NOT THINK WOULD HELP

Scott McCloud, *Understanding Comics: The Invisible Art*. Although this book is not about the movies at all, it is fascinating. McCloud is attempting to, well, understand comics: what happens when we read them, what a comic does inside our brains as we read it. His insights might get you thinking about what happens when you read a screenplay, or what happens when you see a movie. Don't be scared. It's a comic book.

Joseph Campbell, *The Hero with a Thousand Faces*. Movies are mostly Very Old Stories wearing Very New Outfits. Joseph Campbell was an anthropologist who studied Very Old Stories. He proposes that hero myths all over the world have one basic pattern. There is a whole mini-industry of screenwriting seminars based on Campbell's theory of the hero's journey, and George Lucas took inspiration from him. Campbell might get you thinking about stories: why we tell them and why they last.

Writing Groups

A writing group is a bunch of writers who read what each member is working on and then get together and talk about it. Writing groups give writers some things that are otherwise hard to get: urgency, encouragement, criticism, and people to bitch to.

URGENCY

If five other people are eager to read your pages, you'll write them sooner.

ENCOURAGEMENT

Praise from fellow writers will mean more to you than praise from your mom.

CRITICISM

Your fellow writers know what you're capable of, and they won't let you get away with so-so work. Also, civilians may criticize the wrong thing. Writers can pinpoint exactly what needs fixing.

PEOPLE TO BITCH TO

When one producer mistreats you, it's humiliating. When packs of producers mistreat all of you, it's a bunch of funny stories.

WHO SHOULD BE IN YOUR WRITING GROUP?

No one should be in the group who isn't writing. Girlfriends, colleagues, friends who are kicking around the notion of writing something one day: these people, while no doubt fun to go to a movie with, are not doing what you're doing. Their criticisms may be on the money, but they are readers' criticisms, not writers'.

Also, if someone's in the group who's not a writer, then he doesn't ever get criticized. It's much easier to take criticism from someone you tore into last week, and you're going to be that much more precise in your criticisms if you know he's going to get his turn to tear into you.

You don't have to all be screenwriters, but everyone should be at roughly the same level of craft. In my writing group, the rule was that everyone had to be a professional writer, so we had a TV writer, a comics writer, three novelists, and a feature film writer. You don't have to be friends already; if things work out, you'll probably become friends.

HOW TO FIND FELLOW WRITERS

Most writing groups probably start with a few friends who are writers, then add friends of friends. What if you don't know any writers at your level?

If you're taking a writing class, seminar, or workshop, ask some of your fellow students whose writing you like if they'd be interested in working together after the class is over. Whether or not you're a student, you can always ask writing professors if they know any students in their classes whom you might contact.

Put up a notice at the local coffee shop where writers hang out. You know the one: there are always a couple of people sitting alone, nursing their one cappuccino for hours, writing. In the notice, describe what flavor of writing group you want to start. You can also put up your notices at the local art-house movie theater, the film-fan video store, the English department at a local college, your bookstore, and so on.

It's a long shot, but check out the various Internet newsgroups (rec.movies.*), chat boards, websites, and so forth. Post a message asking if anyone in your hometown wants to join a writing group.

It might be a good idea to meet with each potential member yourself, alone, before letting him or her into your group. That way it's "your" group, and you also can screen out anybody who might make the rest of the group uncomfortable.

HOW TO RUN A WRITING GROUP

Meet in person so that everyone can hear everyone else's criticisms. The free-for-all that develops in a good writing group meeting can save you a month of frustration. While it's possible to have an Internet chat-room writing group, you can't have the same creative give-and-take, and you can't go out and get a beer afterward.

If you can set a regular monthly or biweekly meeting time, people can organize their schedules around it, and it encourages people to get their writing done. Whoever is going up next time should e-mail out his pages early enough that everyone has a couple of weeks to read and think about them.

Each meeting should be devoted to one piece of work. That way, everyone gets a full evening devoted to his or her script, and no one needs to feel shortchanged. Some people write more slowly than others, so some people may go twice before another person has anything to show. But it's probably good if no one brings their own material more than twice before everyone else has had their turn. Even if you only have half of a rough draft, bring that in.

If you just want to pitch an idea, then you can bring that in to someone else's meeting. You should give your pitch after the group has discussed the evening's main work. Don't schedule a whole night of pitches, because it will feel like a competition. You're not competing against each other. You're competing against all those other guys out there.

Don't talk with each other about the material before the meeting. Otherwise people start to refine their opinions and come to a consensus, and you only get one group opinion at the meeting. A good meeting is like a brainstorming session: the meeting generates ideas that two people talking might never have thought of.

The moment everyone has arrived, start the meeting. Don't waste energy gossiping. After you're done talking about the work, then you can go to the pub and gossip.

Go around the room and make sure everyone says one positive thing about the evening's script before you start criticizing. That way people don't get suicidal. Then go around once again while everyone gives their overall opinion of the work. Our group came up with a "talking beer": a can of Guinness Stout with feathers tied to it. Whoever held the talking beer was allowed to talk. Anyone else was only allowed to make brief catty comments. After everyone had their say once, we left the floor open and people could say whatever they liked. Then, if necessary, we went to page-by-page notes.

When you're in the hot seat, don't argue with the criticisms the group gives you. Don't explain what you were trying to do, unless you're really trying to figure something out, or the group really wants to know. If your material didn't work, it doesn't matter what your explanation is. You just have to fix it. You're not obliged to agree with anyone or do what they say, but you are obliged to listen quietly and take notes.

A USEFUL PHRASE

When people are pounding you with a criticism you think is all wrong, the phrase you use is, "I'll be sure and take a look at that." It's not a lie. You will. And a week later it may make a whole lot more sense than it does now, which is why you write it down now and don't waste energy disagreeing with everybody. It might seem all wrong, or more likely, it might seem like excellent criticism *if you wanted to write an entirely different movie*. But while they're pounding on you, acknowledge what they're saying without getting into a fight. This phrase is, incidentally, the phrase you should use when a producer is making a criticism that makes you want to run your head into a brick wall.

Getting Feedback

Your goal is to make your screenplay as transparent as possible. How do you tell if you've succeeded? You get people to read it. Aside from your writing group, three sets of people can help you:

1. Friends
2. Film fans
3. Professionals

All feedback is *valuable*. Your script exists only to be read and eventually turned into a movie. If anyone thinks it's confusing, it is obviously not as clear as it could be. If someone doesn't like or care about your main character, then the character is not as compelling as he might be.

But that doesn't mean that all criticism is *correct*. It's your job to listen carefully to what people are saying. If they have a problem, you have to figure out how to rewrite your script to solve it. Then you have to decide whether you want to make that fix.

For example, someone may tell you your screenplay starts off slowly. In an action movie that may be a problem. But maybe to make your story really score, you need to set up quite a few things: you need to introduce us to many characters, or communicate some important information. You have to decide whether you can set up some of those things later, or whether starting off slow is an acceptable price to pay for setting everything up properly.

Criticisms may also focus on the wrong thing. A scene may feel "slow" because it's a slow scene, but it may also feel slow because it comes too early in the story's development, or too late, or because we don't understand what it has to do with the characters' goals, or because it is exactly the scene we were expecting.

The same is true for compliments. Some compliments may hide a useful criticism. For example, you may hear, "I really like the villain!" Does that mean you've done a good job with the villain? Or that he is the only character who really stands out, and the others are not compelling enough?

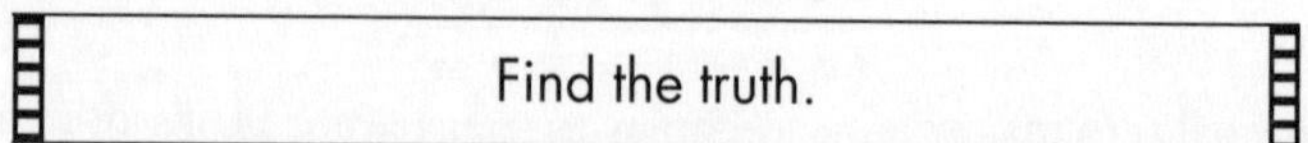
Find the truth.

My acting teacher, Joanne Baron, probably one of the finest acting teachers alive, used to say, "Find the truth." By that she meant that when you look at a performance or a work of art, don't look first for what's wrong with it. Look for what's right. So, if you get a criticism, don't look for what's wrong with it. Look for what's right about it. Finding the truth means forcing yourself to accept that even the silliest feedback is, at some level, true and useful.

Unless someone else is paying you to write, then it's up to you and only you what direction you want to go in. You will sometimes hear clever suggestions that will fundamentally change your story. It may become a more commercial story, or a more consistent story, or have a better hook. But it may not be the story you intended to tell. It may have a different ending or even a different theme. Do you stick with the story you envisioned? Or do you write a different movie than you intended? Only you can decide.

FRIENDS

Your friends may say, "But I don't know how to read a screenplay." That's actually one of the best things about getting your friends to read your work. Assuming they like to see movies, they should be able to see the movie in their heads. Friends are your stand-in for the mainstream audience. If you confuse them, your story is confusing. If they don't get it, the audience won't get it.

The down side to having friends read your script is that reading dialogue and hearing it in your head is a skill that takes time to learn. So you'll have to work twice as hard to figure out which criticisms are on the money and which are just because your friends aren't experienced readers.

FILM FANS

Film fans may be even more helpful than your friends. Anyone who really cares about movies, who sees lots of them and thinks about them, can give you useful feedback. The guy at the video store who's seen every movie they have at least once, the women having the argument about Bergman in the revival house, people who write intelligent reviews on the IMDB website (http://www.imdb.com), people who write to the various movie newsgroups: these people probably have useful things to say about your movie, and because they don't know you, they're less likely to praise something that doesn't work.

Many of them would probably be willing to read your script and tell you what they think, for free. Why? People like to be asked their opinion, especially when you take it seriously. People love it when you treat them as an authority on a subject that they, personally, think they know something about even though they have no credentials. Moreover, they want to become involved in the process of making pictures, and this is an easy way to do it. Also, they, too, are probably "thinking about" writing a screenplay, and reading your script may encourage them to get to work on their own.

Start reading one of the many rec.movies.* newsgroups, and see whose opinions seem smart, reasonable, and true. Write them a gracious note saying you like what they have to say and wonder whether they would be willing to read your screenplay and tell you what they think. Not everyone will have the time or willingness, but quite a few of them will. Who knows? You might even make a new friend.

Be careful, though. Many film fans have very strong prejudices about what is good and bad in cinema. They may have vigorous theories about, say, the value of voice-overs, or flashbacks, or Dogma 95. They may decide that you've written your screenplay all wrong because it doesn't match the theories they're fond of. Only you can decide whether someone's criticisms are right. Only you can decide how to respond to them.

PROFESSIONALS

If you're lucky enough to know people who work in development in the entertainment industry, they're the best people to give you advice. They've read thousands of scripts. They understand what a movie project faces trying to get made. They will be able to tell you not only how your script could be better, but how it could be more commercial.

Most of us are used to judging a script within its own genre and by what it's trying to be (is this a *good* zombie slasher picture or a *bad* one?), but bear in mind that everyone has prejudices. You should take a professional's advice more seriously than a civilian's, but you still have to make your own decision.

Remember, too, you're asking them to do for free what they do for a living. It's a favor. They'll read your next script if they like this one, but they probably won't read this one again. If you have someone in the business who's willing to read your script, hold off on sending it to her until you've made it as good as you know how. Don't blow it. If she's willing to read it now, she'll be just as willing to read it in six months.

Other Kinds of Help

SCREENWRITING SOFTWARE

There are two kinds of screenwriting software:

1. Screenplay formatting programs
2. Screenplay plotting programs

Screenplay formatting programs such as Final Draft, Scriptware, Movie Magic Screenwriter, and so on, are intended to make it easier to write a screenplay in proper format. Among other things, they

a. make it easy to shift between various styles, such as sluglines, action, dialogue, parentheticals, and transitions.
b. break dialogue correctly over a page break, inserting "(MORE)" and "(CONT'D)" as appropriate.
c. guess which character name or location you're trying to write, so that you only have to type *T* and hit return to have the character name "THOMAS" appear.
d. keep sluglines consistent, so that

```
INT. MILLER HOUSE – TOM'S ROOM – DAY
```

doesn't become

```
INT. TOM'S ROOM – DAY
```

and later

```
INT. TOM MILLER'S ROOM – DAY
```

which will get confusing for the people in the production office later.

A typical screenplay formatting program will have a viewer program that anyone can download from the Net for free. So, for example, if you want to send someone a Final Draft file, they can download the free Final Draft Viewer program and read your file.

The viewer won't allow you to create a script on it, which is why you need to shell out for the real program.

Many screenplay formatting programs have handy extra functions. For example, Final Draft allows you to look at your scenes on virtual index cards and move them around.

Screenplay formatting programs are 100 percent necessary during a production. You need to be able to number your scenes, lock pagination, mark changes from revision to revision, and create A and B pages in a locked script. If that sounds like gibberish, don't worry: You don't need to know about any of these things unless you are a script coordinator or production coordinator. If you're writing a selling script, screenplay formatting programs are *not* necessary, they're just convenient.

(In case you're interested, during preproduction the script's pagination and scene numbering are locked. This means that if the big love scene, scene 22, starts on page 57, it will always start on page 57. If it is rewritten so that it's longer than it was, it will spill over onto pages 57A, 57B, etc. If it is deleted, there will still be a page 57, but it will contain nothing but an "omitted" scene that looks like this:

```
22. OMITTED
```

That way when three scenes are cut in the beginning of the script, the production office doesn't have to hand out complete new scripts. They only make copies of the revised scenes, on colored paper, and people can swap out the appropriate pages in their copies of the script.

Individual lines that are changed are marked with *'s in the margins. If the word *cute* got changed to *adorable*, the script would look like this:

```
                    JACKIE
          Oh, I don't know. I think he's kind of
          cute.                                        *
```

That way it's easy to see which lines have been changed and which are the same. A heavily rewritten scene may have asterisks all down the side.)

Personally, I use an occasionally flaky screenplay formatting program called Final Draft. But I didn't have to pay for it. A production I was on bought me the program; before that I was happily using an ancient version of Microsoft Word. If you don't want to shell out the couple hundred bucks a copy of Final Draft costs, you may find that you can create a convenient style sheet in your word-processing program that takes care of most of the formatting you need. It won't automatically add `(MORE)`'s and `(CONT'D)`'s, but it can prevent a page break between a character name and dialogue, or between a slugline and the action that follows, and so forth. (A sample Word style sheet can be downloaded from my website, http://www.craftyscreenwriting.com.)

By the way, the best way to e-mail scripts is to use Adobe Acrobat to turn them into PDF files. Almost everyone has Acrobat Reader, or if not, they can download it for free. PDF files keep the original formatting, so that the pages you're looking at are exactly the same as the pages they're looking at. Acrobat is a few hundred bucks, though. Check it out at http://www.adobe.com, or buy somebody's spare copy cheap on the Net.

I've only tried one screenplay plotting program. Dramatica attempts to formalize the process by which a crafty screenwriter creates a story. It boils down story structure to a "branching tree" of thirty-two thousand possible "storyforms." By answering questions like "Does the main character succeed or fail?" and "Is this a good or bad thing?" you settle on one "storyform." That is supposed to help you crystallize your story. It is supposed to take about a week to learn how to use Dramatica. I have no idea whether Dramatica is worth the money, but the company has some happy reviews on their website. If you have trouble figuring out why your stories come out wrong, or just have trouble creating story structure, Dramatica or something similar might help.

WRITING WORKSHOPS, SEMINARS, AND CLASSES

Writing is lonely work. If you're just starting out, you probably don't know a lot of other writers, and you may not know a lot of people who even respect writing. Screenwriting workshops enable you to meet lots of other aspiring writers and get encouragement and camaraderie from them and from your teacher.

Many people like the urgency and discipline involved in a writing workshop. It provides a structure. Instead of just writing whenever you have the time, you'll be writing to deadline for a teacher who's going to read and comment on your work, so you make the time. Make sure the classes are small enough that you're getting personal attention. If the teacher is only lecturing, you might as well just read his book. If he's reading your script and giving comments, or if there's a lot of interaction in the class, you may learn something that you couldn't get from a book.

Workshops can be expensive, so be sure you're getting your money's worth. Who's the teacher? Is he an industry professional with credits? Has his screenwriting been produced, or is she a veteran development executive? Does he have experience as a studio exec? Does she have producer credits? You can look up any producer or writer's credits on the Internet Movie Database, http://www.imdb.com. But bear in mind, for each credit a writer has, you can assume he's written four to ten scripts that didn't get produced. For each credit a producer has, he's worked on a dozen projects that didn't get made. Script doctors don't normally get any credit for the short, focused rewrites they do, and it's rare for development executives or agents to get any credits at all.

If the teacher has no credits, and can't point to years working in the industry as an exec, but seems to be making a living giving workshops, then on what authority is he teaching? On the other hand, if a teacher without credits has written a book that makes a lot of sense to you, then you may very well get something out of her seminar or workshop.

A very important question is: Who are your fellow students? Part of what you're paying for in a workshop is the opportunity to meet fellow writers with whom you might, for example, be able to form your own writing group. If the other writers are not as advanced as you, then they won't be much help in a writing group, and the class may be pitched down to their level. If they're far more advanced than you, then it may be difficult to develop a writing relationship with them.

Don't become a workshop junkie! If a workshop helps you gets started, then great. But if you're spending time in a workshop that you would otherwise be spending actually writing, then why not save the money and just write?

If it's comments you're looking for, by the way, you may find that a script consultant can give your finished script much more attention than you can get in a workshop where you're one of many students. A workshop will introduce you to fellow writers and give you encouragement; a consultant will give you more specific and in-depth comments. See below.

Writing classes, at a school or university you're already enrolled at, have the same pluses and minuses as writing workshops. But you're not shelling out extra money for them, and you get course credit. So why not?

There are two seminars that are quite popular in the entertainment industry. Both John Truby and Robert McKee run very popular independent seminars that look at story in a structural way, based partly on the theories of Joseph Campbell. Personally I find that theory is fun, and can sometimes highlight problems in your story, but it is dangerous to use theory to construct a story. Instead of coming up with fresh discoveries as you tell your story, you may fall back on cliché. If you're interested, buy McKee's book or Truby's audiocassette course before you pay for the seminars.

STAGED READINGS

In a staged reading, actors sit on chairs and read your script, either to you or to an audience. Each actor speaks the dialogue of one or more of the roles, and someone reads the action.

If your actors have had a chance to read and understand the characters they're playing, you can hear your dialogue coming to life. You'll know which scenes work and which don't. You'll hear where the dialogue seems too on-the-nose or awkward or hard to say or just plain wordy. Actors may also come up with a different understanding of a character than you have, which either means you need to rewrite the part, or you can go with the actor's take on it and rewrite with the insight you've gotten from the reading.

A staged reading really only works for dialogue-heavy scripts, particularly dramas. That's why plays typically get staged readings before being chosen for production: It's much easier to appreciate the play when it's read out loud than when it's just words on a page. Dialogue can come alive in a staged reading. Action can't: You'll just be reading a lot of description in an enthusiastic voice.

Good actors don't like to work for free, although they'll sometimes do a reading if you can convince them that the director or some casting directors will be there: it's another chance to be seen. The reason staged readings aren't on my list of best ways to get help is just that they are an awful lot of work to organize. Most people hold them only after the screenplay is polished, as a showcase for potential investors in the motion picture.

If you're getting a sense that I'm not a devout believer in writing classes, you're right. I have found that the most effective way to learn writing is to do writing. If a class helps you, great, but it's not necessary. But directing, editing, acting, financing, and packaging—all these are much harder to do by yourself, so it makes sense to take classes. Any knowledge of the industry and art of filmmaking can be enormously useful to you as a crafty screenwriter.

(As an aside, I found acting classes enormously valuable to my writing. Acting training can give you an understanding of what an actor does when he gets your dialogue. How is writing drama different from writing prose? What is the creative process an actor goes through to interpret your lines?)

SCREENWRITING CONSULTANTS

A consultant reads your script and tells you what's wrong with it and how to fix it. A consultant might charge anywhere from $100 to $1,000 or more.

Some consultants out there are brilliant screenplay analysts. They will read your screenplay carefully. They'll think about it. They will give you detailed comments, nailing exactly what needs fixing and giving you a fresh, clever, original way to fix it. A good script consultant will also explain the general rules that apply to the script's specific flaws.

Some other very successful consultants will farm your script out to a bevy of film students who check off boxes on a form, then give the form to a secretary who cuts and pastes the appropriate paragraphs from a file full of standardized criticisms.

The first kind of consultant is worth serious money. You're spending months writing your script. (At least I hope you are.) If you're barking up a wrong tree, you can waste months of your time. A careful, surgical critique can set your script on the road to health. What is your time worth?

The second kind of consultant may still be useful, because even college students can provide useful feedback, especially ones who are reading dozens of scripts a week. But the criticism will probably be shallow. That's worth the price of a screenplay coverage, say fifty bucks, not the hundreds of dollars many consultants charge. (A screenplay coverage, remember, is what studios pay readers to do: a brief synopsis and a few pages of evaluation.)

If you decide to invest in a script consultant, treat it as a whole learning experience. What steps went wrong in your writing *process*? Did you spend too little time on the hook? Did you jump right to pages instead of polishing your story? How can you do better next time? Make the most of the fee you're being charged. If you have a follow-up question, try to answer it yourself, but either way, don't be afraid to ask the consultant.

Just Write It

All the methods mentioned in this chapter can help you write your script. But none of them will write it for you. Only you can write your script.

No matter how you do it, what gets the screenplay done is actually sitting down and writing it. You may occasionally solve a dramatic problem by going out with friends, sleeping on it, or vacuuming, but by and large you'll only fix it by working on it. Writers write.

Force yourself to finish projects you start, or at least bring each phase to completion. If you have a hook, finish the story outline. If you start writing pages, finish writing them. You'll feel better, and you'll learn more. I often get discouraged in the middle of a script that later turns out pretty well. If I stopped, I would now own a bad half-script instead of a good whole script.

Don't be afraid to write something bad. Your first draft may be terrible. Sometimes you just need to get something written down. There's no point to writing something that you know is wrong, but if you're stuck in a scene that just isn't singing to you, sometimes you need to write the "bad version" of the scene so that you can move on. Once you're done, you can come back and rewrite.

8

REWRITE

"You must kill your darlings." —Eudora Welty

Never, ever show an agent, producer, director, or actor your material before it's as good as you can make it. No, not even if they're begging for it. A producer who *urgently* wants to read your unpolished script because "I've got a director who's screaming for something exactly like this" will forget you told him it was unpolished. The director won't cut your script any slack, and the producer will think of you as a writer who doesn't know how to polish. Show people like to create artificial urgency. They want to read your script *now*. But they will reject sloppy work blindingly fast, while good material will always open doors for itself. Besides not having a brilliant hook, the most common cause of screenplay death is that the screenwriter didn't put in the time rewriting, reworking, rethinking, and polishing. Make your shot count.

Time will give you perspective. When you're writing, it's hard to step back from what you've written. You may need to put the script down from time to time.

> Never ever show an agent, producer, director, or actor your material before it's as good as you can make it.

But keep rewriting. Nobody writes a perfect first draft. You have to look at every scene to see if it's doing everything it is capable of doing. Reexamine the pacing, the story logic, the characters. Pretend you're a producer and read it. Pretend you're an agent and read it. Pretend you're a star and read it.

Expect to spend as much time rewriting your script as you did writing it, and maybe much more. You must question and requestion everything about the script. This is devilishly hard to do, because when you've got something you like, you don't want to risk losing it.

> All drafts are first drafts.

All drafts are first drafts. You may have polished your script to a fine gloss. All the dialogue is great. All the action is clear and transparent and jumps off the page. All the scenes flow smoothly into each other. And then some horrible person gives you an idea that would mean rethinking the whole script. The main character should be a woman, not a man. It should have a sad ending, not a happy one. The lover should be a traitor. And this horrible idea *is a much better movie than the one you've written*.

You have to be willing to dump overboard all that good polished stuff. Otherwise you're stuck polishing a steam engine to a high gloss when you could have an ugly, dirty, smelly new *jet* engine.

You must keep rewriting your script until you can see no way to improve it, and none of your readers can see any way to improve it, or you can't figure out how to use their comments. Only then should you send the script out to agents and producers.

Before you consider your script completely polished, go through and make sure it is in proper format and properly bound.

Screenplay Format

If you are using a screenplay formatting program, then you can skip this section. You automatically have correct screenplay format. Otherwise, make sure you're using the proper screenplay format. If you don't, you'll look like an amateur. You will get shunted off to a minion, and you know what I think about minions, right? The basics are as follows (a few sample pages are included in Appendix B).

- It must look typed. No font other than `Courier 12`. No boldface. No justified text.
- The title page has the title and your name in the middle, and where to find you (including your e-mail address) in the lower right-hand corner.
- Never put a date on your script, or what draft it is. If someone digs it up after four months or four years, you don't want them to toss it out because it's old.
- Do not put in blank pages anywhere.
- Do not have a dedicatory quotation, especially not in a foreign language.
- No dramatis personae, that is, no page telling us who the characters are. This is a theater convention that is also used in TV scripts *in production*, but should not be used in any selling script.
- The first page starts with `FADE IN:`.
- Don't repeat the name of the screenplay or the screenwriter on the first page.
- Margins are at 1.25 inches and 7.25 inches.
- On every page except the first, put the page number in the upper right-hand corner, about an inch from the right, about a half inch down from the top.
- Transitions should be all caps, margins at 4.25 inches and 7.25 inches. `CUT TO:`
- Sluglines should be in all caps, and take the form

`INT. JOE'S STORE – BACK ROOM – DAY`

or

```
EXT. GRASSY FIELD — NIGHT (STORM)
```

- Don't number your scenes.
- Character names should be in all caps. Margins at 3.25 inches and 6.25 inches.
- Parentheticals should have margins at 2.75 inches and 5.75 inches.
- Dialogue should have margins at 2.25 inches and 6.25 inches.
- Put one blank line after every transition, slugline, line of action, or line of dialogue. Never put a blank line after a character name or a parenthetical. Never use more than one blank line.

Where the same character speaks again after some scene description, put (CONT'D) next to the character name.

```
                    JOE
          This is a good place.

      He looks around.

                    JOE (CONT'D)
          Could use a coat of paint, though.
```

Otherwise a careless reader may blip over the second "Joe" and think your second character is responding. The same goes for a page break:

```
                    ABE
          Four score and seven years ago, our
          fathers brought forth on this

      - - - - - - - - page break - - - - - - - -

                    ABE (CONT'D)
          continent a new nation, conceived in
          liberty and dedicated to partying . . .
```

(CONT'D) is the only formatting cue that belongs in a selling script. Screenplay formatting programs will often add additional cues that you don't really need; you can set your preferences so they don't add them. You do not need to put `(MORE)` at the bottom of the page where a scene continues on the next page, or a `(CONT'D)` at the bottom of the page where dialogue continues, or a `(CONTINUED)` at the bottom or top of pages where scenes continue. These, along with scene numbers, are formatting cues used in scripts that are actually in preproduction or production, so that scene breakdowns can be done efficiently. They only clutter a selling script.

Don't write "Title Sequence" or "Main Credits" even if you think it is a good sequence over which to place the main credits. That's up to the director.

If your script is way too long or too short, changing the margins will not help. We'll notice.

> Please spell-check you're script; its important!

Spell-check your script. Not just with a spell-checker, but by eye. If I see *you're* for *your* or *its* for *it's*, I tend to recycle the script for scrap paper. Many people who read for a living find it physically painful to read bad spelling. I have also never read a badly spelled script that turned out to have a good story. The best way to spell-check is to read the script *backward*, sentence by sentence. That way you can pay attention to the spelling and not get swept up in the flow of the story.

SCREENPLAY LENGTH

If your script is too long, you will need to trim it. A spec feature screenplay should be from 100 to 115 pages. Anything over that gives readers one more excuse to reject it. If you have a subject of great epic scope (you're adapting *War and Peace*), you may go over 120 pages, but anything over 125 pages is asking for trouble. After you've handled a few thousand scripts, all printed on 20 lb. copier paper, you know instantly when you pick up a script that's too long or too short. A 130-page script just looks and feels fat.

The reason you have so little leeway is that standard screenplay format clocks in at a page a minute. The scripts I've worked on that got produced really did come in at about a page a minute after editing. So a 130-page script means a two hour ten minute movie. Worse, rewriters and directors almost always add scenes without taking them out, so if a script starts plump it will end up obese.

Exhibitors dislike any picture over two hours. Think about it. They have two really busy shows on a weeknight, say at 7:30 and at 9:45. They need maybe ten minutes in between shows to sweep out the theater and ten minutes for advertisements and trailers. A show longer than two hours pushes the second show past 10 P.M., which is a psychological barrier for people who have to work in the morning. Or, it pushes the 7:30 show back to 7:00, which doesn't give people enough time to come home from work, put on jeans, eat some dinner, and go out for a movie. So the exhibitors put pressure on the distributors (the studios), who put pressure on the producers not to have overlong pictures. So keep your feature script to 115 pages if you possibly can.

A low-budget spec screenplay, something intended for straight-to-video production, should be no more than 99 pages. Video distributors require movies to be a minimum of 92 minutes long. More pages take more days to shoot, and days cost money, so few low-budget commercial pictures are much longer than 95 minutes.

Comedy scripts may also be shorter. Comedy movies are rarely over 100 minutes long. Woody Allen once said that the ideal comedy length was 87 minutes. Bear in mind that a shorter comedy is easier to keep funny. If you have a comedy script that's over 110 pages, cut out the least funny 10 pages of gags.

How to Bind Your Script

Unorthodox screenplay binding gets you off on the wrong foot. If your script looks much different from all the scripts coming in from the studios and agencies, then people feel you're an amateur and . . . yes, give it to minions.

Screenplays should be on three-hole 20 lb. plain white paper, bound with two 1¼″ brass brads (ideally Acco #5 brads), with brass washers in back, and card-stock covers. You should be able to get brads at larger office supply stores such as Office Depot. Brass washers are a little harder to find. If you can't find them, okay, but they help prevent the back cover from ripping off.

Why two brads and not three? Because you only need two to bind a script, one each in the top and bottom holes, and when you're making thousands of script copies a week, as the studios and agencies do, the cost and time of putting in an unnecessary middle brad adds up.

Don't use 3″ brads (too long) or those skimpy #7 brads (they don't hold the script together). A few people use aluminum screw brads ("Chicago screws"), but it's not normal, and they tend to be slightly too long for 120 pages. Please never use those funny folding metal strips with sliders to bind the script. Personally, I like to take the bottom brad out when reading so I can flop the pages over. That's impossible with metal strips. Don't spiral-bind your script either. If we like your script we're going to run it through a copy machine so multiple people can read it. Ever tried to rebind a spiral-bound script by hand?

Flatten the points of the brads back against the back of the script so they won't catch on people's clothes. Bashing the brads with a hammer will accomplish this nicely if you have brass washers; otherwise, fold each brad point backward on itself, and then flatten it with a hammer.

Covers should be card stock, that is, 80 lb. paper. Any copy shop should have card stock. They can probably punch the top and bottom holes in them for you, too. Don't use clear plastic covers. For extra credit, use precreased 9½-by-11-inch covers that fold over and cover the points of the brads. My printer, L.A. Print & Copy—(310) 445 3200—made fold-over covers for me out of my chosen card stock. Maybe they'd make some for you.

If you live on another continent, try to get 8½-by-11-inch paper. Scripts on A4 paper look outlandish. But if you can't conveniently get standard American paper, don't stress about it.

Don't photocopy your title onto your cover.

Some caring people (including the William Morris Agency) were copying scripts onto both sides of each page to save trees, postage, and schlepping, but they stopped doing it. People found double-sided scripts hard to read, and assistants hated copying them, so I can't recommend it.

There's one last thing you need to do. I hope you've been doing it all along, but now's your last chance to make sure your title is as good as it can be.

Your Title

When you came up with your hook in chapter 1, you also came up with a temporary title. I recommended that you keep working on your title at least 10 percent of the time you are working on your script. Until you send your script out, it doesn't matter whether your title is perfect or not. But it's about to matter enormously.

A bad title can kill your project any step along the way. I refused to see *The Shawshank Redemption* for three months, in spite of rave recommendations, because I couldn't imagine how a prison movie with *redemption* in the title could be anything but preachy. If Frank Darabont had sent me a query letter asking if I wanted to read "*The Shawshank Redemption*, a prison movie with a clever twist," I would have tossed the query letter out. I would have been making a terrible mistake, but that wouldn't have helped him.

A good title can get someone to pick up your script when he's sitting in someone's office waiting for that person to get off the phone. I picked up a script called *Hello, She Lied* because the title was so clever, and by the time the producer was off the phone I had read five pages. If those had grabbed me, I would have called the writer's agent.

A title can work on multiple levels. It can tell literally what the movie's about. It can suggest the feeling we're supposed to get from it. It can comment on the movie, raising a simple story to the level of myth or fable. It can simply grab our attention and make us want to read the script or see the movie. A truly brilliant title might do all these things. Here are the basic types of titles as I see them:

EXPLANATORY TITLES

Most titles tell you basically what the movie's about:

Names of famous people: *Bonnie and Clyde*, *Gandhi*, *Lawrence of Arabia*, *Henry V*, *The Adventures of Robin Hood*
Premise: *Shakespeare in Love*, *How the Grinch Stole Christmas*, *Mr. Smith Goes to Washington*, *The Great Escape*, *The Day the Earth Stood Still*
Type of Protagonist: *Clerks*, *Gladiator*, *The Insider*, *The Graduate*
Situation: *Stagecoach*, *On the Waterfront*, *Star Wars*, *The Boat*
The MacGuffin (Hitchcock's term for "the thing everyone's chasing after"): *The Treasure of the Sierra Madre*

A script called *Gandhi* is going to be about Mahatma Gandhi, no doubt about it. *The Graduate* is presumably about a guy who just graduated. An explanatory title lets your potential reader know what you're offering him. Anyone who was offered the script for *Gladiator* assumed she was going to be reading about a fighter in an arena. Anyone who was looking for an arena movie would have therefore known she should read the script, or at least glance at it. Anyone looking for another big ancient Rome movie as a follow-up to *Gladiator* who gets a script called, say, *Spartacus*, knows to read it right away, since it must be about Spartacus, the slave who led a slave rebellion against Rome. If I'm looking for an occult thriller and I get a script called *The Exorcist*, I'll read that. An explanatory title sells the meat and potatoes of the script.

An explanatory title is most useful when it sums up your hook: *Shakespeare in Love; Honey, I Shrunk the Kids; The Madness of King George;** *The Attack of the 50 Ft. Woman*. But the old salesman's proverb

---

*The original British title was *The Madness of King George III*, but there was concern that American audiences might be put off if they thought they'd missed the first two.

says, "Sell the sizzle, not the steak." Telling straight out what your movie's about isn't as good as hinting. A hint gets the reader involved; he'll try to figure out what you're hinting *at*. Which leads us to the opposite end of the spectrum.

MYSTERIOUS TITLES

Mysterious titles don't tell you much at all about the movie. They might make sense by the end of the movie. They might not. You'll have to read the script or see the movie to find out. Each of the following titles begs a question:

The Matrix	What is the Matrix?
Blade Runner	What's a blade runner?
A Clockwork Orange	How can an orange have clockwork?
The Green Mile	Where is the green mile, and why is it green?
The Wrong Trousers	What can be wrong about trousers?
The Good, the Bad, and the Ugly	Who are they?
Sling Blade	What is that?
The Opposite of Sex	What is the . . . ?
Close Encounters of the Third Kind	What are . . . ?
Seven	Huh?
M	What?
Reservoir Dogs	What the hell?

These titles all sell pure sizzle. What makes them work is that even though they don't say anything straight out, the words in them carry emotional weight. *Blade Runner* suggests someone running, and a blade. The reader is thinking action, the threat of violence: an action thriller. (The title of the Philip K. Dick story on which the movie was based, "Do Androids Dream of Electric Sheep?" would have been too goofy.) *Trousers* is a funny word, and *wrong trousers* is a very odd phrase. The movie is a quirky comedy. *Matrix* is a high-tech word, slightly threatening with that "x" ending, which is perfect for a science-fiction thriller. *Sex* is . . . well, it sells tickets, doesn't it?

A mysterious title is really helpful when your subject matter might turn people off but you think they'll get over it once they read your movie. *A Clockwork Orange* is about a psychopathic thug who hurts people for kicks. *Sling Blade* is about a retarded murderer. *The Green Mile* is about guards and prisoners on Death Row. *M* stars a homicidal child molester. An explanatory title could have wrecked any one of these. The subject matter doesn't have to be negative to be a turnoff. *The Wrong Trousers* is about an inventor being hustled by a criminal penguin. I don't know how many people would pay to see that unless they knew from the title that it's a quirky, oddball comedy. Even a single well-chosen word can be extremely evocative, hinting what flavor of movie it will be without giving too much away: *Alien*, *Jaws*, *Psycho*, *Predator*, *Unforgiven*.

NEUTRAL TITLES

Chinatown
The Bridge on the River Kwai
Fargo
Amadeus
Annie Hall
Yojimbo
Miller's Crossing
Forrest Gump

Like mysterious titles, neutral titles don't give away much about the movie. But unlike them, they don't really sell the movie at all. They're names or people or places we don't know anything about. The names will probably come to mean something in the movie. Most people won't know until they see the picture that Amadeus is Mozart's middle name or that it means "loves God" in Latin. In the movie, the antihero Salieri hates God for giving his childish, spoiled rival Mozart the talent he thinks should have been given to himself.

Chinatown, we find out, is where the hero, Jake, last made a futile stand for decency; at the end of that picture, he loses again.

You may use a neutral title if you're afraid of giving away too much. A title creates expectations, so if you don't want to define your movie up front, a neutral title will keep the reader's and the audience's minds open for the experience. Woody Allen originally wanted to give *Annie Hall* the title *Anhedonia*, an impenetrable word that means "inability to experience pleasure," which is the hero's tragic flaw. Aside from frightening off moviegoers, it would have made the movie too focused on that one issue. So might a catchier title like *Groucho's Club*. *Annie Hall* didn't scare anyone away, and it didn't define the picture too strictly.

The problem is that your title and your hook are the two things that get people to read your script. If no one reads your script, your title has failed, and it's no consolation that you've avoided overdefining your story. I doubt any of the above titles were spec scripts; they were probably all developed by the filmmakers themselves. I don't recommend neutral titles for anyone writing a spec script.

SUGGESTIVE TITLES

Raging Bull
Singin' in the Rain
Run Lola Run
In Cold Blood
It's a Wonderful Life
Touch of Evil
Dog Day Afternoon
Splash!
The Lion in Winter
Apocalypse Now

These titles don't give away much of what the movie's about, either. Oh, sure, there's somebody named Lola and she's obviously running, but that's not much to go on, is it? But more than mysterious titles do, they tell you what kind of *feelings* the movies are about. *Raging Bull* must be about someone very angry and very powerful; perfect for a boxing movie. *Singin' in the Rain* and *It's a Wonderful Life* guarantee you a happy movie. *Splash!* just seems like fun. *Braveheart* implies courage and guts. The movie might not end happily, but you're going to see someone put himself on the line to do something important. *Dog Day Afternoon* suggests heat and exhaustion. These titles sell not only the sizzle, but the scent of the steak. They're even catchier when based on a familiar expression: "in cold blood," "dog day afternoon," or for that matter "all that jazz," "bananas," etc.

LITERARY TITLES

By basing your title on a quotation, you get to poach an already well-crafted, time-tested phrase and take advantage of all the associations people have with that phrase. (For our purposes it doesn't matter if the title was originally a book title or not; either it's a good title or it's not.)

Once Upon a Time in the West: from the traditional opening to a fairy tale, suggesting this is in some sense a fairy tale about the West.

All the President's Men: . . . couldn't put Richard Nixon back together again. A reference to Humpty Dumpty, it also brings to mind *All the King's Men*, an earlier movie about another would-be American autocrat, Louisiana governor Huey Long.

The Grapes of Wrath: From the Battle Hymn of the Republic: "He is trampling out the vintage where the grapes of wrath are stored." Raises this story about a poor family in the Dust Bowl to the level of a myth.

One Flew Over the Cuckoo's Nest: From the nursery rhyme Tingle Tangle Toes: "One flew east, one flew west, one flew over the cuckoo's nest." Plays on a familiar word for "crazy," while foreshadowing the strange destinies of the various characters. (I think.)

The Sixth Day: On the sixth day, God created man. A good title for a movie about a man who has just discovered he's been cloned, it adds moral weight to an otherwise by-the-numbers science-fiction thriller. Similarly, *End of Days* uses a biblical term for the end of the world to add gravity to an occult thriller.

In the same vein, many good titles come out of loaded phrases from popular culture:

Unlawful Entry
Rules of Engagement
Enemy of the State
Basic Instinct
The Right Stuff
Boys Don't Cry
First Blood
Internal Affairs
High Fidelity

The best of these titles are not only catchy because they're familiar, they say something about the story. *An Officer and a Gentleman* comes from the military crime, "conduct unbecoming to an officer and a gentleman." Zack Mayo (Richard Gere) is neither an officer nor a gentleman in the beginning. He is training to become an officer, but only his love for Paula (Debra Winger) will make him into a gentleman. (The title *Conduct Unbecoming* was used seven years earlier in a picture about British officers misbehaving.) *High Fidelity* is not only about the owner of a record shop (fidelity as in "hi fi"), it's about the hero's relationships (fidelity as in "faithfulness"). *American Beauty* is not only the name of the variety of roses one character cultivates; it is a reference to the underage woman the protagonist has the hots for, as well as a mocking reference to the American way of life in general.

I can't stress enough how important your title is. Your title is the first thing anyone reads or sees, whether in your query letter or when they grab it off the shelf. (Someone will write the title on the spine of your script with a marker pen, but you shouldn't do that yourself.) It is the handle by which people carry around your movie in their minds. If your project goes into development, it will be the only thing that gets written on the whiteboard on the list of projects. It will be the first thing anyone sees in a newspaper ad for your movie, along with the star's face.

For every time someone reads your script, people will read your title fifty times. Make sure it scores.

9

GET IT MADE!

You've done the fun, hard part and written the screenplay. Now you come to the part that's just hard: getting your screenplay into the hands of someone who will pay you for it and make it into a movie.

Access

Your mission is to get your screenplay read as carefully as possible by as many people who can help you as possible.

As many people: The more people read it, obviously, the more likely you'll reach someone who'll love it. The best possible outcome is to get it read at the same time by two people who love it, and they get into a bidding war. If your only offer comes from me, you'll probably end up taking it; but if I'm competing with somebody else to give you the best deal, you could get something wonderful.

Who can help you: Your script will go through many middlemen before it reaches someone who can say yes. Middlemen can only say no, or pass the script up the ladder. "Yes" means someone pays you money to option or buy the script from you, and eventually "yes" means someone finds the financing to make the movie. The fewer middlemen your script goes to before it gets to someone who can say yes, the more likely you hear yes.

As carefully as possible: By the time it reaches producers and executives who can pay you money for it, your script will be competing with other projects that have elements attached: a director, a star, a coproduction partner, 50 percent financing. Most companies have rivers of scripts coming through their doors in manila envelopes and going out in big blue recycle bins. You don't want someone to take your script to the washroom, read a few pages, and toss it aside. You want everyone to sit down, read it, and consider it seriously.

Agents

Unless you know a bankable director or star, the best person to put your script in the hands of someone who can buy it is an agent. A literary agent is someone who represents you, and takes 10 percent of whatever you make from your screenplay, and is therefore highly motivated to get you as much money as possible. If you don't get paid, she doesn't get paid. (In the book business, someone who represents books is called a literary agent whether the books are literary or not. But in show business, a screenwriter's agent is called a literary agent and someone who represents books is called a book agent.)

What a literary agent does all day is

a. Call development people and producers and try to get jobs for her clients.
b. Call development people and producers and try to get them to read and buy her clients' spec screenplays. (A "spec" screenplay is any screenplay the writer wrote without getting paid by a producer to do it. You're writing a spec screenplay.)
c. Have breakfast, lunch, cocktails, and dinner with industry people and try to do (a) and (b).
d. Negotiate deals for her clients when they have succeeded at (a) or (b).
e. Go to screenings of movies her clients wrote.

f. Go home and read scripts to see if they, and the writers who wrote them, are worth representing, so she can do more of (a) through (e).

What she is looking for is a well-crafted script with a great hook. If she thinks you've got one, she'll sign you.

Here's how it's supposed to work:

A good literary agent knows a big chunk of all the people your screenplay should go to. She has built up a reputation with them for sending good material, so that if she tells them your script is really good, they'll read the script quickly.

Once she signs you, she is going to spend a week or two talking up your script to all the development people she knows at the major production companies. Then on the appointed day, she'll "go out" with it. That means she has a stack of thirty copies of your script sitting in a box, each in a 9½-by-12½-inch envelope with her agency's logo on it, each with a cover letter introducing you and your script. Go Between, a courier agency, picks up the box and delivers all thirty of the scripts to the various recipients within about three hours.

Then she waits for the phone to ring. Well, actually, she makes about a million other calls for other clients, waiting for the phone to ring on your script.

What she hopes is that two production companies will love the script and want to buy it. A bidding war is the only way you get those big paydays you read about in *Variety* and *The Hollywood Reporter*. If all goes perfectly, within a week she has a buyer or two, and you make a deal.

If no one buys your screenplay, your agent will try to get it set up somewhere on an option deal. (I'll explain what that is in a moment.) Now she's sending your script out one copy at a time. Depending on how much she believes in you, she may keep you on as a client for six months to two years, hoping she can sell or option your script or get you a writing job, or that you'll write a new and better spec script she can go out with. In the meantime, she will keep your script in the back of her mind, so whenever a producer or executive mentions that he's looking for something like it ("right now we're looking for edgy children's movies" or "I need a thriller that can be shot in Puerto Rico for a price") she can say, "I've got the perfect thing" and send your script.

If you live in L.A., or can come to L.A. for a few weeks, she'll try to set up meetings for you with producers and development people who liked your script but didn't buy it. At these meetings, you talk about your upcoming projects and hear about what they're doing. You may be considered for writing work. They'll give you some material—a novel that needs adapting or a script of theirs that needs rewriting—and ask you to read it and think about and come back with your take, the theory being that if your take is the best they'll hire you to do the rewrite. (I have my doubts about how many times they actually do hire the person with the best take if he's not someone who's already sold a spec script, so you'll need to decide for yourself whether working all week on a take for a producer is really worth your time.)

You can't do any of this yourself. You can't send out thirty scripts all at once. You don't know to whom you should be sending them, and you probably can't get thirty development people to read your script even if you have a superb hook. You don't know how much money it's realistic to ask for. You'll ask for too little or too much. You won't know when to take the money offered and when to hold out for more. You can't create a bidding war. You don't know when it makes sense to accept an option deal and when you should insist on a purchase deal.

Here's why even an unsuccessful agent is better than no agent:

1. An agent takes 10 percent of your screenwriting income. Until you have income, it's a free service. You might have to pay for photocopies, but you don't have to type the addresses or schlep to the post office yourself.
2. Many producers will not read a script that isn't sent in either by an agent or a lawyer. People claim this has something to do with protection against lawsuits. I'm not quite sure how your having an agent protects them, but that's the custom of the

industry. If you don't have a representative, they may give you release forms to sign, but they may also just refuse to read your script.

3. Having an agent means that at least one person likes your script for purely greedy reasons. She isn't in the business for her health. She must think your script is marketable. Having even a so-so agent validates your writing to other people.
4. If you sell your script, you really shouldn't negotiate on your own behalf. Most writers aren't good negotiators; producers are. Even if you are a good negotiator, the person negotiating needs to be able to say things that upset the producer without getting the producer mad at you. You can't do that. You want your agent to be the bad cop, so you can be the good cop.
5. If you're thinking of writing a new script, she can tell you whether there are other projects like it already in the works, or whether your idea isn't as marketable as you think, saving you time and frustration.

So, you need an agent.

How Do You Get an Agent?

The best way, of course, is to get recommended by someone who knows her personally, or whose name she recognizes. Catch-22? Sure.

The usual way is to send an agent a query letter. It's exactly the same query letter as discussed in chapter 1, but it says that you are looking for representation. You probably want to send out dozens and dozens of query letters to different agents at different agencies, hoping that at least one will spark to your material.

The usual way to get the names and addresses of agents is to get the Writer's Guild's list of signatory agencies. You can either send a stamped, self-addressed envelope and a dollar to the WGA at 7000 West Third Street, Los Angeles, CA 90048-4329, or you can go to their website, http://www.wga.org, and get it for free.

The WGA list notes which agents will accept unsolicited scripts. "Unsolicited" doesn't mean that you just mail the script in; you never do that. It means that the agents don't know you, and you weren't recommended by someone. However, these agencies tend not to be the hottest and most powerful agencies, so you may as well send query letters to everyone.

Don't bother with any agencies not on the WGA list. I don't believe that any agent who hasn't signed with the WGA can possibly help you, and I think they could hurt you.

Don't bother with any agencies not in Los Angeles County (including Santa Monica, Beverly Hills, and West Hollywood) or in New York City. If you're Canadian, add Toronto to the list. There are also a few agents with primarily local practices in Montreal and Vancouver. I have 335 literary and talent agents in my Rolodex. Except for a handful in London and Paris, they are all in the following area codes:

(310) Santa Monica, Beverly Hills, L.A.'s West Side
(323) L.A., to the east of La Cienega Boulevard
(818) L.A.'s San Fernando Valley
(212) New York City
(416) Toronto
(514) Montreal

Over two-thirds of these are in (310).

Agents elsewhere can't help you because they don't go to lunch with the right people. If I get a letter from an agent or lawyer in Arizona, it gets no more attention than I would give to a letter from a long-haul trucker in Arizona.

Don't bother with anyone who runs seminars, teaches extension classes, offers screenplay analysis, or does anything else for a living. Anyone who's a real agent should be supporting herself on her 10 percent commission on all the money she's getting for her clients. Someone who runs seminars is probably making most of his money giving seminars. He might send your script to one or two people, but the important thing in his mind, I think, is to get you to take his seminar so he can collect the $500 fee. You can make a *lot* of money giving seminars at $500 a head.

(That doesn't mean you shouldn't take seminars if you feel you'll learn useful things. It just means you want to be represented by someone who only gets paid when you get paid.)

Don't just send a letter addressed to the agency in general. You must send your letter to someone in particular, or it will get shunted off to a nameless minion. (It bears repeating: *at every step of the way, you want to avoid minions*, because they can only say no.) Take the trouble to find out who is the hungriest young literary agent at each agency. She's the one who will give your script the most attention, because she is still building her client list.

To get the name of the hungriest young agent, try calling the agency. Be perky and gracious and brief. Ask who'd be the most interested in reading your script and representing you. If the receptionist doesn't know, you can either try to dig out the names of agents from the trade papers (*The Hollywood Reporter* and *Variety*) in the weekly "spec sales" column, or you can get the Hollywood Creative Directory's *Agents & Managers Directory*. You can buy it on-line at http://www.hcdonline.com, by phone from (310) 315-4815, or from your friendly local movie bookshop.

The *Agents & Managers Directory* won't tell you explicitly who's young and hungry, but the lowest names on any agency's listing of their agents will be those with the least clout and experience. Practically anytime you run across a list of people in show business, if it's not in alphabetical order, then it is in strict order of who's got the most clout. People get irritated if someone with less clout is above them in a list, so people making lists are very careful about that sort of thing.

The top agents get the top assistants. So another way to find out to whom you should send your query is to ask for one of the top agents by name. His assistant will pick up the phone. Ask the assistant to which *other* agent at the agency you should send your query.

You don't absolutely have to send all your query letters out at once. If you don't, you might occasionally get some feedback from a friendly agent who's willing to talk to you after rejecting your script.

Then you can revise. On the other hand, if you do shotgun your query letters all at once, you stand a greater chance of getting two agencies interested at the same time. That way you can choose the one you like best.

If you are incredibly lucky, two agents will want to represent your material instead of just one. Choosing between them is a simple formula:

```
Enthusiasm × Enthusiasm × Clout =
  the value of the agent to you
```

A wildly enthusiastic middle-level agent is better than a mildly enthusiastic high-level agent; but an agent who isn't taken seriously is not going to be helpful, no matter how enthusiastic. I doubt any agent working out of her apartment in Minneapolis can help you much. But a wildly enthusiastic agent at a small working agency (assistant, but no receptionist) can be more helpful than a semi-interested agent at even a top agency.

How do you know if someone has clout? You can look for material success. The more layers you have to go through to talk to your agent, the more real her agency is. If you talk to a receptionist, and then an assistant, and only then the agent, you're dealing with an office with at least a handful of agents and enough income to hire staff. Agents only get income if their clients make money, so layers of staff mean their clients are working. At the opposite end of the spectrum, if your agent is answering her own phone, or voice mail is, then she's not doing that well.

If your agent wants you to pay for copies, she's probably not doing that well. If you're a client of even a B-ranked agency, your sole responsibility is to deliver her a clean copy of your script, or e-mail her a digital copy. The agency's minions make copies, put on covers, and courier the scripts out. A not-so-successful agent might ask you to reimburse her for photocopies. A very not-so-successful agent might ask you to pay for postage. If an agent asks you for any other payments—reading fees, consultation, or anything else—immediately call the WGA and blow the whistle on them. Agents are allowed to charge for photocopies and postage, but nothing else.

Anyone who wants to represent your script who is not an agent, whether they charge money or not, will probably not be able to help you. There are on-line services that claim they will, for a substantial fee, read your script and, if they like it, pass it along to important people. These "services" make their money from the fees you pay them, not from a commission from the money you make selling your screenplay. Save your money.

If an agent wants to represent you, you can and should also ask her whom else she represents, or what scripts she's sold in the past year. Write the names of the clients down and check their credits on the Net and see if they're successful people. If she has no successful clients, what are the odds she's going to be able to help you? It's also a good idea to look her up on the Internet. Did *Variety* report two months ago that she sold someone's first script for $500,000 against $1.5 million? Or is her only mention on the Net an article in the UCLA student paper three years ago?

I should tell you that practically no one gets a good agent through query letters. You get good agents through contacts in the movie industry. (Yes, Virginia: It is not what you know, it's who you know. Everything they say about Hollywood is true. What makes it possible to survive here is that everything they say is also not entirely true.) But you have to start somewhere. I did get my first agency through the WGA list of agencies that accept unsolicited scripts. Those guys didn't sell my script or get me a job, but they sent me on some meetings and I got some exposure. That made it easier to get my next agent, who was a step up, and she made it easier to get my next agent, who was another step up, and so on.

How do you make contacts in the film industry from scratch? Leverage. You use a faint contact to work your way into a stronger contact, and the stronger contact to work your way in the door somewhere. Let's say you've already sent one script out, and someone liked it, though he didn't buy it. Ask him if he can recommend an agent who'd be right for you. He can probably tell you the name and number of an agent who makes up for her lack of clout by hard work and cheerful perseverance, who keeps sending him good scripts from "baby writers." That's the kind of agent you want at this stage. Now you can write her a query letter that starts with, "Joe Thalberg at Whahoo Productions suggested I contact you." As soon as you get a positive response to your query, you can send your script to the interested agent.

By the way, you don't need to live in L.A. to get an agent. Just make clear that if your agent wants to set up meetings after your script goes out, you'll be able to come to L.A. for a few weeks. You don't need to live in L.A. unless you want to get a sense of what you're up against, in which case getting a day job in the industry, such as being an agent's assistant, might not be a bad idea. (For more information about that, see my on-line FAQ, http://www.craftyscreenwriting.com/FAQ.html.)

Copyright

"Talent borrows. Genius steals." —Alex Epstein

Many writers are concerned that someone will steal their work. Agents are not going to steal your work; that's not their business. Producers are generally not going to steal your work, either; they're far too busy. If they like your script, they're going to option it for a little money now and then use someone else's money to buy it later, so why would they open themselves up to a lawsuit? But it's a good idea to protect your script before you send it out, just in case. You can even copyright it when you only have an outline, although this will not protect your dialogue.

WHAT IS COPYRIGHT?

Copyright is the right of the author to control who can publish his or her work. It exists from the moment he creates something copyrightable that can be sold, licensed, or given to another party. In copyright law, "publish" doesn't just mean books; it includes any means of reproducing it for the public, such as exhibiting a film or play based on it.

In ancient Greek times, there was no copyright. Authors wrote for fame. They had no hope of getting royalties when their books were copied by hand. With the invention of the printing press came the possibility of getting paid royalties. But Elizabethan England had no copyright laws. Rogue publishers would regularly send people with extremely good memories (memories were much better then) to see plays by popular authors such as Shakespeare. They would come home, write down as much of the dialogue as they could remember, and the publisher would try to print and sell an edition of the play before the legitimate owner of the work published a clean copy. Publishers also bribed actors to steal scripts. But the moment you published a complete copy of your play, anyone could produce it elsewhere without paying you.

So, copyright was invented to make sure authors got paid.

WHAT CAN BE COPYRIGHTED?

There are four main criteria for determining what is copyrightable:

- The work must be original. If you stole your plot from Shakespeare, you can't copyright that plot, only the ways you departed from Shakespeare's work.
- It must be the independent expression of an author. Only the expression, not the underlying ideas, are protected. For example, your specific dialogue, the sequence of scenes or visual images, your characters, all can be protected. Your concept cannot be protected. What's an idea that can be gleefully stolen, and what's the expression of an idea, is a matter the courts decide case by case, but if it can be told in two sentences, it's an idea.
- The work must be of a nonutilitarian nature. You can't copyright a contract or instruction manual.

- The work must be fixed in a "tangible medium of expression," that is, it has to be recorded on paper or on a computer disk; it cannot just be something you said over lunch.

HOW DO I ENFORCE MY COPYRIGHT?

There are two ways people protect their copyright in the entertainment industry.

The Writer's Guild of America will, for your $30 check, archive a copy of your work (screenplay or synopsis) and send you back a slip with a registration number on it, providing independent proof that you wrote a screenplay or story at a certain time. This can be useful if someone later steals your idea or screenplay, but:

- The registration lasts only five years, then has to be updated.
- The registration has no legal force, except as evidence.

A better way to protect your screenplay is to register it with the Registrar of Copyright at the Library of Congress in Washington, D.C. It is then archived in the Library of Congress *forever*, which is why the LoC is the largest library in the world.

There is an important legal distinction between the two services. The WGA provides a private-party service with no legal effect. Your WGA registration will help prove in a court of law that the screenplay is yours. It's like having a contract to buy a house and a canceled check to go with it. The LoC registration has its own legal force. It is like having a title deed to your house that has been registered at City Hall.

The legal difference is that if someone infringes your copyright—steals your stuff—then you will have to sue him. If you have registered at the WGA, then you will have to prove that your stuff was stolen and that you were hurt by having it stolen. If you have registered at the LoC, you are entitled to what are called *statutory damages*, meaning you don't have to prove you were hurt, only that your stuff was stolen.

To register a work at the LoC, you need a Form PA, which you can order by phone at (202) 707 9100. You can also download a Form PA in PDF format at http://www.loc.gov.

Note that popping a script in the mail and mailing it to yourself (so-called poor man's copyright) is useless. What's preventing me from mailing myself an empty envelope today and then putting any script I like in it ten years from now?

You do not need to be a U.S. citizen to copyright a work at the Library of Congress. However, if you copyright your work in most nations, your work is automatically considered copyrighted in the United States. For example, if you copyright your work in Belgium, it is protected in the United States by treaty. If you live in a new nation such as Croatia, or a nation on poor terms with the United States such as Cuba, Iran, North Korea, or Libya, then you will need to copyright your work here in order to be protected. Of course if you're a writer, you'd better get out of Cuba, Iran, North Korea, or Libya before you write the wrong thing, y'know?

You can't copyright an idea, only your dialogue, characters, and plot, that is, the way that idea is expressed. However, you *can* protect your idea *contractually*. If you come to an agreement with someone that, if they use your idea, they have to pay you for it, then you have a contract. If they steal your idea, you can sue them for breach of contract—even if it isn't an original idea and you never wrote it down.

A written contract is the safest way to do this. Technically you can create a legal oral contract by saying, "If you use this, I wanna get paid, okay?" in front of witnesses, but they may not remember what you remember, and then everybody gets upset. As Samuel Goldwyn is supposed to have said, "An oral contract ain't worth the paper it's written on."

You only have to copyright your work once. Even if you revise it later, it will still have much the same characters and plot, so if someone steals from a revision, they will run afoul of your copyright. If you change the work so completely that someone could steal from it without stealing from the original, then you need to copyright the work again.

Sending Your Script

The best way to physically send a script to anybody is by U.S. Mail. Priority Mail arrives in two or three days and costs under four bucks. The U.S. Post Office gives away free Priority Mail envelopes, made out of nice strong cardboard, in patriotic red, white, and blue, that are perfectly sized for a script. If you'd like to save a little money, send your script Special Fourth Class rate. This costs a little less than six first-class stamps. It'll get there in a week or two, which is plenty fast, considering most people will take four to twelve weeks to read it. Don't overnight your script. It just makes people nervous.

You do not need to protect your script inside file folders or use bubble-wrap envelopes. It's a pile of paper, for heaven's sake, not bone china.

Include a nice cover letter saying that per their request, you're sending them your script. Remind them what your hook is. Thank them for their time and consideration, and hope to hear from them at their convenience.

Now you wait and hope.

E-MAILING YOUR SCRIPT

Some of the younger, more wired agents are accepting electronic submissions these days. The best way to send in a script electronically is as a PDF file. PDF files are created by Adobe Acrobat Exchange, a not-cheap but very easy-to-use program. You can buy it in stores or on the Net at http://www.adobe.com. (eBay often has a few copies at heavy discounts.) PDF files can be read by Adobe Acrobat Reader, a free program that many people already have on their computer, or can be downloaded from the Net. PDF files look *exactly the same* on any computer or printer.

The second-best way to make an electronic submission is using a screenplay formatting program or word processor. The risk here is that pagination will not come out the same on the agency computer as on your computer, especially if one of you is on a Mac and the other is on Windows. This is not a big issue if you're using a screenplay formatting program, because it will still break pages properly, but if you're using a word processor, it is likely that the script won't print out quite right on the other end. Also, if someone has your word processing file, they can easily change your script without your permission, whereas with a PDF file it's a major pain.

The third-best way, and it is really not a good way, is as a Microsoft RTF file. Rich Text Format enables you to send word processing files over e-mail in cases where your Internet service provider is screwing up your attachments; often RTF is the only way to get a script through to AOL. It's readable, but page breaks will occur in unpredictable places, and there may be even worse formatting errors.

Waiting

A couple of weeks after their script goes to the agent, many people like to call the agent to see what the response is. Sometimes they say they're just checking to make sure the script arrived safely. The idea is that this gets the agent to read the script a little faster. Also, if the agent read it and didn't like it, and can remember why, you might get some feedback. That can be quite valuable since it's feedback from someone who could have done something with it.

On the other hand, it is never *necessary* to call. If you find it is too painful to hear rejections and evasions, keep in mind that if they read and like your script, they *will* call you, assuming you put your contact information on your cover page. If they're not calling you, they either haven't read it yet or they didn't like it.

If they haven't read it after three months, your script is dead there. It's lost or has been tossed. They no longer care about it, or they were never really serious about reading it. They are not going to read it, and they are not going to send it back. It is no longer useful to call.

Getting It Back

Some people like to include a stamped, self-addressed envelope (SASE) with their script. Me, I've never understood the point of getting scripts back. It costs less to copy a script if you shop around a bit for a cheap copy shop than it does to buy the stamps and the envelope for the SASE. So if you get your script back, you're losing money. Moreover, even if the agent actually saves your SASE, and can find it much later when he's read the script, your script is now smudged and coffee-stained, and you're getting it back four months later when you've rewritten it. What's the point? Let 'em recycle the paper. No muss, no fuss, no bother.

Some agencies will, as a courtesy, send your script back to you at their own expense. (I once even got a script mailed to me that I'd never sent. They'd printed my script out from a PDF file I e-mailed and were kind enough to mail me back the copy!) Most don't, even when you are also an industry professional. Personally, I tend to mark scripts up when I'm reading them, bend the pages over, occasionally even hurl them across the room in frustration or elation, so they're pretty well thrashed by the time I'm done. Skip the SASE, is my advice.

An Agent Says Yes

If you've got a crafty script with a good hook, an agent will say she's interested in representing you and the script. At that point you can call the other agents who've already asked to read your script and give them a week or so to read it.

If two agents like your script, you generally want to choose the more enthusiastic one. Enthusiasm is precious stuff. If they're enthusiastic to you, they'll be enthusiastic to other people.

Occasionally, agents will offer to take you on as a "back pocket" client. That means they're not willing to commit the agency to representing you as a client, but they will personally rep your script.

This is not very satisfactory, since they're not really committed. But it's better than nothing.

Your agent may send you a contract right away, or not. The standard deal is 10 percent of whatever you make from your writing over the course of the next year or two. You can fire your agent after any four months in which she hasn't sold anything or gotten you any bona fide job offers. Agents are regulated by the laws of the state they're in. The State of California limits agents to a 10 percent fee. They are not allowed to act as producers. They are allowed to package your script with other clients' (directors', stars'), but only if you've agreed to it. Only the bigger agencies have enough clients to do this usefully.

If You Don't Have an Agent

If you haven't been able to get an agent, then you have to do the agent's job for yourself. You have to send query letters to producers.

How do you get a list of producers? The Hollywood Creative Directory publishes a *Producers Directory* that lists every production company with any kind of credits. As with agents, you want to address your letter to a specific person at each company. You want to send it to someone with a title like Vice President of Development, Director of Creative Affairs, or Story Editor.

If you have an agent, but she has run out of steam after a few months, it's all right to ask if she would be comfortable with you sending out query letters on your own to supplement the submissions she's made. She will probably be comfortable with that, because she can only benefit if you get interest from a producer; then she can negotiate your deal and collect her commission. If she doesn't want a confusion of efforts, respect her decision. But in general, you should always be hustling to promote your own work; use your agent only to complement your own efforts. No one cares about your material as much as you do. Meet with as many producers as you can. Try never to leave a meeting with anyone in show business without having figured out which of your scripts he'd be most interested in, and getting permission for your agent to send it.

Know the producers to whom you're submitting your stuff. Check the company's list of credits before you send a query letter or meet. A company that has made ten children's movies will not want your horror film. A company that only makes art films will not want your $80 million science-fiction spectacular.

Sending query letters to producers is quite a chore. There are more producers than agents. Mostly they will not bother to respond to your query letters, even to say no. But if your hook is good (remember your hook?), then you will get some positive responses, and you'll be able to send your script out to them.

Screenwriting Competitions

Many people send their screenplays to screenwriting competitions in the hopes that it will get them attention. Personally, I feel about screenwriting competitions the way I feel about the lottery. In order for one person to win $1,000, two hundred (or more) people are submitting their screenplays and paying $50 for the privilege. That means the people running the competition are taking in $10,000 and paying out $1,000. I feel the $9,000 profit accounts for the large number of screenwriting competitions. While winning a screenwriting award may get your screenplay read by a few more people, I do not believe it will contribute much to the likelihood of your movie getting bought or produced. There are a few screenwriting competitions worth taking seriously, such as the Nicholl Fellowship, Project Greenlight, and Francis Ford Coppola's "Virtual Studio," Zoetrope Studios. But I think most competitions exist because someone wanted to run a competition, probably not someone making a living from producing movies. I don't think I've ever read that a movie got made because the screenplay won an award. If you want to spend money on your writing habit, send your script to a script consultant (see the previous chapter). That way you'll at least learn something, and if your script is superb, it probably will get passed along to people who can buy it, just the same as if you had lucked out and won a competition.

A Producer Says Yes

If a development executive or producer is interested in your script, he will try to make a deal with you. If you don't have an agent, you'll have to negotiate on your own.

However, if there's an agent that expressed some interest but didn't sign you, now might be a good time to go back to that agent and ask if he or she would like to negotiate on your behalf. That means very little work for the agent, in exchange for 10 percent of your money (*compensation* is the legal term). It's worth it, because your agent can easily get you more than 10 percent more than you would have gotten yourself, and you won't have a nagging feeling that you misnegotiated your deal.

If you do have an agent, you won't be negotiating directly with the producer, but you shouldn't just leave it all up to the agent. Be clear with your agent how much money you want and how much you'll settle for, and whether there are any issues you need her to raise with the producer. You're the one who's going to have to live with the deal you make. Your agent, for example, will care whether your script has a purchase price of $50,000 or $100,000, but she won't care much whether you get paid $500 or $1,000 for an option, because to her it's a difference of only $50. Your agent won't care whether you have creative involvement in the project, or the right to be on the set, or an invitation to the premiere, because none of these puts money in her pocket. But you may care.

The Deal

There are two usual kinds of deals for your script, an option deal and a straight purchase deal. In a *purchase deal*, the buyer is immediately buying all rights to your screenplay. From now on, they own it.

They can do anything they like with it, subject to the terms of the deal. Purchase deals put a lot of money in your pocket fast. You will never be offered an outright purchase deal unless you have competing offers or the "heat" or "buzz" on your script is tremendous.

In an *option deal*, the buyer is paying you a small amount of money now. In return, at any time during the option period, which might be anywhere from three to eighteen months, he can purchase your screenplay according to the terms set forth in the deal. The option deal contains all the same contractual terms and conditions as the purchase deal, but the buyer doesn't have to pay you the big money until and unless he decides to purchase the script.

The deal is a negotiation. You don't get what you deserve, you get what you negotiate. As with all deals, unless the other side believes you're willing to walk away without making any deal if you don't get the terms you want, you'll get very little.

If you are a member of the Writer's Guild of America, the writer's union, you cannot accept less than certain minimum payments, called WGA scale, or just scale. Producers who have signed the Writer's Guild's Minimum Basic Agreement (MBA) can't offer you less than scale. In practice, though, all studios own subsidiaries (legal companies) that are not members of the WGA, companies that exist entirely so that the studios can make less-than-scale deals. If they can get away with paying you less than scale—for example, if you don't have a good agent—they will.

Thus, under the MBA, a purchase price for a regular-budget feature film can't be less than around $60,000, and an option payment must be no less than 10 percent of the purchase price, that is, $6,000. (For the latest figures for scale, check out the Writer's Guild website at http://www.wga.org.) But if you're not a WGA member, a producer might offer $500 or $1,000 or nothing for the option, and if you agree, that's what you'll get. There's nothing immoral about doing a deal for a $1,000 option. There are many producers who are never going to do a deal for more than that because they don't have much cash; they're making movies entirely with Other People's Money, and until they get investment in your movie project, they don't have any money to give you. They can't shop your script to generate investment in it until they have an option. So don't feel terrible if you accept a $1,000 deal. That's $1,000 more than you had before. Either your producer will manage to make his money back by producing your picture, or you'll get your script back after the option period expires.

A typical purchase deal will have a purchase price and a production bonus. You get the purchase price whenever the producer decides he wants to own your script permanently. Usually this isn't until the first day of production, but it could be earlier.

You get the production bonus when the picture goes into production. This might be a flat fee, or a percentage of the budget. If it's a percentage, there is usually a ceiling, or cap. Anything you've been paid up till then counts against the bonus. Thus if your deal is 200 against 500, you'll get paid $200,000 for the purchase and $300,000 on production, for a total of $500,000. Thus, the main deal points for a screenplay might be:

Option: $2,500
Option period: 12 months
Purchase price: $75,000 against 3 percent of budget. Cap of $250,000.

If the picture is made for $1 million, you get	$ 75,000
If the picture is made for $2.5 million, you get	$ 75,000
If the picture is made for $5 million, you get	$150,000
If the picture is made for $8 million, you get	$240,000
If the picture is made for $8.5 million, you get	$250,000
If the picture is made for $10 million, you get	$250,000
If the picture is made for $100 million, you get	$250,000

That's a very fair deal if you're dealing with an independent producer. What you consider an acceptable deal is up to you, but I would never recommend taking less than the following:

Option: $500 for six months, renewable for an additional twelve months for another $1,000.
Purchase: $50,000 against 2 percent of budget. Cap of $200,000.

Most deals also include standard payments for any sequels, prequels, remakes, and TV spin-offs based on your script. Writers usually also get 5 percent of the net profits; this is called *net profits participation* or *points*. Points are practically never worth anything, which is why they're sometimes dubbed monkey points. Every once in a blue moon, a picture is made for *so* little and does *so* well that they can't hide all the profits and the writer gets a nice chunk of money. For example, *Four Weddings and a Funeral* was shot for about $4 million and made over $100 million in box office. I suspect the writer did very well from his points. It is worthwhile to insist that you get paid your net profits "according to the best definition of Net Profits accorded by any Net Profits participant in the Picture." That means that if there are, by some miracle, net profits, no one else will get them ahead of you. (See the Sample Option Deal in Appendix A, paragraph 3b.)

If a studio or major production company wants your script, then you should be able to find an agent who will represent you. She will insist on a minimum of a WGA deal.

An important deal point is the right of first refusal to rewrite. If you get this right, they are under no obligation to have the script rewritten, but if they do want it rewritten, they must give you the chance to do it. The rewrite fee is specified in your contract.

If they like your writing, they'll probably give you this right if you insist. If they only like your hook, and they're planning to rewrite your script immediately, then they won't be inclined to give you this right. On the other hand, if they despise your writing but absolutely love your hook, then if you insist, they'll have to give you this right anyway, won't they? 'Cause they can't *force* you to accept their terms. So long as you're willing to walk away, you have ultimate control of the negotiation.

Aside from not having your project mangled by another writer, there are two good reasons to insist on the first rewrite. One: you'll share credit with another writer, depending on how much of your script he changes. Say the producers want to add a few characters (for example, a love interest) and move the story to a new location. If a new writer makes these changes, and also polishes the dialogue, he might be entitled to share credit with you. If you make these changes, and then he polishes the dialogue, you'll be entitled to sole credit.

Two: the most likely outcome for *any* script under option is that it gets rewritten once or twice, and then gets put on the back burner until the option runs out. If you did the first rewrite, you have now gotten paid for the option and then for the rewrite. If you didn't, you only got the option money, and somebody else got the rewrite fee. A typical rewrite fee is about ten times the value of a typical option.

Whatever you negotiate, never, never kick yourself for making a bad deal. There's no future in it. If you asked for too little and got it, just do your best, consider the project an investment, and resolve to cut a better deal for yourself the next time.

FREE OPTIONS

Producers will ask you for a *free option* if they think they can get away with it. The idea is that they don't pay you any money now, but they negotiate what they will pay you to buy your script if and when they get the project set up. In return they will spend their time and effort trying to get your movie made.

I am of two minds about free options. On the one hand, if nothing else is happening with your script, why not? I have seen the occasional script go into production based on a free option, so the writer who gave the free option did better than he would have if he hadn't given a free option.

On the other hand, if a producer is serious about setting up your script, he should be willing for fork out at least some money to option it. If he won't, maybe he's not really so serious. Or, maybe he's too poor to pay you—and if he's such a successful producer, why is he poor?

Certainly, you should never give a free option for longer than four months, with the right to renew the option for another year by paying money. For example, free for three months, plus an additional year for a couple thousand bucks. If inside four months the producer can't get your project in good enough shape to be willing to pay you money, then he's not going to do it in more time. You don't get anything out of having the project sit on his shelf and you may as well move on.

If a producer is asking for a free option, you can instead agree to give the producer a letter saying that for a limited period of time, such as six months, if the project is set up somewhere, that producer is attached to the project. The letter does not specify the details of your deal. That means that if the producer gets the project set up at a studio, he negotiates *his* deal with the studio, but you negotiate *your* deal separately. If you negotiate your deal only after the project is set up somewhere, it is worth much more money. It is already a project with studio interest. The producer isn't going to want to walk away from a project with interest from a studio, so you can ask for more money. Producers won't like this proposal, but if the producer isn't prepared to pay you up front, then it's only fair you keep more control. You want to play, you got to pay.

FREE REWRITES

A producer will often tell you that your script is pretty good, but that you need to rewrite it a bit before he'll take it on. For free. Should you?

If you've got someone else who will option or buy the script without a rewrite, then of course the answer is no. Except in rare circumstances, go with the bird in the hand.

On the other hand, if that producer is the only interested party, then ask yourself if his critique seems right. Will the producer's comments make the script better if you rewrite it? Then why not do the rewrite? You've taken the script this far. Why not get it to the point where someone can do something with it?

But if the producer's comments take the script in a direction that will only benefit that producer ("I really need this skiing movie rewritten for Puerto Rico"), then you should not do the rewrite unless you're paid for it.

There's an ancient joke in show business:

Q. How do you tell when a producer is lying?
A. His lips are moving.

I used to work for a producer who would say he had "practically all the money" to finance a movie project. That meant that he thought he knew where he might be able to get the money. You can never trust anything a producer tells you about whether he has all his financing in place, stars interested, studios just waiting to read your script, blah blah blah. What you can trust is the producer's self-interest. He's not going to ask you to rewrite the script in a given direction unless he thinks he can do something with it. So, if he knows what he's doing, his comments will make your script more marketable. What you need to decide is whether or not it's worth your time and effort to do the changes. Treat his feedback as you would any other feedback. If it makes the script better, great. If not, tell him you think his ideas are very interesting and you'll take a look at it. ("I'll take a look at that" is how writers politely say "I think that's the dumbest idea I ever heard, right now, but maybe I'll like the idea better later, and I really don't want to upset you.")

THE OTHER KIND OF FREE REWRITE

Sometimes a producer will ask you to rewrite a script he owns, or to develop a script based on his idea, for free. He will especially do this if he thinks you haven't got a clue about show business. He will promise that the movie is practically in preproduction, and you'll get a credit and a big fee when, not if, the picture goes.

Hah hah hah hah hah hah hah hah hah.

How do you tell when a producer is lying?

Never, ever work on someone else's material for free. This is what the WGA calls writing on spec—confusingly, it is entirely different from writing a spec script—and it is banned by the WGA. Follow their lead. It costs the producer nothing to ask, so you have no way to know if this is a project that will definitely go ahead or something the producer thought up this morning and will have forgotten all about by the time you've written what he wanted. (*N.B.*, there is no such thing as a project that will definitely go ahead.)

If a producer has a truly brilliant idea, then you can make the following deal: He assigns you all rights to his idea. In exchange for that, you write the script and grant him a one-year free option to buy the script from you. That's fair. You get a brilliant idea, he gets a script, and after a year, you're free and clear.

Otherwise, working on other people's projects for free is just a big fat time-waster. Never, ever do it.

Writing for Hire

Don't turn down a writing job unless it doesn't pay enough, or you don't trust that the people hiring you will pay you, or you are sure you can't do the project justice creatively. (I can't write a sitcom.) Professional writers almost never turn down a paid gig unless they're working on another paid gig.* Sure, it's more fun to write your own ideas, but spec scripts don't go on your résumé unless they get bought.

Suppose someone wants to hire you to write. How much should you charge?

As a bare minimum, here's a formula for how much you must charge in order to avoid getting burned. You must be *guaranteed* this amount, no matter whether good things happen with the projects or not. Assume that anything you hear about whether the project is going to get made or not is a big fat lie, at least for the purposes of this calculation.

Take the amount of time you think it will take to do the work. Triple it. (Writing always takes longer than you think it will, especially when you are responding to a producer's vague, contradictory, whimsical comments.) Now double that. (Half the time, you're not writing, and you have to make the time you spend writing pay for the time you're not writing.) Now figure out how much your time costs you. If you are making a living writing, that's how much money you spend. If you're making a living doing something else, that's how much you get paid an hour in your job. Multiply six times the amount of time

*To tell the truth, several other paid gigs.

you think you'll spend by the cost of your time: that's the minimum amount you can charge. If you charge less than that, you're not writing for the money, you're writing for the sheer enjoyment, or as part of your education, or you're investing in the picture. That's okay, too, just be clear on what you're doing.

Yes, this formula means that a writer who does something else for a living can profitably charge less than someone who writes full-time.

As a rule, you shouldn't write a treatment for less than $500, or a script for less than $5,000. These are very, very low figures. Anyone who insists on paying you less isn't serious about hiring a writer.

In addition to the amount you must be guaranteed for the work, you should also get a substantial bonus if the project gets made, and if enough of your script survives in the movie that you are granted credit. A reasonable percentage is 2 percent of the budget of the picture, reducible to 1 percent if you don't have sole credit.

Television

The development process for television is slightly different. In television, you are not trying to sell your spec script, though it's not impossible. You're writing a spec episode in the hopes that you'll get hired to write an episode of another series, or even get hired as a member of the show's writing staff.

TV is a different market for a number of reasons. First, the writer is king. Directors are hired hands. Many powerful TV producers worked their way up as staff writers on various other shows.

TV has an enormous appetite for scripts, and they get made fast. TV writers do far more writing and less waiting than feature-film writers. They get paid less per script, but they are paid far more per year because they work more. TV writers often say, "I'd love to work in features, but I can't afford it."

TV agents know an entirely different world of buyers than feature agents. Most agencies with more than a few agents will have both kinds of agents. Some agents cross over.

TV shows almost never buy scripts or ideas from the outside

world. If they don't get all their ideas and scripts from their staff writers, they will ask freelance writers whom they know to come and "pitch the show" (i.e., to present ideas for possible episodes of the show). They are extremely unlikely to buy a TV series idea, "bible," or pilot episode for a new series, at least in the United States. (A TV show's "bible" is the blueprint for the series, usually created before any episodes are written.) TV shows are typically developed from the concept onward by many writers and writer-producers, with much input from the network or production company and from the star and her representatives. Short of a miracle, your pilot will not match their needs because you are not in the loop.

If you want to get into TV, what you must do is write a sample ("spec") episode of one of the hottest, most respected, popular, Emmy-award-winning shows on television now. The hot shows change every year. Call an agency and ask an agent's assistant for which series they're recommending their clients write sample scripts. ("What shows are you telling your clients to spec?") You want to pick a show that you think will be around for at least a few years.

Your spec should be ready at least four months before staffing season, which begins around the end of March. It takes time to get TV agents to read scripts, and as staffing season approaches, they start working feverishly to get jobs for the writers they already represent. They don't have time to fool around with new talent.

Before you write your spec, it's a good idea to see every episode you possibly can of the show you're writing. Check out the official website if one exists, and the fan sites. They may have backstory on the characters. Some fan sites have show synopses, quotes, transcripts, and even actual scripts.

Your objective is to prove that you understand the unwritten rules of the show. Prove you can write the show's main characters in fresh circumstances. Don't introduce important new characters, because that's not the point. (New bad guys are okay.) Don't be afraid to make your episode more intense or more outrageous than a TV show dares to be. You're not going to sell your spec script; you're trying to show your ability.

The most important thing is to get the voices of the characters right and follow the beats of the typical show. You're not trying to innovate; you're trying to show you understand the structure and world of the show.

When you've written a great spec, find out which of the agents who accept unsolicited manuscripts are TV agents, and query them.

Suppose for the moment, though, that you have an idea for a show burning in your brain and, feverish, you must absolutely write a pilot episode for a show that does not yet exist. In other words, suppose you have not understood a word I just said. After you have written it, what should you do? Get it to James Van Der Beek's agent? Nope.

What you need to do is get your show idea to a showrunner, one of the blessed few writers whom the networks allow to create shows for them. They're the ones who get the "created by" credits. Gene Roddenberry (*Star Trek*) was a showrunner. Chris Carter (*X-Files*, *Millennium*, *Harsh Realm*), J. Michael Straczynski (*Babylon 5*), Steven Bochko (*Hill Street Blues*, *NYPD Blue*), Aaron Sorkin (*The West Wing*), Joss Whedon (*Buffy: The Vampire Slayer*, *Angel*), and David Kelly (*Dawson's Creek*) are all showrunners. Watch the shows that impress you, that are in the same genre as your pilot, then send a query letter to the showrunners who created those shows. Tell them (or have your agent tell them) that you have a five-page pitch that you'd love to send them, and what the concept is.

It is unlikely that you will get a positive response. But at least you are knocking on the right door. If your premise is brilliant, and your characters are amazingly real and fresh and compelling to the lucky peon who gets to read your manuscript, your work might get passed up the ladder—using the word *might* as in, "It might snow in July," or "Microsoft might make nonbuggy software." A showrunner can make your show a reality if he deigns to try. An actor's agent or network executive will not touch it.

Note that in Canada (and maybe other countries, too) it is entirely possible for a "baby writer" to get her TV series pitch optioned, and then get paid to write a show bible and pilot episode. I got a TV series idea optioned in Montreal after having written a grand total of one

TV episode. But the Canadian government subsidizes the development of Canadian TV shows, so the North is different.

Never Write from Hunger

You have now written a script, polished it, and gone out with it. If you did everything right, and you're lucky, you made some money and you're waiting to see if they make it into a good movie. If not, you learned a lot and had fun.

What's next?

If you're really a writer, the answer is always more writing. A writer writes. For me, it's an addiction. If I don't write, I'm unhappy. I start snapping at people. I growl at dogs. I eat too much.

Every script is a learning process. You never stop learning. After the first dozen or so scripts you start to think you really know something, and then after the second dozen you decide that *now* you really know something. John Boorman recounts that when he went to see David Lean on his deathbed, the eighty-three-year-old Oscar-winning director of *Lawrence of Arabia* and *The Bridge on the River Kwai* told him, "You know, John, I was just beginning to get the hang of it."

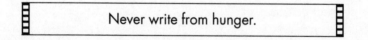

> Never write from hunger.

Write what you love. Write a movie you'd like to see. Or write a movie you enjoy writing, even if you'd never pay money to see it. If you think there's an aspect of writing you're bad at—dialogue, action, plot—write a movie that will strengthen your ability in those areas, as a writing exercise, to develop your craft. But never write from hunger.

Writing from hunger means writing purely for money. Some people make a lot of money writing commercial scripts. But don't be fooled. They're not writing purely for money. They love what they're doing, they have a gift for it, and they are writing at the top of their ability after years of learning their craft. They are not condescending to the material. If you are writing from hunger, your script will suffer. The reader will know that you don't care, and she won't care either. Let's face it. The odds of selling any given script are not that good, to put it mildly. If you write from love and don't sell it, you get to keep the love. If you write from hunger, all you're left with is the hunger.

Write from your soul. If you're fortunate enough that your imagination gives you terrific hooks, and your soul loves extremely commercial high-octane thrillers, then write those. If your soul loves sad, twisted little art films, then write those. Write what you love. At least, of all the addictions you could have, there are few things cheaper than writing, and few that do more to make the world a better place.

Good luck, and tell the truth.

APPENDIX A

A Sample Option Deal

The following is a simplified version of a deal memo I have used myself. Everyone has their own standard deal memo, but most deal memos cover more or less the same points.

OPTION AGREEMENT

between Eric Gould ("Writer") and Crafty Productions, Inc., a California company ("Producer"), regarding that certain screenplay entitled *Firewall* (the "Screenplay"), which may be used as a basis for a motion picture film project currently entitled *Firewall* (the "Picture").

1. GRANT OF OPTION

In consideration of the nonrefundable payment to Writer of the sum One Thousand Dollars ($1,000.00) (the "Option Fee"), to be due and payable on execution of this Agreement, and other good and valuable consideration, Writer hereby grants to producer an option to purchase (the "Option") all motion picture, television and allied, subsidiary and ancillary rights in and to the Screenplay including, but not limited to, the sole, exclusive, perpetual and worldwide rights to make feature-length theatrical and/or television motion pictures based on the Screenplay, and the right to exploit, distribute, exhibit and turn to account the same, theatrically and through television, and by all other means, manner and media now known or hereafter developed. All rights excluded by the Writer's Guild of America 2001 Theatrical and Television Minimum Basic Agreement (the "MBA") are hereby excluded.

They pay you a thousand bucks. They have the right to buy all rights to your script, except for a few "excluded" rights, such as the right to publish a novelization of your story.

2. COST AND TERM OF OPTION

The Option Period shall commence upon complete execution of this agreement and shall terminate on July 31, 2010 (the "Option Period"), unless extended as follows:

The Option Period may be extended, prior to its expiration, to July 31, 2011 (the "Extension Period") by sending written notice thereof to Writer, accompanied by payment of the sum of Two Thousand Five Hundred Dollars ($2,500) (the "Extension Price"), which payment shall be applicable against the Purchase Price.

They have about a year (from July 31, 2009, the date the deal memo is signed, to July 31, 2010) to buy your script. If they want another year after that, they have to pay you an additional $2,500. If the option expires before they've bought the script, you keep the money and they have no rights anymore.

3. EXERCISE OF OPTION

a. The Producer shall exercise the Option, if at all, before the earlier of the commencement of principal photography, and the end of the Option Period, by making written notice to Writer and by making payment of Seventy Five Thousand Dollars ($75,000) to Writer as the purchase price ("Purchase Price") for the Screenplay. Upon receipt of the Purchase Price, Writer shall forthwith deliver an assignment of Writer's right, title, and interest in and to the Screenplay. The form and content of the assignment shall

> be supplied by Producer and shall be consistent with the standards of the industry.

If they want to buy the script, they pay you $75,000. They are required to buy the script before the film actually starts shooting.

> b. If the Picture is produced, and if Writer receives sole credit for the Screenplay (e.g., in the form of "Screenplay by" or "Written by"), within two months from delivery of the completed motion picture, Producer shall pay Writer the sum of 3% of the production budget, less the Purchase Price; and Writer shall receive 5% of 100% of the Net Profits of the Picture, according to the best definition of Net Profits accorded any Net Profits participant in the Picture.

After the picture is finished, they have to give you 3 percent of the budget, less whatever else you got paid, provided you got sole credit. (See "Credit," below.) You also get 5 percent of the net profits, which probably won't be worth anything.

> c. If the Picture is produced, and if Writer receives shared credit for the Screenplay (e.g., in the form of "Screenplay by" or "Written by"), within two months from delivery of the completed motion picture, Producer shall pay Writer the sum of 2% of the production budget, less the Purchase Price; and Writer shall receive 3% of 100% of the Net Profits of the Picture, according to the best definition of Net Profits accorded any Net Profits participant in the Picture.

If you're rewritten so substantially that you share credit with another writer, you get only 2 percent of the budget and 3 points. Note that this language is a little tricky because if you don't get sole or shared credit, you get no percentage of the budget at all. This is reasonable, though, since if you got rewritten so heavily, you haven't contributed that much to the movie.

> d. The budget shall be determined by the sum bonded by the completion bond, or if there is no completion bond, by the sum insured by the production insurer, subject in

either case to revision after an audit by an independent auditor at Writer's request.

The budget figure will be whatever figure the completion guarantor used for the completion bond; no squirming out of that.

e. Writer's compensation for sequel, remake, television series, spin-off and/or other similar rights shall be according to the MBA.

The standard active and passive payments for sequels and the like are tied to the Writer's Guild standard contract.

5. FIRST REWRITE

Producer and its assigns shall hire no other party than Writer to perform writing services with respect to the Screenplay, before hiring Writer, if reasonably available, to perform one Rewrite for $30,000.

They can't hire anyone except you to do the first rewrite, unless you refuse, or have moved to Nepal. After that they can do what they like.

6. WGA AND CREDIT

Writer shall be accorded a standard "Written by" credit on-screen and on all paid ads and packaging, subject to the customary exclusions; provided however that if Producer engages another writer to rewrite the Screenplay, then Writer's Credit shall be determined according to the credit provisions of the MBA by an independent, mutually approved arbitrator familiar with the WGA procedures for credit arbitrations.

If they hire another writer, that writer will have to make substantial changes to be entitled to share credit with you. The formula is that the second writer must change 30 percent or more of the script. It's a subjective judgment, though, made by a team of other writers. The second writer could change every last line of dialogue and not get a credit; or the second writer could write four really crucial scenes and potentially get credit.

The credit language is the most important language in the document. Don't back down here. The money you get paid will get spent. Your writing credit will build your career. Unfortunately, producers will sometimes find it inconvenient to give you the credit to which you're entitled. If, for example, the producer makes the picture in Canada and you are not Canadian, it might really help the financing to give the entire credit for the screenplay to the Canadian guy who rewrote the last few pages. If the credit language states that your credit is at the producer's discretion, or simply fails to explain what happens in the event of a dispute, then you may not get your credit. (If you're a member of the WGA, this is irrelevant because the WGA will adjudicate credit if there's a dispute.)

7. REPRESENTATIONS AND WARRANTIES

Writer hereby represents and warrants that:

(a) Writer owns all rights in and to the Screenplay as specified in this agreement hereof free and clear of any liens, encumbrances, claims of litigation, whether pending or threatened;

(b) to the best of Writer's knowledge, neither the Screenplay nor any element thereof infringes upon any other literary property;

(c) the production or exploitation of any motion picture or other production based on the Screenplay will not violate the rights to privacy of any person or constitute a defamation against any person, nor will production or exploitation of any motion picture or other production based thereon in any other way violate the rights of any person whomsoever. Writer shall be reciprocally indemnified by Producer to the extent materials other than those contributed by Writer are added to the Screenplay or the Picture by the Producer;

(d) Writer has full right and power to make and perform this agreement;

(e) to the best of the knowledge of Writer, the Screenplay has not previously been exploited as an element in a motion picture, television production, play or otherwise, and (as limited above), no rights have been granted to any third party to do so, except as such rights may have expired. Writer hereby indemnifies Producer against any loss or damage incurred by reason of any breach of the foregoing representations and warranties. The term "person" as used herein shall mean any person, firm, corporation or other entity.

You haven't stolen the screenplay from someone else (it's okay if you stole the idea), you haven't sold it to someone else already, and you're not making up lies about real people.

8. NOTICE

Notice to Producer shall be in writing, by certified mail, to the address below:

PRODUCER
125 Arroyo Caldo
Beverly Hills, CA 90212

Notice to Writer shall be in writing, by certified mail, to the address below:

WRITER
Eric Gould
914 Seventh Street
Santa Monica, CA 90403

All payments to Writer shall be made by wire transfer to a bank account or entity to be designated by Writer, or by cashier's check delivered in person to Writer.

9. MISCELLANEOUS

This agreement shall be binding upon and inure to the benefit of the parties hereto and their respective heirs, successors, administrators, and assigns.

Writer agrees to execute at Producer's request any and all additional documents or instruments necessary to effectuate the purposes of this Option Agreement.

This Option Agreement is the sole agreement between the parties, and supersedes all prior and contemporaneous agreements. Any change to this agreement, in order to be effective, must be in writing and signed by both parties.

The prevailing party in any litigation or dispute shall be entitled to recover from the other party hereto, all costs and reasonable attorney's and/or auditor's fees.

Writer shall not be entitled to rescind this agreement or to seek or receive any injunctive or other equitable relief for any breach thereof, Writer's sole remedy in such instance being the right to bring an action at law for money damages.

This agreement shall be governed and construed in accordance with the laws of the State of California, whose courts shall have exclusive jurisdiction herein.

Standard legal language ("boilerplate") that's part of all option contracts.

Agreed to and accepted as of the 31st day of July, 2009

PRODUCER	WRITER
____________________	____________________
By Z. Gesundheit	Eric Gould

Put your John Hancock here.

APPENDIX B

Sample Screenplay Pages

The Wine Dark Sea

by Alex Epstein

[my address]
[my phone number]
[my eddress]
www.craftyscreenwriting.com

FADE IN:

A MAN

stares into the distance with tremendous longing. In the moonlight, on his face, the wisdom and sadness of years of war. He is ODYSSEUS.

BOY (O.C.)
Sir?

EXT. SEA SHORE – NIGHT

Behind Odysseus, GALLEYS are drawn up on the stony beach, sails furled, black hulls glistening in the moonlight. The water laps gently at the shore. The BOY is 14, and out of breath:

BOY (CONT'D)
They're fighting again, sir, in the council. Eurylokos told me to, uh . . .

ODYSSEUS
– drag me into it. Thank you.

Odysseus turns, already walking.

BOY
It sounds bad, sir.

Odysseus strides up the beach, passing into the sprawl of dirty tents and guttering torches that is the GREEK CAMP.

ODYSSEUS
Diomedes wants to go home again?

SOLDIERS carouse around a PIG roasting over a campfire –

BOY
And King Menelaos is calling him a coward.

TWO FOUR-YEAR-OLDS run past them, dragging a toy on a string.

ODYSSEUS
And Dio is saying, if Menelaos had been as good in bed with his wife as he is at shooting off his mouth, all the warriors of Greece wouldn't've had to sail halfway across the world to die in front of the walls of Troy, just to get her back for him.

A SOLDIER smooches with his MISTRESS in shadows –

BOY
Something like that, sir.

MORE SOLDIERS drinking and laughing. They nod at Odysseus with the proud respect veterans give to a commander who's earned it.

ODYSSEUS
Think he's right? If we can't get over those walls – and we've been trying since you were four – we might as well go home. Right?

The Boy looks at Odysseus.

ODYSSEUS (CONT'D)
Think your mother misses you?

The Boy starts to smile hopefully –

Then his smile drops.

BOY
It's honor, sir.

ODYSSEUS
Oh yes. Honor.

Someone MOANS. Odysseus turns:

INSIDE A TENT, a dozen MEN are stretched out on the dirt, some moaning, others dead. A

DOCTOR puts two copper coins on the eyes of a dead man.

ODYSSEUS (CONT'D)
Doctor?

DOCTOR
It's Euryades, milord.

ODYSSEUS
From Zakynthos?

(The doctor nods.)

His father was killed last year, at the Scythian Gate. He had a brother, too, didn't he? . . . Oh yes. Hector killed him, just before Achilles killed *him.* The brother's name was . . .

DOCTOR
Elpenor.

ODYSSEUS
No. Canthus.

DOCTOR
He was a good man.

ODYSSEUS
They were all good men.

He looks at the doctor, at a loss for words.

Then staggers slightly. And looks down.

ODYSSEUS (CONT'D)
HEY!

One of the KIDS has slammed into his legs. The Kid starts CRYING. Odysseus leans down, picks the kid up.

ODYSSEUS
What are you doing up? Where's your mamma?

KID
Horse!

Odysseus looks down. A wooden horse on a string leans, tilts, and falls over in the dirt. Odysseus bends and picks it up, hands it to the child, who stops crying.

BOY
Sir? The council . . .

Odysseus looks over the TOY HORSE, its little wooden wheels, suddenly fascinated. And, for the first time, he *smiles* . . .

CUT TO:

A RAVEN

wheels in the blue sky. Then banks, dives down toward the level plain, landing right by:

A SEVERED HAND

The big, jet-black bird pecks at the hand, jiggling it. As we circle the Raven and the jiggling hand, we discover:

GLEAMING WHITE STONE WALLS rising forty feet up from the plain, stretching for hundreds of yards in either direction. Castle TOWERS rise fifty feet on either side of thirty-five-foot WOODEN GATES. A THOUSAND SOLDIERS line the walls, the Sun reflecting off their bronze helmets and spear points.

This is

TROY

1184 B.C.

ON A TOWER

A sentry points:

SENTRY
Look!

IN THE DISTANCE,

a forty-five-foot WOODEN HORSE groans slowly forward on six-foot wheels, pulled by a HUNDRED MEN, dust rising from the plain.

THOUSANDS MORE SOLDIERS, Greeks, march forward on either side, the Sun gleaming off their helmets and spear points. They are CHANTING a war song punctuated by WHOOPS. WAR CHARIOTS roll in front of the soldiers. Drums THUNDER. Horns BLAST.

ON THE WALLS,

Trojan soldiers YELL and CLASH their shields and spears together, SINGING their own war song. Their trumpets BLAST.

HUGE WOODEN WHEELS

CREAK as the huge wooden Horse rolls down the plain.

A HUNDRED MEN

heave at thick ropes, sweating, straining.

THE HORSE

picks up speed as it approaches the walls.

ON THE WALLS

The Trojans stare at the Horse, amazed, their song faltering.

THE WOODEN HORSE

RUMBLES faster toward the walls, the infantry YELLING and CHANTING alongside it as they begin their charge—

GREEK SKIRMISHERS

in loincloths run forward, whirling slings, firing off stones that WHISTLE up at the gates.

THE TROJANS

raise huge oxhide shields, the stones THUDDING against them.

ON THE HORSE'S HEAD

A dozen GREEK HEROES, all as big as football tackles, *stand on a platform,* twenty-foot-long lances pointed at the sky. Their eight-foot-high shields gleam with silver and gold. Bright Mohawk-style crests rise from their helmets, making them seem eight feet tall.

At their head is AGAMEMNON, gray-bearded, sturdy. Next to him, his golden shield glistening, a handsome man: MENELAOS. He SHOUTS back:

MENELAOS
ODYSSEUS! GOOD IDEA!

ODYSSEUS smiles for Menelaos's sake, but his wise eyes hold a touch of sadness. As the Horse shudders forward toward the Trojan walls, Odysseus slams his gleaming bronze helmet down over his face.

THE GREEK HEROES lower their twenty-foot-long lances until they are level, pointed at the Trojans on the walls—

THE TROJANS step back, frightened, as—

THE HORSE'S HEAD smashes into the wall, bashing stones aside, Greek lances skewering Trojans—

THE HEROES charge onto the walls, jabbing with spears and hacking with swords, shoving Trojan soldiers SCREAMING off into space.

Index

About the Author

Alex Epstein has over a decade of experience turning screenplays into movies. A graduate of Yale University and the UCLA School of Film and Television, he has been vice president of production for three independent production companies, where he optioned and commissioned screenplays, hired writers, and worked with all the major studios and agencies to develop and package projects. Also a produced screenwriter for film and television, Epstein has worked with veteran directors such as John Badham (*Saturday Night Fever*) and Richard Attenborough (*Gandhi*). His award-winning website is www.craftyscreenwriting.com.